THE COMEDIES OF
MACHIAVELLI

THE COMEDIES OF

MACHIAVELLI

THE WOMAN FROM ANDROS

THE MANDRAKE

CLIZIA

BILINGUAL EDITION

EDITED AND TRANSLATED BY

DAVID SICES AND JAMES B. ATKINSON

PUBLISHED FOR DARTMOUTH COLLEGE BY
UNIVERSITY PRESS OF NEW ENGLAND
HANOVER AND LONDON, 1985

Printed in the United States of America

LIBRARY OF CONGRESS CATALOGING IN PUBLICATION DATA
Machiavelli, Niccolò, 1469–1527.
The comedies of Machiavelli.
English and Italian.
Contents: The woman from Andros—The mandrake—Clizia.
I. Sices, David.   II. Atkinson, James B., 1934–
III. Title.
PQ4627.M2A25   1985   852'.3   84–40595
ISBN 0–87451–329–4
ISBN 0–87451–330–8 (pbk.)

CONTENTS

ACKNOWLEDGMENTS

We would like to thank all those who, by their criticisms, suggestions, and encouragement, have contributed to the publication of the present volume. In particular, we are grateful for the aid toward publication of the bilingual text furnished by the Ramon Guthrie Fund, by the office of the Dean of the Faculty, and by the Committee on Research of Dartmouth College. A special expression of thanks is due Errol G. Hill, Willard Professor of Drama and Oratory at Dartmouth College, for his role in the inception of the project.

AN ESSAY ON
MACHIAVELLI AND COMEDY

The name of Niccolò Machiavelli is not generally associated—
at least by English-speaking audiences—with the drama. According to a tongue-in-cheek prologue written for a recent production of *The Mandrake*,

> The man, of course, was known far more
> For his wicked *Prince*, and for his *Histories*,
> As well as for an *Art of War*,
> But he also mastered theater's mysteries.

Many readers may be surprised to learn that the author of *The
Prince* is also responsible for a trio of comedies, one of which is
considered by Italians to be the earliest—and by knowledge-
able authorities such as dramatists Carlo Goldoni and Luigi
Pirandello to be the greatest—of their country's theatrical classics. More than half a century before Shakespeare established
the tradition of English-speaking comedy that has prospered
and endured to the present, *The Mandrake* was entertaining audiences with its racy vernacular language. Audiences marveled
at its contemporary character, and the play became a model for
dramatic construction and comic characterization. *The Mandrake* provoked delight and thoughtful bemusement because of

its representation of serious—if not seriously treated—ethical questions. These features have continued to inspire admiration more or less uninterruptedly until our day. Indeed, the play's linguistic and dramatic verve have made it more immediately accessible—and to a wider range of audiences—than are the comedies of Shakespeare.

Machiavelli's serious dramatic efforts date only from the last ten years of his life. At the beginning of this period he was poverty-stricken, disillusioned, and embittered. His wit and intelligence had won him great political success, proximity to power, and the friendship of strong leaders. When the Medici returned to power in Florence in 1512, overthrowing the republic that Machiavelli had served since its inception in 1498, they were suspicious of his loyalty and kept him on the periphery of power. Although history has cleared the record, Machiavelli was rumored to have been involved in a conspiracy to expel the Medici and was briefly imprisoned for his alleged complicity. Later, in the 1520s, the Medici relented and restored him to their favor; they granted him several commissions—notably, *The Florentine Histories*—but they permitted him no real access to the seats of power.

During the last decade of his life Machiavelli was thus writing some of his most significant analyses of political and historical events. Nevertheless, he was keenly aware that there was an alternative means for getting his ideas across to others. Machiavelli seized upon comedy as a useful tool for hammering out his political message so that it reached a more immediate audience. Comedy succeeded in a more resounding fashion through what we may call the politics of pleasure: Machiavelli politicizes the laughter he arouses, so that when the laughter dies down, the message can better be grasped by the alert members of the audience. Like Aristophanes, Machiavelli unsettles his audience with incongruity, distortion, and other techniques bordering on the grotesque. Hence, one cannot derive pleasure from Machiavelli's plays without also having one's political values shaken.

It is not surprising, therefore, that the ideas preoccupying Machiavelli when he writes about politics or history should thrust their way into his explanatory and theoretical statements on the nature of his comedy. The connection on the theoretical plane, be it in the prologue to *Clizia* or in his treatises, is clear. Translating this connection between comedy and politics so that it comes alive on the stage is a major endeavor. Comedies about love ruled the day—then as now—and one of the givens of the romantic love convention is that the lovers are subject to "unforeseen events." For someone acutely aware of the problems of *fortuna*, the abstraction that Latin and medieval thinkers devised to represent the arbitrary forces at work in the universe to impede a person's use of intelligent foresight, the parallel between the literary and political spheres is instructive. Thus, Machiavelli is intrigued with writing about the same type of problem, but in a context different from his customary political one. He makes of love and its attendant issues a testing ground where many of his political and theoretical interests can assume a new phase. Moreover, these issues become the point of balance between the traditions of comedy and his practice of the art.

Little needs to be said about Machiavelli's lesser theatrical endeavors. He is credited by some of his contemporaries with having adapted *Aulularia* by Plautus, but verifying this claim involves too tortuous a path to follow here. In 1960 a hitherto unknown holograph copy made by Machiavelli of *Eunuchus* by Terence was detected in a Vatican codex that also included a copy of *De rerum natura* by Lucretius. Careful examination of the handwriting suggests that the Terentian play was probably copied early in the 1500s. Because these years are not the period of his known theatrical activity, scholars have unconvincingly proposed later dates.

Concerning another of his theatrical ventures there is even more confusion; if we knew anything more substantial about it, the text could prove to be one of his most interesting dramatic efforts. Giuliano de' Ricci, Machiavelli's literary execu-

tor, claims to have seen among his uncle's manuscripts—to paraphrase him—a damaged, imperfect draft of a *ragionamento* in a comic vein, reminiscent of *The Clouds* and other Aristophanic comedies. Ricci notes that Machiavelli had called it *Le Maschere*, "The Masks"; he editorializes, however, that it was so full of reckless accusations, of both ecclesiastics and laymen alike, that he decided not to copy it. He also adds the tantalizing aside that the people thus slandered were still alive in 1504. Posterity has no way of judging whether or not it was literary taste or political prudence in the face of the Counter Reformation's militant morality that dictated Ricci's regrettable decision not to copy it and hence to rob posterity of a potentially fascinating text. Because of the similarity in political and aesthetic views, it would be tempting to construct a theory, based however hesitantly on Ricci's evidence, about Aristophanic influences on Machiavelli. But rather than to lament what we lack, it is more to the point to examine what we have.

THE WOMAN FROM ANDROS

There are two versions of Machiavelli's translation of Terence's charming play *Andria*. According to handwriting analysts, the first version is found in a hastily prepared manuscript dating from late 1517 or early 1518. Some scholars have suggested that because Machiavelli was in such dire financial straits then, he translated the play solely to make money. The second version, contained in a more meticulously prepared manuscript, was probably completed in 1520. In this work, Machiavelli has gracefully and wittily re-created an elegant, formal comedy of manners by lacing it with pungent and fast-paced dialogue. He was especially careful to modernize and localize the deftly executed Latin comedy so that it might more readily appeal to early sixteenth-century Florentine audiences. In his translation, Machiavelli made clear which Florentine values he believed his contemporaries needed to improve.

The sparkling patina of Terence's play glows over a typical

New Comedy plot, with its conflict between an austere, ortho-
dox father who objects to his son's intended because of her un-
acceptable social status, and a son whose passion compels him
to fly in the face of filial obligation. A third typical figure is
the slave Davus—Davo in Machiavelli's translation. Through
the devices he contrives, Davus tries to earn his stripes as a *ser-*
vus callidus, a "tricky slave," a character made popular by Plautus. Yet Terence is not trying to compete with Plautus through
this character. Rather, Davus exists to elicit laughter and to
intensify the father-son conflict. Because Davus allies himself
with the son and devises strategies for him, he finds himself
exposed to the father's reprisals. All three characters act out the
clash between social duty and private desire. Another typical
element is the recognition scene, with its heavy reliance on co-
incidence—that is, *fortuna*—to resolve the conflict between
the individual, whose values are centered on romantic goals,
and the society, whose values are translated on stage by the
blocking measures concocted by the father. The recognition
scene allows the marriage of the young couple to take place according to the demands of society, its conventions and laws.
The stability and order of society as a whole are reaffirmed at
the same time as the earlier threats to social union, particu-
larized in the interests of the father and son, are harmonized.
This reconciliation is an important factor in Machiavelli's appreciation of *Andria*: He holds in the highest esteem the com-
munal spirit asserted in Terence's play. This quality is not the
focal point for the two most famous reworkings of the story:
Richard Steele's sentimental comedy *The Conscious Lovers* (1722)
and Thornton Wilder's lambent, gossamer fable *The Woman of*
Andros (1930).

Machiavelli's play omits Terence's topical prologue and opens
on a street in Athens. Simo, Panfilo's father, is engaged in a
discussion with the elderly freed slave Sosia. Through this conversation we learn that Panfilo has been frequenting the house
next door, where a woman named Criside, from the island of
Andros, has set herself up as a hetaera. Simo is worried that his

plans for Panfilo to marry Filomena, the daughter of his rich friend Cremete, may be foiled by this intimacy. Indeed, he should be worried, because Panfilo has met Glicerio, Criside's ward, fallen in love with her, and made her pregnant. Glicerio's relation to Criside is never made clear until the end of the play, but throughout the first several acts the key fact important to the plot—and the reason behind Simo's resentment of her—is that Glicerio is a foreigner without any Athenian legal status. Shortly before the play opens, Criside has died. We learn that Criside has handed Glicerio over to Panfilo, who valiantly swears to marry her and to acknowledge publicly that he is the child's father. A hint at a double plot develops with the entrance of Carino, Panfilo's friend, who is in love with Filomena and wants to marry her. Meanwhile her father, Cremete, comes to suspect that Panfilo is in love with Glicerio, and he therefore terminates the wedding agreement. Simo refuses to inform his son of this fact because he wants to discover the depth of Panfilo's feelings for Glicerio. In addition, he wants to test Panfilo; obedience to paternal commands is one of the play's important themes. According to the custom, Cremete's contractual offer of marriage contains a dowry for Filomena, and the motive of greed thus plays among the father's feelings.

Davo is aware of all of these issues and could easily lead the play into broad comedy, but his character is kept under control so that the play can depict a wider range of human emotions. Machiavelli, in turn, is mindful of Terence's original intention and the role of Davus in that play. Davo does not govern as much of the action as we might expect—Simo does that handily—but his contrivances ensure that Panfilo does not lose Glicerio. Davo deftly manipulates the events around her lying-in. As matters build to a showdown, Crito enters, on the lookout for any property of Criside's that might be lying around unclaimed. Crito's entrance signals the beginning of the sequence of events that will lead to the recognition scene. He turns out to be an old friend of Cremete, but he also knows all

about how Criside adopted Glicerio and, more importantly, who Glicerio's real father was. With the opportunity at hand, marriage between Panfilo and Glicerio is finally permissible. To complement the sense of symmetry in plot, action, and characters, Carino is also allowed to marry Filomena.

The ultimate emphasis of the play is on masculine values and interests; the father-son relationship serves, not to illustrate the contrast between right and wrong, but rather to further the education, one might even say the social "initiation," of Panfilo. The son struggles with the father; rather than defeating him, he becomes like him through his acceptance of the father's values. The play thus presents the duties and responsibilities that a young Roman man must learn—and these are the values of the society as a whole.

It is impossible to know whether Machiavelli decided on his own to translate this play or the choice was forced on him by need. If the decision was clearly his, then scholars could more easily argue that his purpose was to urge his audience to take stock of its values. We cannot be certain, and, therefore, to determine the author's goals we must look more closely at how he focuses on the narrative element and how he uses language to localize the story and thereby predispose his audience to react positively to the values the *Andria* implicitly asserts.

At several points Terence insists that his audience realize that they are in the presence of a *fabula*. The word is multivalent in Latin: it refers to talk or conversation as well as to a narrative story, tale, or fable; by extension, the term can refer to the plot of a drama, specifically, of a comedy. Terence plays on the overtones in the "stuff and nonsense" flavor of the word; he is not above self-consciously dragging in the connotation of plot to get a laugh. Davus cries out, *Quae haec est fabula?* (v. 747). Similarly, because Machiavelli can achieve an equal degree of multivalence with the Italian word *favola*, he consistently translates *fabula* literally (*Che favola è questa?*). Thus, he gets precisely the right effect. In English, the subtleties of the play on words in Latin and Italian are blunted; yet a similar

line in English—"What kind of comedy is this?"—would still elicit a laugh. Machiavelli takes a cue from Terence and elaborates a line in order to emphasize his point even more. In act 5, scene 4, Simo ironically comments *fabulam inceptat* (v. 925) just as Crito is about to launch into a narrative pivotal for the recognition scene. The line means simply "now the pack of lies is about to begin." But Machiavelli extends that brief phrase to read *egli ha ordito una favola da capo* ("he has composed a comedy from the ground up"); this slight alteration serves to intensify the self-consciousness of the art—that is, the awareness of art calling attention to itself.

In act 3, scene 5, through another addition to Terence's text, Machiavelli reminds his audience that there is a narrator behind the scenes. Panfilo has just learned from his father that Cremete will allow Filomena to marry him—information that delights the father and depresses the son. Panfilo is prepared to vent his anger on Davo, who mutters in an aside, "I'm thinking of telling him that I've come up with some clever idea" (Machiavelli's *io penso di dire di avere trovato qualche bel tratto* translates the skimpy Latin *dicam aliquid me inventurum*, "I'll tell him I'll think of something" [v. 615]). Although Davo is not an arch manipulator like the typical "tricky slave" in Plautus, he is nevertheless trying to control the action at this point in the play. He serves as a "narrator" propelling the story forward. Thus, the narrator's point of view is paramount. Machiavelli's amplification of the text gently underlines Davo's function, thereby making the audience more acutely aware of the sense of story as well as of a storyteller.

Although Machiavelli persists in translating *fabula* faithfully, he is not above manipulating language—especially by relying on Tuscan idioms—in order to capture a Florentine audience's attention. The addition of the Italian equivalent of four-letter words occurs in both the original 1517–1518 version and the one finished in 1520. His revisions of certain passages indicate hesitancy about how spicy he ought to be, but

he shows no reluctance to enliven the text scatologically. Furthermore, he is adept at finding equivalents for Terence's polished rhetoric. Aware that literary critics would be particularly attuned to this quality, because the Renaissance greatly admired Terence's rhetorical skill, Machiavelli worked hard on this facet of his translation. His ability to come up with aural puns that highlight grammatically parallel or antithetical clauses is a measure of his success as a translator. Taking his cue from Terence, Machiavelli frequently resorts to figures of speech that emphasize repetition to achieve a play on words. Polyptoton, a reiteration of words derived from the same root, but with different endings or forms; paronomasia, a reiteration of words that sound alike but differ in meaning to create a pun; and antimetabole, a reversal in the order of words in a sentence that produces a reverse in logic, are among his favorite figures. It must be admitted, however, that Machiavelli is no match for Terence in the use of such rhetorical tropes.

By far the most felicitous example of Machiavelli's use of language combines this kind of wit with his skill at particularizing and localizing the play so that it emerges from the Roman past into the Florentine present. In the second scene of the first act in the Latin original, Simo berates Davus for being a knavishly poor guide and teacher for his son. Terence thereby accentuates through a negative example his thematic concern with the paternal role. His point is that a surrogate for a father—and, by extension, a proper father—should teach the correct values to his son; thus he acts in an exemplary fashion and may, in the son, produce exemplary results. Davus plays dumb and replies, *Davos sum, non Oedipus* (v. 194). Connecting Simo with the Sphinx, whose enigmatic remarks Oedipus must decipher, would have brought a laugh from a Roman audience. Machiavelli's search for an equivalent is an interesting illustration of his witty response to the translator's perennial headache of finding the proper word. Originally he wrote *Io son Davo, non propheta vel non el frate* ("I'm Davo, not a prophet,

especially not the Frate"), and thus he took a direct jab at Fra Savonarola, whose prophetic powers had been proven to be severely limited. (Although Charles VIII of France had in fact descended on Italy and wreaked havoc, Savonarola's predictions of a Florence purified of all evil had failed to materialize.) Florentine audiences would have appreciated the irony involved. But by the time he came to write the 1520 version, Machiavelli had become more circumspect; he translates the line merely as *Io son Davo non propheta*. The audience is forced to supply any prophet it wishes, from David the prophet-king to, perhaps, Savonarola. Machiavelli consistently seeks to intensify the audience's involvement with his writing whether he writes for the stage or for the reader. Nevertheless, the line in the later version probably would not get as much of a laugh as the line in the first version might.

The theme of the paternal role that Simo obliquely reinforces in this scene is one Panfilo announces broadly three scenes later in the opening line of his first appearance on stage (I, 5). Machiavelli is prudently literal: *È questo cosa umana? È questo ofizio d'un padre?* ("Is this a humane thing? Is this a father's duty?"). He is railing against his father's highhanded decision that, like it or not, he will marry Filomena. Machiavelli painstakingly preserves Panfilo's ironic expression of the theme fundamental to Terence. In fact, he delicately accentuates it by tampering with the nature of the responsibility Panfilo accepts for Glicerio's child. Terence has his hero say merely *nam pollicitus sum suscepturum* (v. 401; "for I've promised to acknowledge the child"). Machiavelli's *perché io ho promesso d'allevarlo*, through its use of the verb *allevare*, implies a stronger commitment on Panfilo's part to raise and care for the child. Although the Greeks and Romans had an official ceremony during which the father decided whether a baby was to be brought up in the family or to be exposed, and the verb *suscipio* was frequently used in that context to signal the choice of keeping the child, the connotation of nurturing is greater in the Italian. Machiavelli's choice of words emphasizes the ritual

aspect less and stresses the substantive, human contribution that the daily care of a child necessitates.

The theme of paternity reverberates sharply for Machiavelli. He is probably not as interested as Terence in sounding the interior, psychological depths of the characters. But he is concerned to create a trenchant analysis of two profound types of accountability. Both types inhere in relationships, but one exists between father and son and moves in a downward direction, whereas the other exists between son and father and moves upward. Consequently, the "growth" Panfilo undergoes in *Andria* is not so much that of a boy becoming a man but rather that of a youth coming to terms with the responsibilities of fatherhood. What Machiavelli, given his concerns for civic affairs, sees in this interaction can be expressed in terms of an analogy of vital significance. The analogy helps to clarify some of the reasons motivating the political Machiavelli to read Roman comedy with heightened interest. Just as a father is responsible for a family, so a leader is responsible for a city. Someone with true civic responsibility must see to it that the city nurtures its future leaders while they are still "sons" so that they, in turn, will have the proper values to instill in the citizenry they will eventually lead. Machiavelli saw in the Roman *paterfamilias* an example of these principles and their acknowledgment by society. It is no wonder, then, that Machiavelli felt affinities with Roman comedy.

The conflict between the characters over their desires and responsibilities comes to a head in the third scene of the last act as Simo chides Panfilo for what Simo believes to be actions tantamount to a usurpation of the role of father without his sanction. Significantly, Cremete, also a spokesman for paternal authority, closes the scene on a conciliatory note: "Even for a major crime, a father can go easy on the punishment." By this line, Machiavelli deepens the audience's understanding of the role of authority. Compassion, when appropriate, is a value that authority must know how to demonstrate. This is the moment—obvious to the dramatist—for the recognition scene.

Machiavelli does not disappoint us: Crito appears to provide the details necessary for a full reconciliation between father and son—and son and father. Thus, the play closes on an appropriate, festive note with not only Panfilo getting Glicerio but Carino getting Filomena. The recognition scene in turn facilitates the long-awaited comedic resolution.

The ending of a Roman comedy conventionally seeks to break the stage illusion of reality and remind the audience of the essentially fictive nature of the play. To do so, one actor usually urges the others to return to the stage for a final set of speeches. Terence respects this convention; he ends the play with a simple appeal to the audience for applause, spoken by a singer-musician-actor. Machiavelli modifies the convention of the ending only slightly. He dispenses with the *cantor*, thereby throwing all the weight of the ending on Davo's final speech. Davo urges the audience to go home, confident that all will be well in the ongoing lives of the characters as they return to their separate houses. Furthermore, "everything else that's wrong will get fixed up inside too." This alteration brings to light the full impact of the comedic resolution. Moreover, it puts the brunt of the responsibility for the final reconciliation squarely on the audience's shoulders. The line "May God be with you; enjoy yourselves" is not in Terence; Machiavelli adds it to Davo's speech in order to press the audience to attend to the comedic conventions. Davo exacts a commitment from the audience to replicate the harmony achieved on stage in their own lives. Thus, the play's ending coordinates the values inherent in comedy with those Machiavelli would like to see flourishing in society.

Emphasizing values in this way suits Machiavelli's temperament. First, the twist at the end accords with his conception of values and, second, it accords with how he believes values should be instilled. Consequently, comedy in general—and *Andria* in particular—is justified. Machiavelli will go on to pursue the values comedy asserts, not merely by translating them, but by creating them. In the process he will discover

that within the constraints of farce lie values that are even more temperamentally congenial than those he has encountered in comedy.

THE MANDRAKE

Machiavelli's reputation as a playwright rests on *The Mandrake*. Evidence from manuscripts, printed books, and contemporary comments about various performances proves that the play was acclaimed during his lifetime. Yet for all that certainty, we do not know exactly when it was written. Scholars have suggested various dates for the composition of the play, from 1504, the play's fictive date, to 1520. The more moderate of these voices would place the *terminus a quo* in the period between 1512 and 1520 because of evidence in the first printed edition. Guessing more narrowly, these voices would place it in the latter part of this period because of indications in an early manuscript of the play. What is now regarded as the first printed edition, in which the play is called *Comedia di Callimaco: & di Lucretia*, has no date. Nevertheless, the frontispiece provides a lead. It shows Chiron the centaur playing on a stringed instrument; in the center of the spiraled embellishment at the top of the ornamental border surrounding this image there seems to be a clumsy representation of six balls—the device of the Medici family. Thus, this edition was probably printed some time after the Medici returned to Florence, that is, after September 1512. An allusion in the fifth quatrain of the play's prologue would also seem to indicate this period in Machiavelli's life, one he refers elsewhere to as the *post res perditas* period. None of this evidence establishes precisely when the play was written, and we must therefore look elsewhere. In addition to our presumptive evidence, we possess a codex of the works of Lorenzo the Magnificent. Buried in it, and unknown to scholars until the 1960s, is a manuscript version of *The Mandrake* copied and duly dated in 1519.

The *terminus ad quem* provided by performance history brings

us closer to this date than to the earlier ones. As with *Clizia*, in fact, information about performances is more extensive and more precise than that from the printed editions or manuscripts. The excitement stirred up by a Florentine production of *The Mandrake* caused Pope Leo X, the former Giovanni de Medici, to insist that the same scenery and actors used in Florence be transported to his court in Rome. The evidence for this command performance is not datable, but a letter to Machiavelli from a friend in Rome, dated April 26, 1520, refers to a forthcoming production of the play; it is generally agreed that this letter refers to the command performance. The evidence for subsequent performances, and thus for proof of the play's popularity, is ample, although sixteenth-century Italian standards of success differ considerably from modern-day standards. There is a diary entry indicating that two performances were given in Venice during the Lenten carnival season in February 1522. Vasari records that a performance, for which Andrea del Sarto helped paint the sets, was the high point of an evening's entertainment at a private party in Florence—probably late in 1524. If Guicciardini, Machiavelli's friend and would-be political patron, had had his way—and had both he and Machiavelli not been preoccupied with foreign affairs at the time—there might have been a production in Faenza during the carnival season of 1526. We know Machiavelli was anxious for this performance to occur, and for it to be good, because he composed a canzone on a *carpe diem* theme for nymphs and shepherds to sing, rhymed a prologue to answer some of Guicciardini's remarks about the play, and added four short canzoni to serve as intermezzos within it. Two of these songs were picked up from *Clizia*; the other two were written expressly for *The Mandrake*. Their dulcet musical line runs counter to the caustic irony with which they comment on the scene just completed. They are appropriately pungent additions to the text. One performance was given—once more in Venice—during the 1526 Lenten festivities. Thus, although no date has been established for the composition of the play, 1519 seems to be

the likely year. The record of performances indicates that the play's reputation spread widely and developed quickly throughout Renaissance Italy.

The tightly constructed plot is one facet of the play's excellence. For all its lively characterization and dazzling speech, the play is thoroughly classical in its fidelity to the pattern prescribed by Donatus in his fourth-century commentary on Terence's *Andria*. The prologue of *The Mandrake* is followed by a protasis, a statement of the situation, the necessary exposition, and the start of the action; an epitasis, in which the plot thickens; and a catastrophe, the final comedic resolution. The play opens with the young hero, a merchant named Callimaco, explaining to his servant Siro why he has recently returned to his native Florence after living in Paris for twenty years. Some of Callimaco's comrades there, in discussing the relative virtues of French and Italian women, made extravagant claims for the beauty of Lucrezia, the wife of a Florentine lawyer named Nicia Calfucci—claims that Callimaco has found to be more than justified. The balance sheet Callimaco draws up to evaluate his chances of amorous success with Lucrezia weighs, on the credit side, the stupidity of her husband, the compliant nature of Lucrezia's mother, Sostrata, and especially the couple's desire for children, against such debits as Lucrezia's reputation for virtue, her ability to rule her husband, and her remoteness from social interaction. Callimaco has cultivated a parasite, Ligurio, who in turn has wormed his way into Nicia's good graces and is urging him to take his wife for treatment of her sterility to a warm springs resort, where it would be easier for Callimaco to meet her than in Florence. The first act ends with Ligurio hatching a conspiracy: Callimaco will pretend to be a doctor in order to recommend that the couple visit a certain spa.

In the second act, Ligurio has a better idea: Callimaco will claim to be the creator of a potion, extracted from the mandrake root (*la mandragola*), that will cure Lucrezia's sterility. The only problem is that the first person to sleep with her after she has taken the draft will inevitably die within a week; there-

fore, a "sacrificial victim" must be found. Callimaco persuades
Nicia that even the king of France has resorted to this strange
expedient. Nevertheless, as Nicia quickly points out, the task
of prevailing upon Lucrezia to go along with this scheme will
be a formidable one. Ligurio proposes to overcome Lucrezia's
reluctance through the assistance of her confessor Friar Timoteo. Ligurio is confident that the friar can be persuaded to join
the conspiracy by "me, money, our villainy and theirs"—and
that Lucrezia's mother will prove willing to be the final link in
the seduction plan. These are the kinds of friends surrounding
Lucrezia, and it is not an accident that her name recalls Livy's
story of the Roman matron who committed suicide after Col-
latinus raped her, rather than live a life of shame (I, 57–59).

Sostrata opens the third act by noting in Machiavellian fashion that "the wise person chooses the lesser of two evils."
Hence, because she wants her daughter to become pregnant,
she will bring Lucrezia to the friar. Thus, she exemplifies, as
will her daughter, an aspect of Machiavelli's notion of *virtù* that
consists of readily adapting one's reactions to fit new situations.
Meanwhile, Nicia and Ligurio visit the confessor, after Ligurio
requests Nicia to play deaf, in order to keep him from spoiling
the delicate negotiations by his stupidity. Ligurio first establishes with an invented story that, given the proper bribe, the
friar can be enlisted in any cause. Once the friar is sure of
his remuneration, he never balks at any request. To Lucrezia
the friar proffers an enticingly fallacious deduction: Because
"your end is to fill a seat in Heaven and to make your husband
happy . . . there is no more sin . . . in this case than there is
in eating meat on Wednesday." Lucrezia, little convinced by all
the casuistry, gives in, imploring "God and Our Lady" to save
her from harm. Nicia declares himself to be "the happiest man
in the world," while the friar predicts, "If I am not deceived,
the doctor is going to give you a fine young son."

The fourth act reveals Callimaco striking the conventional
Petrarchan posture of the lover in the throes of antithetical
emotions. Throughout the play he has been ceding his ini-

tiative and control to Ligurio, and he was entirely absent from
the crucial third act. Ligurio now informs him of the success of
their conspiracy; all Callimaco has to do is to put up the required amount of money. Ligurio will even get the friar to pretend to be Dr. Callimaco, so that the real one, disguised, can
be "caught" and then introduced into Lucrezia's bed. From the
friar's soliloquy we learn how he has rationalized his involvement in this affair: "I can console myself with the thought that
when a thing concerns many people, many people have to take
care of it." Once Callimaco has been captured, the friar can
appear alone in the last scene to pique our imaginations about
the bedroom activities and to solicit from us a willing suspension of disbelief at the play's failure to maintain the unity of
time: "And you, dear audience, don't say that we are not observing the classical unities; you had better stick around, because nobody is going to sleep tonight, so the acts will not
be interrupted by the passage of time." (From the perspective
of literary history, this is an interesting admonition. Aristotle's
"unities" were not to become widely known in Italy until 1548,
with the commentary on the *Poetics* by Francesco Robortello.)

As our attention turns to the bedroom in the last act, the
flavor of *The Mandrake* changes. The humor in the events described thus far centers mostly on values we customarily asso-
ciate with comedy; now elements from farce take over the play's
comedic energy. Timoteo's opening soliloquy sets an arch tone
through his preoccupation with lack of sleep: "I couldn't close
my eyes all night long, I have been so eager to hear how Callimaco and the others have made out." Nicia delivers an ironically voyeuristic description of how the "captive" was prepared
and examined, before Nicia, as he puts it, "dragged him after
me into the bedroom . . . put him in bed . . . and poked my
nose into how things were coming." When Callimaco then re-
counts his own version to Ligurio, he quotes Lucrezia's speech
of submission to him: "Since your cleverness, my husband's
stupidity, my mother's silliness, and my confessor's guile have
led me to do what I would never have done by myself, I have to

judge that this comes from a divine providence that willed it so . . . I therefore take you for my lord, my master, and my guide. . . . What my husband has willed for this one night, he shall have for good and ever." The play ends with everyone invited back to Nicia's house for a meal, an invitation that sets a tone of congeniality typical for the end of a comedy. Nicia even provides Callimaco with a house key, so that he "can get back in" whenever he feels like it. Callimaco replies that he "will make use of it whenever the occasion arises."

If the choice of words is not enough to shift the tone to that of farce, then Friar Timoteo's final action must suffice, for he officially sanctions the young couple's adultery. The friar, who has been concerned exclusively with the external forms of religion, provides—if not blasphemes—the *purificatio post partum* rite of the Roman Catholic church that would typically welcome Lucrezia back into communion after childbirth.

Despite all the appearances of comedic resolution and the aura of comedic harmony that permeate the ending of *The Mandrake*, Machiavelli actually resorts to alternative literary conventions to convey his concern for society—be it Florentine or Italian. His manipulation of these conventions, rather than the political allegory that some interpreters have found in it, defines the uniqueness of this play. He realizes that the values asserted by the customary ending of a Roman comedy can be obtained through different catalysts. Before turning to the resources in Roman comedy, perhaps we should recall the ending of *Andria* for comparison. There, the standard comedic devices reinforce the broader social resolution occurring on stage in which the audience vicariously participates. Hence, at the end of the play, what Terence believes to be the stable virtues of the Roman social ethic are reaffirmed by the restoration of family harmony. The euphoria of reconciliation between father and son, culminating in two marriages—thereby linking the main plot to the subplot—also reminds the audience of the austere responsibilities any *paterfamilias* faces. Whether on the family level or the societal level, Roman comedy asserts the need for

unity within the body politic so that these duties can be discharged with all due probity.

But surely one must ask what is the nature of a body politic in which a Friar Timoteo, a Ligurio—even a Callimaco and a compromised Lucrezia—are permitted to triumph? Not only are they allowed to do so, but it would seem that the audience is expected to endorse the society that is to result offstage from the harmony generated onstage during the play. If the audience refuses to examine this fundamental issue, then Machiavelli will have failed. The moral justification behind *The Mandrake* will be vitiated unless the audience questions the ethical premises upon which the comedic resolution is based. To encourage the audience to consider these issues, Machiavelli reverts to two durable dramatic techniques. Satire and farce become the hallmarks of his success in this play.

The satiric vein of *The Mandrake* is clear; the play roots out social corruption and boldly holds it up for our scorn. It should not be surprising that there is a remarkable similarity between the objects of Machiavelli's satire and those in writings of the classical moralists, Renaissance humanists, or even eighteenth-century satirists. Laughter is the fundamental weapon in the satirist's arsenal, and, in the case of Nicia, the satiric butt is often identical with the comic butt. Our laughter at him or at any character who falls short of the ideal is not tantamount to our winking at the evil in the world of the play. On the contrary, our laughter and our ridicule jog us into realizing a significant aspect of the theatrical experience: that the character under scrutiny lacks an adequate knowledge of himself or herself and, by extension, we too may lack this self-awareness.

Machiavelli's satire makes this absence obvious in the portraits of a corrupt friar like Timoteo or even of a novitiate in bawdry like Sostrata, because both of these characters function smoothly only behind the veil of sanctity. The anticlerical satire, particularly in the scenes with Friar Timoteo and Lucrezia, is keenly felt. Ultimately, it is intellectual chicanery that galls Machiavelli. He regards the sophistry represented by the per-

version of the power of reason in Ligurio and Friar Timoteo as an affront to mankind. Callimaco, in his transports of passion, is only partially humorous; for Machiavelli's purpose, it is more important that he, too, has betrayed his rational capacities. Nicia is condemned for similar failures. Someone who is gullible enough to trust in a magic potion drawn from the root of a mandrake is irrational enough to be a danger to the community. Moreover, Nicia's pedantry represents a threat to society because he has misconstrued the proper use of education.

Despite the many recognizable types in the cast of *The Mandrake*, we are not in the presence of Ben Jonson's typical kind of comedy of humours. Because we sense that satire for satire's sake is not the sole reason why Machiavelli puts his characters on stage, we might be tempted to argue that his characters, each with a recognizable satiric valence, exist as mere accessories to the basic love plot of romantic comedy involving Callimaco and Lucrezia. But Machiavelli proceeds more subtly than that. First, he draws on the viciousness of the *alazon* or imposter figure, a character type basic to Greek and Roman comedy, so that he may form Ligurio, Friar Timoteo, and Sostrata into compliant agents in his romantic intrigue. Then, he decides to exaggerate their function as types; given their ostensible roles, their speeches gradually become more intensely at variance with how they should be acting. Machiavelli heightens this sense of disjunction between words and deeds in the soliloquies he assigns to Callimaco, Timoteo, and Nicia in the last two acts. These characters aggressively elbow their way into our consciousness; we become more aware of them not only because of what they say but also because of how frequently they say it. Although they may have started out carrying the play's satiric weight, that is not the function Machiavelli wants them to fulfill by the time they appear in the last act. Rather than merely serving the plot's romantic interest or its satiric impulse, they become the fulcrum upon which rests the play's delicate balance between comedy and farce. Their highly colored speech and even their very presence as carica-

ture vividly shift the play to one or the other of these modes. *The Mandrake* toys with our delight at watching delightful, romantic comedy—will boy get girl?—and with our mirth at watching raucous, boisterous farce. After all, for Callimaco to get Lucrezia, Nicia must be cuckolded and the two lovers must agree to establish their adulterous relationship. Is there any other mode for dealing with these subjects except farce? Thus, elements from farce are the second main dramatic technique that Machiavelli uses to urge his audience to scrutinize the nature of the social fabric formed at the end of the play.

A brief look at farce as a game may help us appreciate how Machiavelli achieves the effects of his final scene. In his chapter on farce in *The Life of the Drama*, Eric Bentley makes two points that are relevant to this discussion. First, he challenges the ideal embodied in Rudyard Kipling's couplet "Teach us Delight in simple things, / And Mirth that has no bitter springs" ("The Children's Song"). Second, with a long glance at Freud on wit and humor, he argues that aggression constitutes an essential ingredient of farce. Given what we know about Machiavelli's sense of humor and the oblique perspective from which he views most matters, we might predict that he would be moved more by "mirth" than "delight." Hence, while we might anticipate the delight of a romantic comedy during the first scene of *The Mandrake*, we should not be surprised when the mirth of farce snares our attention before the first act is completed. Swiftly and deftly, characters and themes aggressively foist themselves upon us. Their farcical boisterousness may make us laugh; their satiric vitriol may make us think—or laugh in uneasy embarrassment. Whether the evidence comes from his life or from his works, it is doubly clear that Machiavelli is poignantly aware that the "bitter springs" of mirth are unavoidable.

Living unheeded in the frustrating solitude of his country estate at Sant' Andrea, Machiavelli is prepared to be both impatient and angry with the world. Yet *The Mandrake* proves that although his mood is one of desperation, it is not one of

despair. Further, there is an escape from this maze of complicated and frequently polar sets of emotional and intellectual directions. Because Machiavelli has a desperate faith that his audience will find it, he does not give in to what we might see as warranted despair. Rather, he channels whatever aggression he may feel, in his neglected isolation, into the aggression inherent in farce. Adultery was never achieved through passivity. The audience has no alternative but to react to the surging energy it feels swirling about the stage—not only throughout the play but especially in that highly charged atmosphere of the final "reconciliation." Because Machiavelli systematically doles out farcical treats to the audience and tantalizes it with deceptions, from practical jokes to mental subterfuge, the audience quickly realizes that it must delve into the ostensible reality of each character, of each situation. Hence, Machiavelli's use of farce has prepared the audience to unmask the final deception: the last scene.

Comedy proceeds differently. Bentley notes, illustrating his point with *Tartuffe*, that comedy nurtures appearances too. Indeed, it hoards them until the climax; then, and only then, can it tell all. Comedy, therefore, seeks to postpone its striptease of understanding until the final moments of the play. For this reason, *The Mandrake* is not a good representative of the comic mode. Nothing is unveiled at the end. On the contrary, everything is dressed up in garments of reconciliation and resolution. Without Machiavelli's meticulous preparations for exposing deception through the elements of farce, the audience might well accept the ending at face value. As Bentley puts it, because farce shatters and reshatters appearances, the audience is alert. It will challenge Machiavelli's version of the happy ending. Because it has been prepared by farce, the audience is ready to accept the invitation to go home ("as for you, dear audience, don't expect us to come back out again. The service is a long one"). There, it may construct a resolution to the play that can only occur offstage, in people's minds. If and when it does so, and in this lies Machiavelli's optimism, the determina-

tion not to permit the resolution of art to become the actuality of life may be what saves Machiavelli, Florence, Italy—indeed, humanity. It is the art of farce that triumphs over the art of comedy.

CLIZIA

Clizia is the last of Machiavelli's plays, and also the least regarded by audiences and critics. As with *The Mandrake*, a manuscript helps to establish the date of composition: Quite recently a beautiful manuscript of the play was found in England. It is surmised that this was a presentation copy, perhaps arranged for by Machiavelli himself, intended as a gift for Lorenzo Ridolfi on the occasion of his betrothal to Maria di Filippo Strozzi in 1526. The information about the first performance is even more precise. During his fifties Machiavelli carried on an extended affair with an actress known to her contemporaries as Barbara Fiorentina and to history as Barbera Raffacani Salutati. It is believed that he fulfilled a promise to her by accepting an opportunity provided by a rich Florentine politician. He wanted to outdo the success of the private Florentine performance of *The Mandrake* in 1524 in order to celebrate his return to active civic life after a brief exile. Instead of mounting a second production of *The Mandrake*, Machiavelli dashed off *Clizia*. (This assumption helps to account for the difference in quality between the two plays.) The festivities for what is presumed to be the first performance, January 13, 1525, were garish and raucous in the extreme. They aroused the indignation of contemporaries, but the fame of the play "inspired everyone with the desire to see it," so that "all the leading citizens" of Florence as well as "the highest ranking members of the government then in power" came to the performance—one that, according to Vasari, "was very pleasing to everyone."

The play opens with a canzone in praise of the story's "harmony," sung by a nymph and shepherds. As it turns out, the

harmony Machiavelli builds into the comedic resolution of this play raises even more doubts about the nature of order than does the harmony that closes *The Mandrake*. The ensuing prose prologue nimbly alludes to the play's sources. The *Clizia* is inspired by—and a few speeches are actually translated from—*Casina* by Plautus, a Roman comedy frequently imitated by later sixteenth-century Italian dramatists. Plautus, in turn, had gone to Greek New Comedy for his model, to a play known now only by its title and author: *The Lot-Drawers* (*Kleroumenoi*) by Diphilus of Sinope, produced in Athens between 332 and 320 B.C. Machiavelli alludes to this fact in his prologue, noting that mankind is always the same—an idea that he repeats at the beginning of both *The Prince* and *The Discourses*. His comic premise, therefore, is that what once happened in Athens should now have occurred in Florence. The play soon establishes as its fictive date 1506, during the carnival season.

After the speaker of the prologue has introduced the main characters, the curtain rises on Cleandro revealing his love for Clizia to his friend Palamede, a figure, like Sosia in *Andria*, whose sole function is to permit Cleandro to fill us in on the background and explain how Clizia became part of the family. The unexpected barrier to his hopes of marrying Clizia is his own father, Nicomaco, who has also fallen in love with her—so desperately that he has arranged "to marry her off to someone who would be willing to share her with him afterward," namely, the family servant Pirro. Meanwhile, Sofronia has countered her husband's plan by proposing Eustachio, the steward of the family's farm. Thus, what initially is a father-son conflict soon becomes one between husband and wife, with servants as pawns. Today is to be Pirro and Clizia's wedding day; therefore, whatever means may exist to foil Nicomaco, they must be brought to bear quickly. After the first in a series of plaintive soliloquies by Cleandro, Eustachio arrives and prepares to aid the young hero.

Nicomaco appears on stage in the second act. After he tries to bolster Pirro's resolve to marry, Sofronia bustles on stage to

berate her husband. She informs us, in a soliloquy, how capricious and irresponsible her once upright husband has become since he fell in love. Her speech incidentally provides an epitome of middle-class life and values that, in its directness and economy of language, surpasses any analogue in Terence, whose views are similar: her sentiments are certainly not found in Plautus. Throughout this act Machiavelli demonstrates his control of Florentine idiom, but especially in the final scene—an exchange of insults between Pirro and Eustachio that surpasses the Plautine scene it imitates.

As the third act opens, father and son openly confront each other. Nicomaco resents the threat to his authority that Sofronia's plan represents: "I intend to be the master in my own house. . . . It is a sad house where the hen crows louder than the cock." From the perspective of the play's ending, it is clear that such petulance works not only to motivate Nicomaco but also to mobilize the play's comedic energy. During this act this energy is going to gather enough steam so that it can eventually "right" the "wrong" Nicomaco laments, yet not in the way he anticipates. The lovesick Cleandro, who is still concealing his real feelings for Clizia from his unsympathetic mother, soliloquizes at length about the pain of having a father as a rival. Nicomaco proposes in exasperation that Clizia's husband should be decided by drawing lots. Sofronia agrees to let chance end the dispute, and the act ends with some sexual punning as Nicomaco and Pirro appear to have won the day.

Act 4 proves that Nicomaco counted his chickens before he knew what plans Sofronia had hatched. Cleandro's lamentation on the fickleness of fortune has strong reminiscences of the twenty-fifth chapter of *The Prince*. He has enough presence of mind, however, to overhear the arrangements that Nicomaco and Pirro are making: Nicomaco has leased a house from his neighbor Damone; Pirro will leave the marriage bed under the cover of darkness, and let the eager Nicomaco take over. In response to Pirro's concern lest Nicomaco be unable to get his "weapon cocked," the old man lets us know that he "will take

a dose of a potion called satyrion . . . that would rejuvenate a man of ninety, let alone a man of seventy like me." Through a servant named Doria, a forerunner of Dorine in Molière's *Tartuffe*, we learn that Sofronia will counterattack, with the help of another servant, Siro: "They took our servant's clothes off him, dressed Clizia in them, and put Siro in Clizia's; and they are going to have Siro take Clizia's place as the bride." Doria keeps Nicomaco at a safe distance by saying that the maddened Clizia is brandishing a knife and threatening to kill him and Pirro rather than marry the latter. Because of the homosexual twist to the bed trick that Sofronia plays, she feels free to set things up as if they were all going to turn out according to Nicomaco's plans. The act closes as Nicomaco breathlessly exits to take his place in the marriage bed, and as the lines from the canzone ring, if not in his ears, at least in ours: "How gentle is deception . . . [It] soothes the blissful dupes we have befriended."

As in the final act of *The Mandrake*, the crucial nocturnal activities occur offstage. They are artfully recounted by one of the principals, Nicomaco himself. In this play, the audience is meant less to approve of the account than to laugh at it; the laughter is at Nicomaco's expense, for he is in tears throughout his burlesque tale of chagrin. Damone finally offers sensible, if unwelcome, advice: "Place yourself completely in Sofronia's hands, and tell her that from now on you will do whatever she says about both Clizia and yourself." Nicomaco agrees to relinquish all his authority to Sofronia, "as long as nobody knows about this business." She, in turn, will happily take over Clizia's affairs. There remains only the question of whether or not Cleandro may marry her. Because Clizia's birth is still clouded in mystery, both parents agree that Cleandro cannot be paired off with her just yet. After Sofronia tells Cleandro about this distressing decision, he speaks his last soliloquy, in which he frets about his fortune. At that timely point, Clizia's long-lost father, the Neapolitan nobleman Ramondo, appears. Touched at the honor and respect shown his daughter, he read-

ily agrees to the match with Cleandro. Confirming her control of the situation, Sofronia shoos everyone offstage, then turns to us: "And you, dear audience, can go back home, because we shall not leave the house again until we have arranged this new wedding. And this time it will be man and wife, not man and man, like Nicomaco's!" As we ready ourselves to obey her, we hear in the closing song an enigmatic remark about there being, beneath "the comic leaven," other truths too numerous to delve into right now: "So, kind audience, we pray / You reap the fruit you merit from our play."

Phrasing the issue in these terms puts the audience on its guard. Shall we rise to the challenge or not? What, in fact, is the nature of the challenge? The meaning attached to the "fruit" and to what we may "merit" is not immediately apparent. What is apparent is the dramatist's ultimate frustration at never being able to be sure of controlling the audience's responses. It shines through this transparent invitation to do our own delving, even though we may unearth the wrong material—or even reject the invitation.

Despite the early stage history of the play, most audiences have refused to enter into any kind of give and take with *Clizia*. Perhaps Machiavelli knew that it was less polished than *The Mandrake* and tried to compensate for his lack of success by passing the responsibility for interpreting the play onto the audience during the last few minutes. Or the issue here may be that Machiavelli has adhered less strictly not only to the values inherent in Roman comedy, which he followed in *Andria*, but also to those inherent in Aristophanic comedy, which he alluded to in *The Mandrake*.

The defects of *Clizia* result from an imperfect blend of literary traditions. The interpretive signals sent the audience are clear, but the elements borrowed from the two comic traditions send confusing messages. Thus, they interfere with the reception of those very signals Machiavelli entreats his audience to heed. If Nicomaco is the butt of the humor, with all the apparatus of farce working throughout the play to make us

ridicule him, then it is hard at the end suddenly to accept him—as Sofronia somehow is able to do—with all the understanding and tolerance that is part of the comedic resolution.

Machiavelli's decision to imitate *Casina* implies a realization that the risks he faces in building toward his ending are analogous to those faced by Plautus. Plautus, too, was trying to maintain an equal emphasis on farce and ethics. Because Plautus frequently uses the former to reinforce the latter, these two aspects of comedy are not mutually exclusive. On the one hand, Plautus is fully aware of the farcical elements in *Kleroumenoi*; he refers to them obliquely in his prologue. Long before he began writing comedies, the Roman taste for farce had been developed and richly exploited by the native Atellan farces, with their lively use of slapstick, obscenity, and typical comic butts. Consequently, Plautus could be selective about what farcical elements he borrowed from the Greek tradition—whether from Aristophanic or New Comedy. On the other hand, *Casina* examines the nature of authority in a Roman family; by extension, it also explores the theme of social authority. To present this theme successfully, Plautus needs to be in complete control of all constituent elements. The example of Aristophanes, and perhaps even Diphilus, proves to him that thematic material like homosexuality, transvestism, the generation gap, the wedding ceremony turned upside down, and the conflict between husband and wife can be handled in a farce. But a balance must be maintained so that the farcical treatment does not outweigh the ethical and social values the play is designed to articulate. That the resolution to the authority dilemma should be provided by the maternal figure is, for a Roman audience, highly ironic. But that a resolution exists, whatever its source, is vital to the final effects—be they social, comic, or both—that Plautus seeks to create.

Because so much haste was involved in the first performance of *Clizia*, we cannot be absolutely certain that Machiavelli actually considered the problems inherent in working with *Casina* in this light. He may merely have had to produce a text

quickly. If we give him the benefit of the doubt, we can see that Plautus's play might prompt in a would-be imitator the kinds of reflections we have been considering. Furthermore, for Machiavelli to create a play consistent with the ethical and social principles that animate *Andria* and *The Mandrake*, he must tread carefully the line between farce and ethics. The artistic problems he faces in adapting *Casina* parallel those Plautus must have confronted when adapting *Kleroumenoi*. Machiavelli seeks to maintain the necessary balance between farce and ethics by radically altering the characterization of Nicomaco and Sofronia. The changes are designed to govern our interpretation of the ending. Nicomaco's analogue in Plautus is the catalyst for the humor, less because of what he does than because of what other people are forced to do in response to him. Machiavelli retains this catalytic function, but he makes Nicomaco less obsessive. Nicomaco's passion, furthermore, is heterosexual in nature, not, as in the Plautine prototype, homosexual. What is important for Machiavelli is that as an old man in love, Nicomaco is ridiculous. Because he is enslaved by his passion, he is unable to rule; his household is divided, not united. This much can also be said for Plautus's character. But Machiavelli permits Nicomaco an aura of dignity—albeit tarnished—that Plautus never grants his protagonist. This air of nobility becomes a crucial factor in engaging our sympathy— or grudging affection—for him at the end of the play.

It is significant that Sofronia attributes this dignity to him during her first soliloquy (II, 4). Nothing like this speech exists in Plautus, whose *matrona* figure is considerably more shrewish, and hence less sympathetic. Because Sofronia's final act of reconciliation with Nicomaco arises from her own *virtù*, it is essential that she appear—not only at the end but also throughout the play—as someone with compassion and understanding. Thus we are meant to interpret her forgiveness of Nicomaco as the result of a genuine concern for him, as well as a change in his character, wrought through her corrective *virtù*, that is as potentially great for him as it is for us. For

many people in the audience, this realization and acceptance will be impossible, because the signs leading to it are blurred. Sofronia clearly articulates Machiavelli's moral, ethical, and social meaning, but the means by which the audience is led to accept this position are not handled deftly.

Perhaps Machiavelli is less successful with this play because his intent at the end of *Clizia* runs counter to his aim at the end of *The Mandrake*. The motivating force behind the earlier play is farce. As we have seen, the play permits, even encourages, a feeling of vicarious irresponsibility while the audience savors the delicious ironies of the finale. If the audience reflects on the reasons for its laughter, it may gradually become aware that something is amiss—for example, that each person on stage participating in the comic resolution is, basically, a comic butt. At this point, and only at this point, can the audience resolve this situation through its own active and clear thinking.

Machiavelli chooses a potentially less risky solution to the question of comic harmony at the end of *Clizia*. Again, farce plays a strong role in making people laugh, but the ending appears to be much more like the customary one of comedy. Sofronia takes over. Into the comedic resolution she thrusts concepts related to *sophrosyne*, the Greek word for temperance and moderation from which her name is derived. *Sophron* means literally 'soundness of mind' and refers to a mastery and a self-control that typify her character and her actions throughout the play. Like Penelope and Andromache, two Greek heroines with this virtue, Sofronia is a good, even exemplary, wife because she is fully aware of herself. Thus, she acts in accordance with her nature and position in life. Because she is self-fulfilling, both in name and in action, she is the model citizen. Hence, she is assigned the speech that reminds Nicomaco of all he is not. It is perfectly right, from an ethical and social point of view, that she does so. But from the point of view of the audience's enjoyment, the laughter as the curtain falls carries with it bemusement. Machiavelli hopes that the laughter at the end of *Clizia* will be tempered by an awareness of the complexities

of the everyday world. The laughter he seeks to elicit is rooted in a tolerance of perplexity, indeed a tolerance of its inevitable impingement upon moments of enjoyment. It is a laughter that accepts the loss of the luxury of a simple response—even to something funny. Machiavelli trusts that the humor of *Clizia* will prepare the audience for the final resolution because he sees this humor rooted in practical experience and therefore immediately pertinent to alert members of his audience. What Machiavelli wants is the laughter of comedy, not of farce.

Unfortunately, here Machiavelli inspires the laughter of farce. All the lasciviousness and voyeuristic pleasure of *The Mandrake* exist in *Clizia*. In fact, because of their shocking quality, they might even be said to be more intensely present in *Clizia*. Once these emotions have been elicited from the audience, it is not easy to submerge and repress them. Through an emphasis on Sofronia's soundness, Machiavelli tries to transmute them into a more acceptable representation, but he fails. While the play titillates us on one level, on another level it seeks our active support for Sofronia's triumphant assertion of control. Furthermore, we must respond on both levels at once; we cannot contemplate these issues at our leisure and in our privacy. Our public participation—in the theater for all to see—in the approval of reunion reinforces our civic sense. But it destroys our appreciation and enjoyment of the story. Taking his cue from Sofronia's assertion of control, Machiavelli proceeds to control us. In *Clizia* Machiavelli sacrifices art for society. In *The Mandrake* he celebrates both art and society—to the detriment of neither.

CONCLUSION

A letter written to Francesco Vettori on January 31, 1515, before Machiavelli began to write plays, according to the view of most scholars, is a significant document for any assessment of what issues were on his mind and of how he presented them. During the final twelve years of his life, neither his attitude

toward the major philosophical issues nor his style for convey-
ing these attitudes remained exactly the same. Nevertheless,
this letter suggests why dramatic writing might be a mode of
expression more conducive to his needs at this time in his life:

> Whoever was to see our letters, my honorable friend, and saw the
> differences in them, might be very astonished, because it would seem
> to him that sometimes we are serious men, totally dedicated to great
> matters, and that no thought could leave our heads that had not pro-
> bity and grandeur in it. But then, turning the page, it would seem to
> him that those same men were frivolous, fickle, and lewd—dedi-
> cated to vanity. This way of carrying on, although it may seem repre-
> hensible to some, seems laudable to me, because we are imitating
> nature, which is variable; whoever imitates nature cannot be blamed.
> Although we customarily have this variety in separate letters, this
> time I want to practice it in a single one, as you will see if you read
> the other side. Now, clear your throat.

In the realm of politics, it has generally been assumed that
Machiavelli's views are best explained as a blending of a knowledge of the classics with experience from the modern world; or,
as he puts it in the dedicatory letter to *The Prince*, "I have
found nothing among my resources that I cherish or value as
much as my knowledge of the deeds of great men, learned
from wide experience of recent events and a constant reading of
classical authors." The ancients were a vital stimulus to him.
Thus, as *The Discourses* would seem to substantiate, he belongs
squarely among the Renaissance thinkers and writers who believed that the cultural rebirth they were experiencing resulted
directly from a revival of antiquity. Yet what he says to Vettori
seems to imply a different priority: Anyone imitating nature
cannot be blamed, for nature is, in a word, "variable." Because
nature is also profuse, it is not odd to have the ridiculous (sex,
lust, and vanity) juxtaposed with the sublime ("great matters"
of "probity and grandeur," that is, the rarefied realm of politics). On the contrary, such contrast is quite normal because
variety and multiplicity define nature; by imitating her, Vet-

tori and Machiavelli are only doing what is right and natural. But if Machiavelli agrees to this kind of imitation in his private correspondence, is there sanction for such a process in his political and historical writings?

To ask this question is to wonder at the same time why Machiavelli turns to comedy between 1515 and 1527, a period when he is also producing some of his major theoretical and analytical treatises. An answer may be found through an analogy with the visual art of his time. The art of this period underwent a "change," according to Giorgio Vasari in his *Lives of the Painters, Sculptors, and Architects*. With some fifty years of perspective, Vasari looks back on the achievements of Michelangelo; he is convinced that Michelangelo is the supreme ruler among artists because he surpasses not only his quattrocento predecessors, "who had almost conquered Nature," but also the artists from antiquity, "who had unquestionably conquered Nature." The accuracy of this judgment is unimportant, but its assumptions are crucial. In Vasari's estimation Michelangelo's incontrovertible artistic prominence marks a significant development in the history of art. Michelangelo is unique because he welds the previously bifurcated sources of artistic inspiration: nature and antiquity. At the very time Michelangelo is in the process of achieving these results, Machiavelli is at work on his comedies.

What Vasari maintains occurs in art suggests the following analogy with Machiavelli. His serious political and historical works reflect his profound commitment to the values of antiquity. But as he acknowledges to Vettori, he is conscious both intellectually and emotionally of harboring another quality, namely, a profound personal commitment to the values of nature. Thus his plays constitute a singular avowal: his willingness and ability to create an art that can combine, and hence contain, a commitment both to nature and to antiquity. Given the terms of this analogy, then, the surface of his plays represents his commitment to nature, while his reliance on the

comic tradition—certainly on Plautus and Terence, and possibly Aristophanes—demonstrates his commitment to antiquity. His turning to a form that could subsume nature and antiquity tacitly implies that such works as *The Prince*, *The Discourses*, *The Art of War*, and *The Florentine Histories* could not. Thus his letter to Vettori justifies the practice of comedy as a means to achieve this goal. Let us go and do likewise.

James B. Atkinson

TRANSLATOR'S NOTE ON
THE WOMAN FROM ANDROS

Translating a translation poses special problems for the scholar. To whom is the second translator primarily responsible—to the original author or to the first translator? If a reader has selected a collection of Machiavelli's plays, then the obvious assumption is that Machiavelli is the focus of the reader's interest. Hence, it would follow that if there is a translation in that collection, the translator's first responsibility ought to be to rendering Machiavelli's text faithfully and readably. But in the case of *Andria*, the fact that the original play is by Terence shifts the balance of responsibility. Historians of the theater generally attribute more literary distinction to Terence than to Machiavelli, and thus would give greater attention to the older author's work. One solution to the problem of translating Machiavelli's version of *Andria* might be to supplement the translation with a scrupulous accounting of all Machiavelli's conscious, and even unconscious, textual alterations. If a discussion of the decisions that went into the translating process complemented the translation, then the reader would be in a better position to evaluate the issues of responsibility and loyalty. This would not, however, be a welcome solution on at least two counts. First, it would produce a lopsided annotation section and thus work against the editors' aim of delighting and entertaining the

reader. Relishing Machiavelli's joy at updating a Roman play for a Florentine audience is hard to do in an edition that deflects the interest in the text to cumbersome, detailed annotations about choices of diction. Second, in accordance with the Horatian formula, learning from someone else's remarks about whether or not a given alteration is conscious or unconscious, or even good or bad, is not necessarily a simple matter. Instructive objectivity may cede to personal interpretation.

My particular conflict arises when I consider that what I am producing in *Andria* is more a text for reading than a script for acting. This fact sharply contrasts my translation of *Andria* with the translations of *The Mandrake* and *Clizia* included in this volume. Although my preference would be to produce a sprightly script, that goal is better served by translating Terence's Latin directly—not through an intermediary. Consequently, I conceive of my primary obligation as providing the reader with a readable text of Machiavelli's translation. Further, since what he wrote was intended to be an acting version, my secondary aim is to produce a translation that comes as close as possible to something that would sound right on stage. This objective must perforce fall short of realization. The fact that Terence wrote first is an influence that produces anxiety for both Machiavelli and me; neither one of us can avoid showing him some respect. Machiavelli's version of *Andria* permits the reader to judge how he relieves himself of his anxiety and renders his homage. Acknowledging that my first obligation is to capture the flavor of Machiavelli, not Terence, is my means of freeing myself from Terence's haunting presence. But it must be obvious that I am not completely absolved of responsibility to Terence. At any rate, knowing his play better is an advantage, even for readers to whom Machiavelli is paramount. Machiavelli's text is merely a screen through which Terence's play may be glimpsed, but not studied. When we read Machiavelli's *Andria*, what we actually are scrutinizing is a fledgling playwright in the process of cutting his dramatic teeth. The sense of completeness that such observation allows us is the

raison d'être for including *Andria* in this edition in the first place.

In my translation of his translation, I believe that I can best fulfill my responsibility to Machiavelli as novice by allowing him enough latitude so that his choices of specific words and idioms may range freely. To satisfy my obligation to the reader, I have effected a compromise based on the solution suggested above. Thus, some of the more salient examples of Machiavelli's lively use of idiom and of his divergence from strict word-for-word translation are discussed either in the Introduction or in the Notes. The guidelines I followed during the actual translation include some additions to and deletions from his text. The additions are mainly in the form of attempts to retain the bite of Machiavelli's idioms. Terence's Latin is elegant, but not without a sense of spirited immediacy. Because no translator can render all the idioms of the original—be it in Latin or Italian—I have tried to keep a rough count of Machiavelli's idioms and to stay within that range in my translation. Hence, an idiom may exist in English where its Italian equivalent is not idiomatic. The reverse is also true. Furthermore, Machiavelli's Italian generally uses more slang than does Terence's Latin; at the risk of producing a translation of Machiavelli subject to the vagaries of slang, I've tried to find some slang equivalent. What has been removed are some of the doublets common in Renaissance prose, some of the causative words ("so that," "thus") frequent in Italian, and some unnecessary expletives (usually "oh").

One final point concerns the text itself. The basic text is the one established by Mario Martelli, "La Versione Machiavelliana dell'*Andria*," published first in *Rinascimento*, second series, 8 (1968):203–274, and subsequently reprinted in his *Niccolò Machiavelli: Tutte le Opere* (Florence: Sansoni, 1971), pp. 847–867. I follow the modifications in Martelli's text made by Guido Davico Bonino in his edition of Machiavelli, *Teatro* (Turin: Einaudi, 1979), pp. 5–61.

James B. Atkinson

TRANSLATOR'S NOTE ON
THE MANDRAKE AND *CLIZIA*

This translation of Machiavelli's *Mandrake* was written in the winter of 1976, when Professor Errol G. Hill of the Dartmouth College Drama Department asked me to serve as "dramaturg" for a production of the comedy, under his direction, by the Dartmouth Players. When I had examined the translations then available, I determined to try my hand at one of my own, hoping to endow it with the qualities that I had enjoyed in teaching the play to undergraduate students of Italian literature, and that the existing versions did not seem to me to express in full measure. I leave to the judgment of the reader whether I succeeded in attaining them myself. Those qualities that I especially sought to achieve included: a close adherence to the Italian text, as embodied specifically in the recent edition of the comedies edited by Guido Davico Bonino, taking account of the important modern textual revisions suggested by Roberto Ridolfi and Mario Martelli; an approximation, in modern English, of the lively vernacular in which Machiavelli's characters speak, avoiding both anachronism and archaism as far as possible (although the former stricture was occasionally broken, for the sake of an irresistible joke or an untranslatable one); fidelity to the spirit of the original, particularly with ref-

erence to humor, to linguistic characterization of the individual characters, to wordplay, and to speech rhythms, in both monologues and exchanges; "speakability" of the lines and exchanges for the actors playing the work; and finally, in the case of verse forms (the opening chorus; the prologue, and the four songs intercalated between the acts), fidelity to the original rhyme schemes and meters, particularly so as to suit the latter to the music that the madrigalist Philippe Verdelot wrote for the 1526 Faenza production commissioned by Francesco Guicciardini, and that Professor Hill included in his lively and imaginative staging.

Whether or not it was thanks in some part to the realization of my own aims in this translation, the success of the Dartmouth Players production—which received excellent notices, played to appreciative audiences, and was revived for a second run during the following summer's repertory season—encouraged me to undertake a similar effort with Machiavelli's *Clizia*. This play, although it is far less well known than *The Mandrake*, struck me as having many of its excellent points, and as deserving wider currency among theater people and lovers of good comedy. I will be happy, indeed, if the present volume contributes to that end.

David Sices

ANDRIA
THE WOMAN FROM ANDROS

TRANSLATED BY

JAMES B. ATKINSON

CHARACTERS

SIMO: an elderly gentleman, father of Panfilo
SOSIA: Simo's elderly freed slave
DAVO: Simo's slave
PANFILO: a young man, Simo's son
CARINO: a young man in love with Cremete's daughter
CREMETE: an elderly gentleman, a friend of Simo
BIRRIA: a slave of Carino
MISIDE: a serving maid to Glicerio
DROMO: Simo's slave; a bodyguard and whip handler
LESBIA: a midwife from the island of Lesbos
CRITO: an elderly gentleman from the island Andros; a friend of Cremete

ATTO PRIMO
SCENA PRIMA

Simo, Sosia.

SIMO: Portate voi altri drento queste cose, spacciatevi! Tu, Sosia, fatti in qua: io ti voglio parlare un poco.

SOSIA: Fai conto d'avermi parlato; tu vuoi che queste cose s'acconcino bene.

SIMO: Io voglio pure altro.

SOSIA: Che cosa so io fare, dove io ti possa servire meglio che in questo?

SIMO: Io non ho bisogno di cotesto per fare quello che io voglio, ma di quella fede e di quello segreto che io ho conosciuto sempre essere in te.

SOSIA: Io aspetto d'intendere quello che tu vuoi.

SIMO: Tu sai, poi che io ti comperai da piccolo, con quanta clemenza e giustizia io mi sono governato teco, e di stiavo io ti feci liberto, perché tu mi servivi liberalmente, e per questo io ti pagai di quella moneta che io potetti.

SOSIA: Io me ne ricordo.

SIMO: Io non mi pento di quello che io ho fatto.

SOSIA: Io ho gran piacere, se io ho fatto e fo cosa che ti piaccia: e ringrazioti che tu mostri di conoscerlo: ma questo bene mi è molesto, che mi pare che, ricordandolo ora, sia quasi un rimproverarlo ad uno che non se ne ricordi. Che non di' tu in una parola quello che tu vuoi?

SIMO: Così farò. E innanzi ad ogni cosa io t'ho a dire questo: queste nozze non sono, come tu credi, da dovero.

SOSIA: Perché le fingi adunque?

SIMO: Tu intenderai da principio ogni cosa, e a questo modo conoscerai la vita del mio figliuolo, la deliberazione

ACT ONE
SCENE ONE

Simo, Sosia.

SIMO: You, there, take these things inside; get a
move on. You, Sosia, wait here; I want to speak to you
a moment.

SOSIA: I know what you have to say—you want me to
do a good job with this stuff.

SIMO: I want something else, too.

SOSIA: What else do I know how to do? How can I
serve you better than I'm doing?

SIMO: I don't need anything like what you know how
to do for you to do what I have in mind. I need the fidelity and discretion that I have always known you had.

SOSIA: I'm eager to hear what it is you want.

SIMO: Ever since I bought you as a little boy, you know
I've treated you with leniency and justice. I got you freed
from slavery because you served me generously; so I paid
you with what coin I could.

SOSIA: I remember that.

SIMO: I don't regret it.

SOSIA: It gives me great pleasure if I've done, or if I
continue to do, anything that pleases you, and I'm grateful
that you acknowledge it. But one thing certainly troubles
me: it seems to me that by bringing it up now it's almost
as if you were reproaching me for overlooking it. Why
don't you tell me straight out what you want?

SIMO: I shall. First of all, I have this to say: this marriage is not, as you suppose it is, for real.

SOSIA: Then why pretend it is?

SIMO: I'll tell you the whole story from the beginning,
so then you'll know my son's way of life, my decision, and

mia e quello che io voglia che tu facci in questa cosa. Poi
che 'l mio figliuolo uscì di fanciullo e che ei cominciò a
vivere più a suo modo (imperò che chi arebbe prima potuto
conoscere la natura sua, mentre che la età, la paura, il
maestro, lo tenevono a freno?). . .

SOSIA: Così è.

SIMO: . . . di quelle cose che fanno la maggior parte
de' giovanetti, di volgere l'animo a qualche piacere, come
è nutrire cavagli, cani, andare allo Studio, non ne seguiva
più una che un'altra, ma in tutte si travagliava mediocre-
mente; di che io mi rallegravo.

SOSIA: Tu avevi ragione, perché io penso nella vita
nostra essere utilissimo non seguire alcuna cosa troppo.

SIMO: Così era la sua vita: sopportare facilmente ognuno; andare ai versi a coloro con chi ei conversava; non
essere traverso; non si stimare più che gli altri; e chi fa
così, facilmente sanza invidia, si acquista laude e amici.

SOSIA: Ei si governava saviamente, perché in questo
tempo chi sa ire a' versi, acquista amici, e chi dice il vero,
acquista odio.

SIMO: In questo mezzo una certa femmina, giovane e
bella, si partì da Andro per la povertà de' parenti, e venne
ad abitare in questa vicinanza.

SOSIA: Io temo che questa Andria non ci arrechi
qualche male.

SIMO: Costei in prima viveva onestamente, guadagnan-
dosi il vivere col filare e con il tessere; ma poi che venne
ora uno, ora un altro amante promettendole danari, come
egli è naturale di tutte le persone sdrucciolare facilmente
da la fatica a l'ozio, l'accettò lo invito; e a sorte, come
accade, coloro che allora l'amavano, cominciorno a menarvi
il mio figliuolo; onde io continuamente dicevo meco mede-

what I want you to do about it all. Ever since my son grew out of his adolescence and began living his own life (for, while he was still being held in check by his youth, his timidity, and his tutor, who could have known what his nature was then). . .

SOSIA: Indeed.

SIMO: . . . he has behaved as do the majority of young men and has been turning over in his mind some diversion or other—like raising horses or dogs, or attending the university. Yet, he didn't pursue any one of these to the exclusion of the rest; in all things he strove for moderation. I was pleased.

SOSIA: You were right; in our lives I think pursuing "nothing in excess" is extremely useful.[1]

SIMO: That describes his way of life: he was tolerant of everybody, humored whomever he talked with, never crossed people, or never considered himself better than others. Anyone behaving like that easily wins praise and friends without arousing envy.

SOSIA: He handled himself wisely; these days humoring people wins friends, telling the truth wins hatred.[2]

SIMO: In the meantime, a certain woman, young and beautiful, left Andros, because of her relatives' poverty and neglect, and came to this neighborhood to settle down.

SOSIA: I'm afraid this person from Andros is the cause of some kind of trouble.

SIMO: At first she lived modestly, earning her livelihood by spinning and weaving; but later, first one lover and then another arrived promising her money. Because it is natural for anyone to slide easily from hard work into leisure, she accepted the offers. It turned out that by chance some of the men who were in love with her at that time began taking my son to her house. Consequently, I kept

simo:—Veramente egli è stato sviato! egli ha auto la sua!—
E qualche volta, la mattina, io appostavo i loro servi, che
andavano e venivono, e domandavogli:—Odi qua, per tua
fè: a chi toccò iarsera Criside?—perché così si chiamava
quella donna.

sosia: Io intendo.

simo: Dicevano:—Fedria, o Clinia, o Nicerato—
perché questi tre l'amavano insieme.—Dimmi: Panfilo
che fece?—Che? Pagò la parte sua e cenò.—Di che io mi
rallegravo. Dipoi, ancora l'altro dì io ne domandavo, e non
trovavo cosa alcuna che apartenessi a Panfilo. E veramente
mi pareva un grande e rado esemplo di continenza, perché
chi usa con uomini di simil natura, e non si corrompe,
puoi pensare ch'egli ha fermo il suo modo del vivere. Questo
mi piaceva, e ciascuno per una bocca mi diceva ogni
bene, e lodava la mia buona fortuna, che avevo così fatto
figliuolo. Che bisognano più parole? Cremete, spinto da
questa buona fama, venne spontaneamente a trovarmi, e
offerì dare al mio figliuolo una unica sua figliuola con una
gran dote. Piacquemi, promissigli, e questo dì è deputato
a le nozze.

sosia: Che manca, dunque, perché le non sono vere?

simo: Tu lo intenderai. Quasi in quegli dì che queste
cose seguirono, questa Criside vicina si morì.

sosia: Ho! io l'ho caro! Tu m'hai tutto ralegrato: io
avevo paura di questa Criside.

simo: Quivi il mio figliuolo, insieme con quegli che
amavono Criside, era ad ogni ora: ordinava il mortoro,
malinconoso, e qualche volta lacrimava. Questo anche mi
piacque; e dicevo così meco medesimo:—Costui per un
poco di consuetudine sopporta nella morte di costei tanto
dispiacere: che farebb' egli, se l'avessi amata? che farebb'

saying to myself, "Surely he's being led astray, he's fallen for her." Sometimes I used to waylay those men's slaves in the morning, during their comings and goings, and demand of them, "Listen here, boy, whose turn was it with Criside last night?" (That was the woman's name.)

SOSIA: I see.

SIMO: Fedria, they would say, or Clinia, or Nicerato—because all three were her lovers simultaneously. "Tell me, what about Panfilo?" "Who, oh he paid his share and ate dinner." That made me happy. Later, on some other day, I asked about it again and still I found out nothing about Panfilo. He really seemed to be a great and rare model of moderation. Because, if anyone consorts with men of such natures and is not corrupted by them, you can bet that he has decided upon his way of life. That pleased me; everybody to a man told me all kinds of good things. They praised my good fortune in having a son endowed with such character. To make a long story short, Cremete, spurred on by this good reputation, came of his own volition to seek me out and to offer his only daughter in marriage to my son—and with a substantial dowry. I liked the match and betrothed him; today is the day we agreed upon for the ceremony.

SOSIA: What's stopping it, then, from taking place?

SIMO: You shall hear. Several days after these arrangements were made, this neighbor of ours, Criside, died.

SOSIA: Oh, I'm glad about that, you're cheering me up; this Criside was making me nervous.

SIMO: Then my son, together with Criside's lovers, was constantly over there making the funeral arrangements; he was melancholy and sometimes he wept. This behavior also pleased me: I said to myself, "If so brief an acquaintance with her produces such great sadness in the

egli, s'io morissi io?—E pensavo queste cose essere indizio d'una umana e mansueta natura. Perché ti ritardo io con molte parole? Io andai ancora io per suo amore a questo mortoro, non pensando per ancora alcun male.

SOSIA: Che domin sarà questo?

SIMO: Tu il saprai. Il corpo fu portato fuora, noi gli andamo dietro: in questo mezzo, tra le donne ch'erano quivi presenti, io veggo una fanciulletta d'una forma . . .

SOSIA: Buona, per avventura!

SIMO: . . . e d'un volto, o Sosia, in modo modesto e in modo grazioso, che non si potrebbe dire più, la quale mi pareva che si dolessi più che l'altre. E perché la era più che l'altre di forma bella e liberale, m'accostai a quelle che le erano intorno, e domandai chi la fussi. Risposono essere sorella di Criside. Di fatto, io mi senti' raviluppare l'animo: ha! ha! questo è quello! di qui nascevono quelle lacrime! questa è quella misericordia!

SOSIA: Quanto temo io, dove tu abbi a capitare!

SIMO: Intanto il mortoro andava oltre: noi lo seguitavamo e arrivamo al sepolcro; la fu messa nel fuoco; piangevasi. In questo tanto, questa sua sorella che io dico, si accostò alle fiamme assai imprudentemente e con periculo. Allotta Panfilo, quasi morto, manifestando il celato e dissimulato amore, corse e abbracciò nel mezzo questa fanciulla, dicendo:—O Glicerio mia, che fai tu? perché vai tu a morire?—Allora quella, acciò che si potessi vedere il loro consueto amore, se gli lasciò ire adosso, piangendo molto familiarmente.

SOSIA: Che di' tu?

boy at her death, then what would he do had he loved her, and what would he do were I to die?" I thought such sympathies were indicative of a humane and gentle nature. Why am I holding you up by talking so long? Even I went to the funeral for his sake—still oblivious of anything being wrong.

SOSIA: What does this mean?

SIMO: You'll see. The body was carried outside and we followed. In the meantime, I noticed, among the women who were present, a young girl whose figure was. . .

SOSIA: Shapely, by any chance?

SIMO: . . . and whose expression, Sosia, was so modest and so gracious—nothing could be more so. It seemed to me that her grief was greater than anyone else's. Because she was more beautiful and distinguished than the other women, I approached those who were attending her and asked who she was. They replied that she was Criside's sister. Immediately I felt my spirit tighten up: aha, that's it! That's why his tears,[3] that's why his compassion!

SOSIA: I dread what this is leading up to!

SIMO: Meanwhile, the funeral procession was moving ahead. We were following it and arrived at the grave. They hoisted her onto the burning funeral pyre and the weeping began. While this was going on, the sister, whom I mentioned, carelessly got dangerously close to the flames. At that moment Panfilo, frightened to death—revealing his concealed, his disguised love—ran up and caught the girl around the waist, crying, "Oh my Glicerio, what are you doing, why are you trying to kill yourself?" Then, you could see that they had become comfortable with one another's love; the woman fell into his arms crying hard, the way close friends might.

SOSIA: What do you mean?

SIMO: Io mi diparti' di quivi adirato e male contento; né mi pareva assai giusta cagione di dirgli villania, perché ei direbbe:—Padre mio, che ho io fatto? che ho io meritato? o dove ho peccato? Io ho proibito che una non si getti nel fuoco e la ho conservata: la cagione è onesta!

SOSIA: Tu pensi bene, perché, se tu di' villania a chi ha conservata la vita ad uno, che farai tu a chi gli facessi danno e male?

SIMO: L'altro dì poi venne a me Cremete gridando avere udito una cosa molto trista, che Panfilo aveva tolto per moglie questa forestiera; io dicevo che non era vero; quello affermava ch'egl'era vero. In summa io mi parti' da lui al tutto alieno da il darci la sua figliuola.

SOSIA: Allora non riprehendesti tu il tuo figliuolo?

SIMO: Né ancora questa cagione è assai potente a riprehenderlo.

SOSIA: Perché? dimmelo!

SIMO: Tu medesimo, o padre, hai posto fine a queste cose: e' si appressa il tempo che io arò a vivere a modo d'altri; lasciami in questo mezzo vivere a mio modo!

SOSIA: Quale luogo ci è rimaso adunque per riprenderlo?

SIMO: Se per amor di costei ei non volessi menare donna, questa è la prima colpa che debbe essere corretta. E ora io attendo che, mediante queste falze nozze, nasca una vera cagione di riprehenderlo, quando ei neghi di menarla. E parte quel ribaldo di Davo consumerà, s'egli ha fatto disegno alcuno, ora che gl'inganni nuocono poco: il quale so che si sforza con le mani e co' piè fare ogni male, più per fare iniuria a me, che per giovare al mio figliuolo.

SIMO: I left angry and very much disturbed. Yet, it seemed as if I had no real reason to give him a hard time, because he would say, "But father, what have I done? Why do I deserve that? Where have I gone wrong? I stopped that woman from throwing herself in the fire and I've saved her life. It was for a good cause!"[4]

SOSIA: You're right, for if you insult someone who has saved a life, what will you say to someone who causes harm or pain?

SIMO: The next day Cremete comes bawling at me that he has heard some horrible thing—that Panfilo had married this foreign woman. I said it wasn't true and he insisted that it was. In short, when I parted from him, he was absolutely opposed to the offer of his daughter in marriage.

SOSIA: Didn't you upbraid your son then?

SIMO: Even this wasn't compelling enough reason.

SOSIA: Why, explain that to me!

SIMO: "You yourself, father, have set a limit on this sort of thing. The time is coming when I shall have to adjust my life to the ways of other people; in the meantime, let me live it my own way."

SOSIA: What basis is there left, then, for taking him to task?

SIMO: If out of love for this woman he shouldn't want to marry Cremete's daughter, then this is the first fault that ought to be corrected. Now, by means of this phony wedding, I'm expecting that a real reason for criticizing him will arise—if he refuses to marry her. Meanwhile, if that rascal Davo has any of his schemes planned, let him carry them out now when his tricks will do little harm. I know that he will do his darnedest[5] to cause trouble—more to hurt me than to help my son.

SOSIA: Per che cagione?

SIMO: Domandine tu? Egli è uomo di cattiva mente e di cattivo animo, il quale veramente, se io me n'avveggo. . . Ma che bisognano tante parole? Facciamo di trovare in Panfilo quel ch'io desidero, che per lui non manchi. Resterà Cremete, il quale dipoi arò a placare, e spero farlo: ora l'ufizio tuo è simulare bene queste nozze e sbigottire Davo e osservare quel che faccia il mio figliuolo e quali consigli sieno i loro.

SOSIA: E' basta; io arò cure ad ogni cosa. Andiamone ora drento.

SIMO: Va' innanzi; io ne verrò.

SCENA SECONDA

Simo, Davo.

SIMO: Sanza dubbio il mio figliuolo non vorrà moglie, in modo ho sentito temere Davo, poi ch'egli intese di queste nozze. . . Ma egli esce fuora.

DAVO: Io mi maravigliavo bene che la cosa procedessi così, e sempre ho dubitato del fine che avessi avere questa umanità del mio patrone; il quale, poi ch'egli intese che Cremete non voleva dare moglie al suo figliuolo, non ha detto ad alcuno una parola e non ha mostro d'averlo per male.

SIMO: Ei lo mosterrà ora, e, come io penso, non sanza tuo gran danno.

DAVO: Egli ha voluto che noi, credendoci questo, ci stessimo con una falsa allegrezza, sperando, sendo da noi rimossa la paura, di poterci come negligenti giugnere al sonno, e che noi non avessimo spazio a disturbare queste nozze. Guarda che astuzia!

SOSIA: Why?

SIMO: You can ask? He's a man with an evil mind and an evil heart, really; if I find out that he . . . But why talk so much about it? Let's try to find in Panfilo what I'm counting on, unless it's missing because of Davo. That leaves Cremete: in the long run, I'll have to calm him down; I hope I can do it. For the moment, your job is to fake this wedding perfectly, to make Davo become discouraged, and to keep an eye on my son's doings and on what he and Davo are plotting.

SOSIA: Fine, I'll take care of everything. Let's go inside now.[6]

SIMO: Go ahead. I'll be right there.

SCENE TWO

Simo, Davo.

SIMO: (It's obvious that my son doesn't want to get married. I noticed how Davo started when he heard about the wedding. But, here he comes.)

DAVO: (I certainly am amazed that things are going along the way they are. I've always suspected what the end result of my master's humankindness would be. Ever since he learned that Cremete didn't want to provide a wife for his son, he hasn't said a word to any of us or seemed to be a bit upset.)

SIMO: (But he will now, and not without causing a great deal of trouble for you, I think.)

DAVO: (This is what he wanted: for us to be trusting and thus to be led on by a false sense of security; once all our fears were laid to rest, he hoped to catch us napping so that we'd have no opportunity to thwart this wedding. Watch out for such cunning!)

SIMO: Che dice questo manigoldo?

DAVO: Egli è il padrone, e non lo avevo veduto.

SIMO: O Davo!

DAVO: O! Hu! Che cosa è?

SIMO: Vieni a me!

DAVO: Che vuole questo zugo?

SIMO: Che di' tu?

DAVO: Per che cagione?

SIMO: Domandine tu? Dicesi egli che 'l mio figliuolo vagheggia?

DAVO: Il popolo non ha altro pensiero che cotesto.

SIMO: Tiègli tu il sacco o no?

DAVO: Che! Io cotesto?

SIMO: Ma domandare ora di queste cose non sta bene ad uno buono padre, perché m'importa poco quello ch'egli ha fatto innanzi a questo tempo. E io, mentre che 'l tempo lo pativa, ne sono stato contento, ch'egli abbi sfogato l'animo suo. Ora, per lo avvenire, si richiede altra vita e altri costumi: però io voglio, e, se lecito è, io ti priego, o Davo, che ei ritorni qualche volta nella via.

DAVO: Io non so che cosa si sia questa.

SIMO: Se tu ne domandi, io tel dirò: tutti coloro che sono innamorati hanno per male che sia dato loro moglie.

DAVO: Così dicono.

SIMO: Allora, se alcuno piglia a quella cosa per suo maestro uno tristo, rivolge il più delle volte l'animo infermo alla parte più cattiva.

DAVO: Per mia fè, io non ti intendo.

SIMO: No, he?

DAVO: Io son Davo, non profeta.

SIMO: (What's the scoundrel saying?)

DAVO: (The master; I didn't see him!)

SIMO: Davo!

DAVO: Yes, what is it?

SIMO: Come here!

DAVO: (What's the prick want?) [7]

SIMO: What did you say?

DAVO: About what?

SIMO: What about? Aren't people saying that my son is in love?

DAVO: People don't have anything *else* to think about.

SIMO: Are you in cahoots with him?

DAVO: Would I do a thing like that?

SIMO: For me to probe into this business now is not the right thing for a good father to do; what he did up until now is of little interest to me. So long as circumstances permitted, I was happy for him to have free reign for his inclinations. From this moment on, a different way of life and a different character are required. Therefore, I insist and, if I may be allowed, I beg you, Davo, that he come back into line now.

DAVO: I don't know what this is all about.

SIMO: As long as you're asking about it, I'll tell you: every man who has a mistress is distressed at being given a wife.

DAVO: So they say.

SIMO: Then, if he chooses a rogue to be his guide in such matters, more often than not, his addled brain gets redirected on a more harmful course.

DAVO: Honestly, I don't get you.

SIMO: Oh, no?

DAVO: I'm Davo, not David. [8]

SIMO: Quelle cose, adunque, che mi restono a dirti, tu vuoi che io te le dica a lettere di speziali?

DAVO: Veramente sì.

SIMO: Se io sento che tu ordini oggi alcuno inganno in queste nozze, perché le non si faccino, o che tu voglia mostrare in questa cosa quanto tu sia astuto, io ti manderò carico a morte di mazzate a zappare tutto dì in uno campo: con questi patti, che, se io te ne cavo, che io abbia a zappare per te! Ha' mi tu inteso o non ancora?

DAVO: Anzi ti ho inteso appunto, in modo hai parlato la cose aperta e sanza alcuna circunlocuzione.

SIMO: Io sono per sopportarti ogni altro inganno più facilmente che questo.

DAVO: Dammi, io ti priego, buone parole.

SIMO: Tu mi uccelli? Tu non mi inganni di nulla; ma io ti dico che tu non facci cosa alcuna inconsideratamente, e che tu non dica anche, poi:—E' non mi fu predetto!— Abbiti cura.

SCENA TERZA

Davo solo.

DAVO: Veramente, Davo, qui non bisogna essere pigro né da poco, secondo che mi pare avere ora inteso per il parlare di questo vecchio circa le nozze: le quali, se con astuzia non ci si provede, ruineranno me o il padrone; né so bene che mi fare, se io aiuto Panfilo o se io ubbidisco al vecchio. Se io abbandono quello, io temo della sua vita; se io lo aiuto, io temo le minaccie di costui: ed è difficile ingannarlo, perché sa ogni cosa circa il suo amore e me

SIMO: So, whatever I have left to say to you, you want me to spell it out?[9]

DAVO: Right.

SIMO: If I hear of you devising any of your tricks today so that this wedding doesn't come off, or if you want to show off how clever you are about this, I'll have you whipped within an inch of your life and packed off to dig ditches with the understanding that if ever I let you out of there, I'll be the one who digs ditches in your stead. Have I made myself understood? Not yet?

DAVO: Oh, yes, I've understood you perfectly; you've spoken clearly, without any roundabout phrases.

SIMO: I'm prepared to put up with deceit more readily in any situation but this one.

DAVO: I beg you, give me your word on that.

SIMO: Are you mocking me? You're not taking me in, not for a moment; but I'm telling you now, don't do anything rash and, later on, never say, "But nobody warned me!" Watch your step!

SCENE THREE

Davo alone.

DAVO: Well, Davo, I understood what the old man was saying just now about the wedding; this is no time to be short on energy or wit. If plans aren't formulated cleverly, then it will mean the end of me or the master. I'm not sure what to do—whether I should help Panfilo or whether I should obey the old man. If I desert Panfilo, I fear for his life. If I help him, I'm afraid of Simo's threats. It's hard to deceive Simo because he knows everything about this love affair and he keeps his eye on me so that

osserva perché io non ci facci alcuno inganno. S'egli se ne
avvede, io sono morto; e, se gli verrà bene, e' troverrà una
cagione per la quale, a torto o a ragione, mi manderà a
zappare. A questi mali questo ancora mi si agiugne, che
questa Andria, o amica o moglie che la si sia, è gravida
di Panfilo; ed è cosa maravigliosa udire la loro audacia; e
hanno preso partito, da pazzi o da innamorati, di nutrire
ciò che ne nascerà, e fingono intra loro un certo inganno,
che costei è cittadina ateniese, e come fu già un certo vecchio mercatante che ruppe apresso a l'isola d'Andro e quivi
morì; dipoi il padre di Criside si prese costei ributtata dal
mare, piccola e sanza padre. Favole! E a me, per mia fè,
non pare verisimile: ma a loro piace questo trovato. Ma
ecco Miside ch'esce di casa; io me ne voglio andare in mercato, acciò che il padre non lo giunga sopra questa cosa
improvisto.

SCENA QUARTA

Miside ancilla.

MISIDE: Io ti ho intesa, Archile: tu vuoi che ti sia menata Lesbia. Veramente ella è una donna pazza e obliàca e
non è sufficiente a levare il fanciullo d'una che non abbi
mai partorito; nondimeno io la merrò. Ponete mente la
importunità di questa vecchia! solo perché le si inobliacano
insieme. O Idio! io ti priego che voi diate facultà a costei
di partorire, e a quella vecchia di fare errore altrove e non
in questa. Ma perché veggo io Panfilo mezzo morto? Io
non so quel che sia; io lo aspetterò per sapere donde nasca
ch'egli è così turbato.

I can't pull off any tricks. If he finds me out, I'm a dead
man. If he chooses to, he'll find a pretext, right or wrong,
for packing me off to dig ditches. To boot, as if these
weren't problems enough, Panfilo has gotten this woman
from Andros—wife, mistress, or whatever—pregnant. It's
amazing to hear their outlandish talk: like lunatics or
lovers, they've decided to raise the child themselves, whatever it may be. Between them they are fabricating some
tall tale about how Glicerio is an Athenian citizen: "Once
upon a time there was an old trader who was shipwrecked
and died near the island of Andros." At that point Criside's
father took in the merchant's little fatherless girl who had
been washed up on shore. Bull! It certainly doesn't seem
to me to be a very likely story, but they are delighted with
their contrivance. Oops, there's Miside coming out of the
woman's house. I'd better get out of here and go to market
so that Panfilo's father won't take him by surprise with
this news.

SCENE FOUR

Miside alone

MISIDE: I heard you, Archile; you want me to bring
Lesbia to you. Lesbia really is a crazy drunk; she isn't fit
to act as a midwife for someone who has never been in
labor—nevertheless, I'll bring her. (Look at that old bag's
pestering, just because they get drunk together. Oh, God,
grant Glicerio the power to have an easy delivery and grant
that bag the power to make her mistakes elsewhere—not
here. But why do I see Panfilo looking like something the
cat dragged in? I don't know what's the matter; I'll wait
and find out why he's upset.)

SCENA QUINTA

Panfilo, Miside.

PANFILO: È questo cosa umana? È questo ofizio d'un padre?

MISIDE: Che cosa è questa?

PANFILO: Per la fede di Dio e degli huomini, questa che è, se la non è iniuria? Egli ha deliberato da se stesso di darmi oggi moglie: non era egli necessario che io lo sapessi innanzi? Non era egli di bisogno che me lo avessi comunicato prima?

MISIDE: Misera a me! che parole odo io?

PANFILO: Cremete, il quale aveva denegato di darmi la sua figliuola, perché s'è egli mutato? Perché vede mutato me? Con quanta ostinatione s'affatica costui per svegliermi da Glicerio! Per la fede di Dio, se questo avviene, io morrò in ogni modo. È egli uomo alcuno che sia tanto sgraziato e infelice quanto io? È egli possibile che io per alcuna via non possa fuggire il parentado di Cremete in tanti modi schernito e vilipeso? E non mi giova cosa alcuna! Ecco che io sono rifiutato e poi ricerco; il che non può nascere da altro, se non che nutriscono qualche mostro, il quale perché non possono gittare adosso ad altri, si volgono a me.

MISIDE: Questo parlare mi fa per la paura morire.

PANFILO: Che dirò io ora di mio padre? Ha! doveva egli fare tanta gran cosa con tanta negligenzia che, passandomi egli ora presso in mercato, mi disse:—Tu hai oggi a menar moglie: aparèchiati, vanne a casa.—E proprio parve che e' mi dicessi:—Tira via, vanne ratto, e impìccati!—Io rimasi stupefatto. Pensi tu che io potessi rispondere una parola o fare qualche scusa almeno inetta o falsa? Io ammutolai. Ché, se io l'avessi saputo prima . . . che arei

SCENE FIVE

Panfilo, Miside.

PANFILO: Is this a humane thing? Is this a father's duty?

MISIDE: (What's this?)

PANFILO: For the love of God and man, if this isn't outrageous! He's decided all by himself that I was to be married today. Shouldn't he have gotten in touch with me about it first?

MISIDE: (Oh dear me, what do I hear?)

PANFILO: Why did Cremete, who had refused to marry his daughter to me, change his mind? Because he realizes that I have changed mine? How hard he works to tear me away from Glicerio! For the love of God, if this happens, I'll absolutely die! Was there ever a man as wretched, as miserable as I am? Is there any possibility for me to escape being a part of Cremete's family—despised and vilified, and in so many different ways? Nothing does me any good. First, I'm turned down, then I'm sought out. There can be only one reason for this: they're harboring some beast they can't dump on anybody else, so they want me.

MISIDE: (This kind of talk scares me to death.)

PANFILO: What shall I say about my father? Ha! Should he have treated such an important matter so off-handedly? Just now in the marketplace he walked by me and said, "Today you are to be married; hurry on home, now, and get ready." He might as well have said, "Run along quickly and hang yourself!" I was stunned. Do you think I could utter a single word or find some excuse, however crude or false? I was speechless. If I had known about it in advance, what would I have done? If somebody

fatto? Se alcuno me ne domandassi, arei fatto qualche cosa
per non fare questo. Ma ora che debbo io fare? Tanti pensieri m'impediscono e traggono l'animo mio in diverse
parti: l'amore, la misericordia, il pensare a queste nozze, la
reverenza di mio padre, il quale umanamente mi ha infino
a qui conceduto che io viva a mio modo . . . Ho io ora a
contrappormegli? Heimè! che io sono incerto di quello
abbi a fare!

MISIDE: Miser'a me! che io non so dove questa incer-
titudine abbi a condurre costui! Ma ora è necessariissimo o
che io riconcilii costui con quella o che io parli di lei qualche cosa che lo punga: e mentre che l'animo è dubio, si
dura poca fatica a farlo inclinare da questa o da quella
parte.

PANFILO: Chi parla qui? Dio ti salvi, Miside!

MISIDE: Dio ti salvi, Panfilo!

PANFILO: Che si fa?

MISIDE: Domandine tu? La muore di dolore; e per
questo è oggi misera, che la sa come in questo dì sono
ordinate le nozze; e però teme che tu non la abbandoni.

PANFILO: Heimè! sono io per fare cotesto? Sopporterò
io che la sia ingannata per mio conto? che mi ha confidato
l'animo e la vita sua? la quale io prenderei volentieri per
mia donna? Sopporterò io che la sua buona educazione,
costretta de la povertà, si rimuti? Non lo farò mai.

MISIDE: Io non ne dubiterei, s'egli stessi solo a te; ma
io temo che tu non possa resistere alla forza che ti farà tuo
padre.

PANFILO: Stimimi tu però sì da poco, sì ingrato, sì
inumano, sì fiero, che la consuetudine, lo amore, la ver-

were to ask me, I should have done *some*thing so as not
to be doing this. But now what should I do? So many
thoughts are holding me back and tugging my heart in
opposite directions: love, sympathy, worry about the wedding, respect for my father, who—up until now—has
been so civilized about allowing me to live in my own way.
Must I now oppose him? Oh, what on earth am I going
to do!

MISIDE: (Oh, dear, I don't know where that "on earth"
might take him. But it's absolutely necessary either that
I reconcile him to her or that I say something about her
that will sting him. As long as he's in a state of doubt, the
slightest effort is enough to make him lean one way or the
other.)

PANFILO: Who's that talking there? Greetings,
Miside.

MISIDE: Hello, Panfilo.

PANFILO: How is she doing?

MISIDE: You can ask? She's laboring in pain; for that
reason she's miserable today because she knows it's the day
that's been set for the wedding and so she's afraid that you
may abandon her.

PANFILO: What! Am I the kind of person who would
do that? Would I let her be deceived on my account after
she has trusted me with her heart and life, when I would
gladly marry her? Would I let her, with her excellent
upbringing, be forced by her poverty to be turned topsy-
turvy again? No, never!

MISIDE: If everything were up to you alone, I shouldn't
worry about it; but I'm afraid you won't be able to resist
the pressure your father will bring to bear.

PANFILO: Do you imagine, then, that I'm so worth-
less, so ungrateful, so brutish, so barbaric that intimacy,

gogna non mi commuova e non mi amunisca ad osservarle
la fede?

MISIDE: Io so questo solo, che la merita che tu ti ricordi di lei.

PANFILO: Che io me ne ricordi? O Miside, Miside,
ancora mi sono scritte nello animo le parole che Criside
mi disse di Glicerio! Ella era quasi che morta, che la mi
chiamò; io me le accostai; voi ve ne andasti, e noi rima-
nemo soli. Ella cominciò a dire:—O Panfilo mio, tu vedi
la bellezza e la età di costei; nè ti è nascoso quanto queste
dua cose sieno contrarie e alla onestà e a conservare le cose
sua. Pertanto io ti priego per questa mano destra, per la
tua buona natura e per la tua fede e per la solitudine in
la quale rimane costei, che tu non la scacci da te e non
l'abandoni. Se io t'ho amato come fratello; se costei ti ha
stimato sempre sopra tutte le cose; se la ti ha obedito in
ogni cosa; io ti do a costei marito, amico, tutore, padre;
tutti questi nostri beni io commetto in te e a la tua fede
gli raccomando.—E allora mi messe intro le mani lei,
e di sùbito morì: io la presi e manterrolla.

MISIDE: Io lo credo certamente.

PANFILO: Ma tu perché ti parti da lei?

MISIDE: Io vo a chiamare la levatrice.

PANFILO: Va' ratta . . . Odi una parola: guarda di non
ragionare di nozze, ché al male tu non agiugnessi questo.

MISIDE: Io ti ho inteso.

love, or honor would not move—nay enjoin—me to keep
my word?

MISIDE: I know only this: she deserves to be remembered by you.

PANFILO: *Remembered!* Oh Miside, Miside, the words
Criside said to me about Glicerio are still written on my
heart. She was almost dead when she called for me; you all
went out and only we stayed. She began, "Oh my Panfilo,
see the girl's beauty and youth; you are not unaware of how
much these two qualities are incompatible with the need
to protect her honor and her property. Consequently, I
implore you by your right hand, your good nature, your
honor, and by the loneliness in which she remains, do not
dismiss her or abandon her. As I have always loved you like
a brother, as she has always valued you more than anything
else, and as she has submitted to you in all matters, so I
give you to her as husband, friend, guardian, father.[10] All
our property I bestow on you and commit to your trust."
She then joined our hands, and at that moment died. I
took Glicerio and I shall keep her.

MISIDE: I certainly believe it.

PANFILO: But why are you leaving her?

MISIDE: I'm going to call the midwife.

PANFILO: Hurry! . . . But listen, take care not to
mention the wedding so that you don't add that to her
suffering.

MISIDE: I understand what you mean.

ATTO SECONDO
SCENA PRIMA

Carino, Birria, Panfilo.

CARINO: Che di' tu, Birria? maritasi oggi colei a Panfilo?

BIRRIA: Così è.

CARINO: Che ne sai tu?

BIRRIA: Davo, poco fa, me lo ha detto in mercato.

CARINO: O misero a me! Come l'animo è stato, innanzi a questo tempo, implicato nella speranza e nel timore, così, poi che mi è mancata la speranza, stracco ne' pensieri, è diventato stupido.

BIRRIA: Io ti priego, o Carino, quando e' non si può quello che tu vuoi, che tu voglia quello che tu puoi.

CARINO: Io non voglio altro che Filomena.

BIRRIA: Ha! quanto sarebbe meglio dare opera che questo amore ti si rimovessi da lo animo, che parlare cose per le quali ti si raccenda più la voglia.

CARINO: Facilmente, quando uno è sano, consiglia bene chi è infermo: se tu fussi nel grado mio, tu la intenderesti altrimenti.

BIRRIA: Fa' come ti pare.

CARINO: Ma io veggo Panfilo; io voglio provare ogni cosa prima che io muoia.

BIRRIA: Che vuole fare costui?

CARINO: Io lo pregherrò, io lo suplicherò, io gli narrerò il mio amore: io credo che io impetrerrò ch'egli starà qualche dì a fare le nozze; in questo mezzo spero che qualche cosa fia.

BIRRIA: Cotesto qualche cosa è nonnulla.

CARINO: Che ne pare egli a te, Birria? Vo io a trovarlo?

ACT TWO
SCENE ONE

Carino, Birria, Panfilo.

CARINO: What's that you're saying, Birria? Filomena is to marry Panfilo today?

BIRRIA: That's right.

CARINO: How do you know?

BIRRIA: Davo told me a little while ago in the market.

CARINO: Oh, that's awful! Until now I've been so mixed up that my heart's been torn between hope and fear: now that hope's been taken away, my mind's worn out and numb.

BIRRIA: Oh Carino, I beg you, if you can't have what you want, want what you can have.

CARINO: I don't want anything but Filomena.

BIRRIA: Ha. You'd be better off devoting your energy to getting this passion out of your system rather than saying things that stir up your desire even more.

CARINO: When one is healthy, it's easy to give good advice to a sick man; if you were in my shoes, you would think differently.

BIRRIA: Do as you like.

CARINO: But I see Panfilo; I want to try everything before I give up.

BIRRIA: (What's he going to do?)

CARINO: I'll beg him, I'll implore him, I'll tell him the story of my love for her. I think I can get him to delay the wedding for a few days. In the meantime, something will turn up—I hope.

BIRRIA: ("Something," nothing, more likely!)

CARINO: What do you think, Birria? Shall I go and meet him?

BIRRIA: Perché no? Se tu non impetri alcuna cosa, che almeno pensi avere uno che sia parato a farlo becco, se la mena.

CARINO: Tira via in mala ora con questa tua sospizione, scelerato!

PANFILO: Io veggo Carino. Dio ti salvi!

CARINO: O Panfilo, Dio ti aiuti! Io vengo a te domandando salute, aiuto e consiglio.

PANFILO: Per mia fè, che io non ho né prudenza da consigliarti né facultà da aiutarti. Ma che vuoi tu?

CARINO: Tu meni oggi donna?

PANFILO: E' lo dicono.

CARINO: Panfilo, se tu fai questo, e' sarà l'ultimo dì che tu mi vedrai.

PANFILO: Perché cotesto?

CARINO: Heimè! che io mi vergogno a dirlo. De! digliene tu, io te ne priego, Birria.

BIRRIA: Io gliene dirò.

PANFILO: Che cosa è?

BIRRIA: Costui ama la tua sposa.

PANFILO: Costui non è della opinione mia. Ma dimmi: hai tu auto a fare con lei altro, Carino?

CARINO: Ha! Panfilo, niente.

PANFILO: Quanto l'arei io caro!

CARINO: Io ti priego, la prima cosa, per l'amicizia e amore nostro, che tu non la meni.

PANFILO: Io ne farò ogni cosa.

CARINO: Ma se questo non si può e se queste nozze ti sono a cuore . . .

PANFILO: A cuore?

CARINO: . . . almeno indugia qualche dì, tanto che io ne vada in qualche luogo per non le vedere.

PANFILO: Ascoltami un poco: io non credo, Carino,

BIRRIA: Why not? If you don't get something, at least he'll know that there's someone ready to make him a cuckold if he marries her.

CARINO: Go to hell with your suspicions, you scoundrel!

PANFILO: There's Carino. Good morning.

CARINO: Oh, Panfilo, God be with you; I'm here to ask you for salvation, assistance, and advice.

PANFILO: Heavens, I've neither the wisdom to advise you nor the power to assist you. What do you want?

CARINO: Are you getting married today?

PANFILO: So I'm told.

CARINO: Panfilo, if you do, you'll never see me again.

PANFILO: Why is that?

CARINO: Oh me, oh my; I'm ashamed to tell you. Birria, you tell him about it—I beg you.

BIRRIA: I'll tell him.

PANFILO: What is it?

BIRRIA: This man is in love with your bride-to-be.

PANFILO: *I* don't share his opinion of her. But tell me, Carino, have you had anything else to do with her?

CARINO: Oh, Panfilo—nothing!

PANFILO: Oh how I wish I you had!

CARINO: For the sake of our friendship and our love, I beg you—above all else—not to marry her.

PANFILO: I'll do everything I can not to.

CARINO: But if that's impossible or if this wedding is dear to your heart . . .

PANFILO: Dear to my heart?

CARINO: At least postpone it for a couple of days so that I can go off somewhere and not have to see it.

PANFILO: Listen to me a minute, Carino, I don't think

che sia ofizio d'uno uomo da bene volere essere ringraziato d'una cosa che altri non meriti: io desidero più di fuggire queste nozze che tu di farle.

CARINO: Tu m'hai risucitato.

PANFILO: Ora, se tu e qui Birria potete alcuna cosa, fatela, fingete, trovate, concludete, acciò che la ti sia data; e io farò ogni opera perché la mi sia tolta.

CARINO: E' mi basta.

PANFILO: Io veggo appunto Davo, nel consiglio del quale io mi confido.

CARINO: E anche tu, per mia fè, non mi rechi mai innanzi cose, se non quelle che non bisogna saperle. Vatti con Dio in mala ora!

BIRRIA: Molto volentieri.

SCENA SECONDA

Davo, Carino, Panfilo.

DAVO: O Idio, che buone novelle porto io! Ma dove troverrò io Panfilo per liberarlo da quella paura nella quale ora si truova e riempiergli l'animo d'alegrezza?

CARINO: Egli è allegro, né so perché.

PANFILO: Niente è; ei non sa ancora il mio male.

DAVO: Che animo credo io che sia il suo, s'egli ha udito a avere a menar moglie?

CARINO: Odi tu quello che dice?

DAVO: Di fatto mi correrebbe dietro tutto fuora di sè. Ma dove ne cercherò io o dove andrò?

it's right for a gentleman to get thanks for something he doesn't deserve. I long to get out of this marriage more than you long to get into it.

CARINO: You've saved my life.

PANFILO: Now, if you or Birria here can do something, do it; think something up, invent it, arrange it so that Filomena can marry you and I'll do everything I can to prevent her marrying me.

CARINO: That's enough for me.

PANFILO: I see Davo coming—just at the right moment; I rely on his advice.

CARINO: As for you, by God, you've never given me any advice, unless it was something I didn't need to know. Get the hell out of here.

BIRRIA: Very happily.

SCENE TWO

Davo, Carino, Panfilo.

DAVO: (Lord, what good news I have! But where can I find Panfilo so that I can take away the anxiety he's in now and fill his heart with joy?)

CARINO: He's pleased, but I don't know what it's about.

PANFILO: It's nothing; he doesn't yet know about my bad news.

DAVO: (If he's heard that he's about to be married, I can imagine what his state of mind is like.)

CARINO: Do you hear what he's saying?

DAVO: (In fact, he's at his wit's end—probably hunting all over for me. Where shall I look for him, where shall I go?)

CARINO: Che non parli?

DAVO: Io so dove io voglio ire.

PANFILO: Davo, se' tu qui? Fèrmati!

DAVO: Chi è che mi chiama? O Panfilo, io ti cercavo! o Carino! voi sete apunto insieme: io vi volevo tutti a dua.

PANFILO: O Davo, io sono morto!

DAVO: Che? De! stammi più tosto ad udire.

PANFILO: Io sono spacciato.

DAVO: Io so di quello che tu hai paura.

CARINO: La mia vita, per mia fè, è in dubio.

DAVO: E anche tu so quello vuoi.

PANFILO: Io ho a menar moglie.

DAVO: Io me lo so.

PANFILO: Oggi.

DAVO: Tu mi togli la testa; perché io so che tu hai paura di averla a menare, e tu ch'e' non la meni.

CARINO: Tu sai la cosa.

PANFILO: Cotesto è proprio.

DAVO: E in questo non è alcun periculo: guardami in viso.

PANFILO: Io ti priego che, il più presto puoi, mi liberi da questa paura.

DAVO: Ecco che io ti libero: Cremete non te la vuole dare.

PANFILO: Che ne sai tu?

DAVO: Sòllo. Tuo padre, poco fa, mi prese e mi disse che ti voleva dare donna oggi, e molte altre cose che non è ora tempo a dirle. Di fatto, io corsi in mercato per dirtelo, e, non ti trovando quivi, me n'andai in uno luogo alto e

CARINO: Why not speak to him?

DAVO: (I've got my feet on the ground.)

PANFILO: Davo, is that you? Stop!

DAVO: Who's calling me? Oh, Panfilo, I've been looking for you. Oh Carino, you're together, as it happens. I
wanted you both.

PANFILO: Davo, it's all over for me.

DAVO: What? Ah! Hear what I have to say.

PANFILO: I'm done for.

DAVO: I know what you're afraid of.

CARINO: Upon my honor, my life's in danger.

DAVO: And I even know what's eating you.

PANFILO: I've got to get married.

DAVO: I know.

PANFILO: Today.

DAVO: Don't bore me with such chatter—I know that
you are afraid you will have to marry Filomena and you are
afraid you won't.

CARINO: You know it.

PANFILO: That's it exactly.

DAVO: There's no danger of that "exactly." Look me in
the eye!

PANFILO: I beg you, take a load off my mind as fast as
you can.

DAVO: Consider it done: Cremete doesn't want you to
marry his daughter.

PANFILO: How do you know?

DAVO: I know. A little while ago your father nabbed
me and told me that he wanted you to get married today—and lots of other things that I don't have time to go
into now. I raced right off to the market to tell you. Not
finding you there, I went to a high spot and looked all
around, but I didn't see you. But it so happened that I saw

guardai atorno; né ti vidi. Ma a caso trovai Birria di costui; domanda'lo di te, risposemi non ti avere veduto: il che mi fu molesto, e pensai quello che fare dovevo. In questo mezzo, ritornandomi io a casa, mi nacque della cosa in sè qualche sospizione, perché io vidi comperate poche cose, ed esso stare maninconoso; e sùbito dissi fra me:—Queste nozze non mi riscontrono.

PANFILO: A che fine di' tu cotesto?

DAVO: Io me n'andai sùbito a casa Cremete, e trovai davanti a l'uscio una solitudine grande, di che io mi rallegrai.

CARINO: Tu di' bene.

PANFILO: Sèguita.

DAVO: Io mi fermai quivi, e non vidi mai entrare né uscire persona; io entrai drento, riguardai: quivi non era alcuno aparato né alcuno tumulto.

PANFILO: Cotesto è uno gran segno.

DAVO: Queste cose non riscontrono con le nozze.

PANFILO: Non pare a me.

DAVO: Di' tu che non ti pare? La cosa è certa. Oltre a di questo, io trovai uno servo di Cremete, che aveva comperato certe erbe e uno grosso di pesciolini per la cena del vecchio.

CARINO: Io sono oggi contento, mediante l'opera tua.

DAVO: Io non dico già così io.

CARINO: Perché? Non è egli certo che non gliene vuol dare?

DAVO: Uccellaccio! Come se fussi necessario, non la dando a costui, che la dia a te! E' bisogna che tu ti affatichi, che tu vadia a pregare gl'amici del vecchio e che tu non ti stia.

this guy's slave, Birria. I asked him about you, but he said he hadn't seen you. That bothered me, so I thought about what I ought to do next. In the meantime, I was on my way back to the house when something about the way things were struck me as being suspicious. I noticed that no one had purchased very many things and that the master was gloomy. Suddenly I said to myself, "This marriage business doesn't check out."

PANFILO: What are you driving at?

DAVO: I went straight to Cremete's house. There wasn't a soul around the front door, which made me happy.

CARINO: You're right.

PANFILO: Go on.

DAVO: I hung around a while: I saw no one enter or leave. I went inside and looked around—not a single decoration or any noise.

PANFILO: That's an important sign.

DAVO: All these things don't jibe with a wedding.

PANFILO: Doesn't seem so to me.

DAVO: "Doesn't *seem* so" to you? It's for sure. Furthermore, I ran across a servant of Cremete's who had purchased some vegetables and a penny's worth of small fish for the old man's dinner.

CARINO: Thanks to your efforts, today I'm a happy man.

DAVO: I shouldn't say that just yet.

CARINO: Why? Isn't it clear that he doesn't want to give his daughter to him?

DAVO: Dumbo! As if it necessarily follows that, if he doesn't give her to Panfilo he'll give her to you! You've got to get on the stick: go around and ask the old man's friends to help you—don't hang around here.

CARINO: Tu mi amunisci bene: io andrò, benché, per mia fè, questa speranza m'abbi ingannato spesso. A Dio!

SCENA TERZA

Panfilo, Davo.

PANFILO: Che vuole adunque mio padre? Perché finge?

DAVO: Io tel dirò: se egli t'incolpassi ora che Cremete non te la vuole dare, egli si adirerebbe teco a torto, non avendo prima inteso che animo sia il tuo circa le nozze. Ma se tu negassi, tutta la colpa sarà tua: e allora andrà sottosopra ogni cosa.

PANFILO: Io sono per sopportare ogni male.

DAVO: O Panfilo, egli è tuo padre ed è difficile opporsegli. Dipoi, questa donna è sola: e' troverrà del detto al fatto qualche cagione per la quale e' la farà mandar via.

PANFILO: Che la mandi via?

DAVO: Presto.

PANFILO: Dimmi adunque quello che tu vuoi che io faccia.

DAVO: Di' di volerla menare.

PANFILO: Heimè!

DAVO: Che cosa è?

PANFILO: Che io lo dica.

DAVO: Perché no?

PANFILO: Io non lo farò mai!

DAVO: Non lo negare.

CARINO: That's good advice. I'll go, although, by heaven, that kind of hope has often deceived me. Goodbye!

SCENE THREE

Panfilo, Davo.

PANFILO: What does my father want, then? Why is he pretending?

DAVO: I'll tell you. If he were to lay the blame on you, now that Cremete doesn't want you to marry his daughter, he would be in the wrong to fly into a rage at you; and he'd be wrong, too, because he hasn't even found out how you feel about the marriage. But, should you refuse, all the blame will be on you. At this point everything will be utter chaos.

PANFILO: I'm ready to put up with any kind of trouble.

DAVO: Oh, Panfilo, he's your father; it's difficult to stand up to him. Furthermore, Glicerio is alone: he'd find some pretext in what she said or did for sending her on her way.

PANFILO: He'd send her away?

DAVO: Immediately.

PANFILO: Tell me, then, what you want me to do.

DAVO: Tell him you want to marry Filomena.

PANFILO: Oh, no!

DAVO: What's the matter?

PANFILO: I should say *that*?

DAVO: Why not?

PANFILO: I'll never do it.

DAVO: Don't say that.

PANFILO: Non mi dare a intender questo.

DAVO: Vedi di questo quello che ne nascerà.

PANFILO: Che io lasci quella e pigli questa!

DAVO: E' non è così, perché tuo padre dirà in questo modo:—Io voglio che tu meni oggi donna—. Tu risponderai:—Io sono contento—. Dimmi quale cagione arà egli d'adirarsi teco! E tutti i suoi certi consigli gli torneranno sanza periculo incerti: perché, questo è sanza dubio, che Cremete non ti vuole dare la figliuola: né tu per questa cagione ti rimuterai di non fare quel che tu fai, acciò che quello non muti la sua opinione. Di' a tuo padre di volerla, acciò che, volendosi adirare teco, ragionevolmente non possa. E facilmente si confuta quello che tu temi, perché nessuno darà mai moglie a cotesti costumi: ei la darà più tosto ad uno povero. E farai ancora tuo padre negligente a darti moglie, quando ei vegga che tu sia parato a pigliarla; e a bell'agio cercherà d'un'altra: in questo mezzo qualcosa nascerà di bene.

PANFILO: Credi tu che la cosa proceda cosí?

DAVO: Sanza dubio alcuno.

PANFILO: Vedi dove tu mi metti.

DAVO: De! sta' cheto.

PANFILO: Io lo dirò: ei bisogna guardarsi che non sappia che io abbi uno fanciullo di lei, perché io ho promesso d'alevarlo.

DAVO: O audacia temeraria!

PANFILO: La volle che io gli dessi la fede, ché sapeva che io ero per osservarliene.

DAVO: E' vi si arà avvertenza. Ma ecco tuo padre: guarda che non ti vegga maninconoso.

PANFILO: Io lo farò.

PANFILO: Don't try to get me to do that.

DAVO: See what comes of it.

PANFILO: I should abandon this girl and take the other?

DAVO: That won't happen because your father will say something like, "I want you to get married today." You'll answer, "Sure." Tell me what reason he'll have to fly into a rage at you then? All his definite plans will become indefinite—and with no risk to you. Because there's no question that Cremete doesn't want you to marry his daughter. But don't let that get in your way, or else your father might change his mind. Tell him you want her so that, even if he does want to fly into a rage at you, he can't reasonably do so. Don't worry, nobody will ever give a wife to someone with your character—he'd sooner wed her to a beggar. Once your father realizes that you're prepared to marry her, he'll become less insistent about getting you a wife. He'll take his time looking for another one. Meanwhile, something good will turn up.

PANFILO: Is that what you think will happen?

DAVO: Without a doubt.

PANFILO: What are you getting me into!

DAVO: Oh, relax!

PANFILO: I shall tell him. He musn't find out that I have a child, because I've promised to raise it. [11]

DAVO: That was foolhardy and rash!

PANFILO: Glicerio wanted me to give her my promise on that score so that she'd know I'd keep my word.

DAVO: It shall be taken care of. But, here's your father; be careful not to look sad.

PANFILO: I shall.

SCENA QUARTA

Simo, Davo, Panfilo.

SIMO: Io ritorno e vedere quel che fanno o che partiti pigliano.

DAVO: Costui non dubita che Panfilo neghi di menarla, e ne viene pensativo di qualche luogo solitario, e spera avere trovata la cagione di farti ingiuria; pertanto fa' di stare in cervello.

PANFILO: Pure che io possa, Davo.

DAVO: Credimi questo, Panfilo, che non farà una parola sola, se tu di' di menarla.

SCENA QUINTA

Birria, Simo, Davo, Panfilo.

BIRRIA: Il padrone mi ha imposto, che lasciata ogni altra cosa, vadi osservando Panfilo, per intendere quello che fa di queste nozze; per questo io l'ho seguitato, e veggo ch'egli è con Davo: io ho un tratto a fare questa faccenda.

SIMO: E' sono qua l'uno e l'altro.

DAVO: Abbi l'occhio!

SIMO: O Panfilo!

DAVO: Vòltati ad lui quasi che allo improviso.

PANFILO: O padre!

DAVO: Bene.

SIMO: Io voglio che tu meni oggi donna, come io ti ho detto.

BIRRIA: Io temo ora del caso nostro, secondo che costui risponde.

PANFILO: Né in questo né in altro mai sono per mancare in alcuna cosa.

BIRRIA: Heimè!

SCENE FOUR

Simo, Davo, Panfilo.

SIMO: (I'm coming back to see what they're up to and what decisions they've made.)

DAVO: He hasn't a doubt that you'll refuse to marry Filomena. He's coming here after ruminating in some solitary place; he hopes that he has found an opportunity to make trouble for you. So keep your head on your shoulders.

PANFILO: If only I can, Davo.

DAVO: You can trust me on this, Panfilo. If you say you'll marry Filomena, your father won't say a single word.

SCENE FIVE

Birria, Simo, Davo, Panfilo.

BIRRIA: (My master has ordered me to drop everything else and keep an eye on Panfilo to find out what his intentions are about this marriage. That's why I've been following him. I see him with Davo. I've only got a moment to do the job in.)

SIMO: (There they both are.)

DAVO: Keep your eyes open.

SIMO: Oh, Panfilo.

DAVO: Turn around and pretend you haven't seen him.

PANFILO: Oh, father!

DAVO: Fine!

SIMO: I want you to get married today, as I said.

BIRRIA: (I'm afraid for our side, now, depending upon what his answer is.)

PANFILO: I'll never disappoint you in anything—not on this score or any other.

BIRRIA: (Well!)

DAVO: Egli è ammutolato.

BIRRIA: Che ha egli detto?

SIMO: Tu fai quello debbi quando io impetro amorevolmente da te quel che io voglio.

DAVO: Ho io detto il vero?

BIRRIA: Il padrone, secondo che io intendo, farà sanza moglie.

SIMO: Vattene ora in casa, acciò che, quando bisogna, che tu sia presto.

PANFILO: Io vo.

BIRRIA: È egli possibile che innegli uomini non sia fede alcuna? Vero è quel proverbio che dice che ognuno vuole meglio a sè che ad altri. Io ho veduta quella fanciulla e, se bene mi ricordo, è bella; per la quale cosa io voglio men male a Panfilo, s'egli ha più tosto voluto abracciare lei che il mio padrone. Io gliene andrò a dire, acciò che per questa mala novella mi dia qualche male.

SCENA SESTA

Simo, Davo.

DAVO: Costui crede ora che io gli porti qualche inganno e per questa cagione sia rimaso qui.

SIMO: Che dice Davo?

DAVO: Niente veramente.

SIMO: Niente, he?

DAVO: Niente, per mia fè!

SIMO: Veramente io aspettavo qualche cosa.

DAVO: Io mi avveggo che questo gli è intervenuto fuori d'ogni sua opinione. Egli è rimaso preso.

SIMO: È egli possibile che tu mi dica il vero?

DAVO: Niente è più facile.

DAVO: That took the wind right out of his sails.

BIRRIA: (What did he say?)

SIMO: You're behaving as you should when I ask you lovingly to do what I want.

DAVO: Was I right?

BIRRIA: (If I've heard correctly, my master is going to do without a wife.)

SIMO: Go into the house now so that you'll be ready when you're needed.

PANFILO: I'm going.

BIRRIA: (It's impossible to trust anybody about anything! The old saw people repeat about how 'every man is his own best friend' is true. I've seen that girl, and, if I remember correctly, she's beautiful; so, I can't hold it against Panfilo if he'd sooner embrace *her* than my master. I'll go and tell Carino about it, and my bad news will get me in bad.) [12]

SCENE SIX

Simo, Davo.

DAVO: (This guy now thinks I've got some trick up my sleeve and that I've stayed behind on account of it.)

SIMO: What are you saying, Davo?

DAVO: Nothing, really.

SIMO: Nothing, huh?

DAVO: Honestly, nothing.

SIMO: I was certainly expecting something.

DAVO: (I can tell something unexpected has happened to him. He's taken aback.)

SIMO: Is it possible for you to tell me the truth?

DAVO: Nothing is easier.

SIMO: Queste nozze sono a costui punto moleste per la consuetudine che lui ha con questa forestiera?

DAVO: Niente, per Dio; e, se fia, sarà uno pensiero che durerà dua o tre dì, tu sai? perch'egli ha preso questa cosa per il verso.

SIMO: Io lo lodo.

DAVO: Mentre che gli fu lecito e mentre che la età lo patì, egli amò; e allora lo fece di nascosto, perché quella cosa non gli dessi carico, come debbe fare uno giovane da bene; ora ch'egli è tempo di menar moglie, egli ha diritto l'animo alla moglie.

SIMO: E' mi parve pure alquanto maninconoso.

DAVO: Non è per questa cagione; ma ei ti accusa bene in qualche cosa.

SIMO: Che cosa è?

DAVO: Niente.

SIMO: Che domine è?

DAVO: Una cosa da giovani.

SIMO: Orsú, dimmi: che cosa è?

DAVO: Dice che tu usi troppa miseria in queste nozze.

SIMO: Io?

DAVO: Tu. Dice che a fatica hai speso dieci ducati: e' non pare che tu dia moglie ad uno tuo figliuolo. Ei non sa chi si menare de' sua compagni a cena. E, a dire il vero, che tu te ne governi così miseramente, io non ti lodo.

SIMO: Sta' cheto.

DAVO: Io l'ho aizzato.

SIMO: Io provedrò che tutto andrà bene. Che cosa è questa? Che ha voluto dire questo ribaldo? E se ci è male alcuno, heimè, che questo tristo ne è guida.

SIMO: Are these wedding plans troubling Panfilo in any way because of his intimacy with that foreign woman?

DAVO: For goodness sake, no! If they were, it would be a problem that would last two or three days, you know, because he has taken this business in the right way.

SIMO: Good for him.

DAVO: He loved her as long as it was allowable, and as long he was of an age to allow it; he kept quiet about it then so that he wouldn't be blamed for this business, as, indeed, a well-brought-up young man ought to. Now that it's time for him to get married, he's turned his attention to marriage.

SIMO: Still, he seemed to me to be somewhat gloomy.

DAVO: Not for that reason; but he certainly faults you for something.

SIMO: For what?

DAVO: Oh, nothing.

SIMO: What the devil is it?

DAVO: Something childish.

SIMO: Come on, now, tell me what it is!

DAVO: He says you're too stingy about the wedding.

SIMO: I am?

DAVO: You are. He says that scarcely ten ducats have been spent and that it doesn't look as if you were marrying off a son of yours to someone. He doesn't know if any of his friends ought to be invited for dinner. And, to tell the truth, you're being so chintzy about this matter that I can't give you much credit for it.

SIMO: Be quiet!

DAVO: (That got a rise out of him!)

SIMO: I'll see to it that everything is nicely taken care of. (What's this all about? What does this rascal mean? If there's any mischief going on here, that wretch is at the bottom of it.)

ATTO TERZO
SCENA PRIMA

Miside, Simo, Lesbia, Davo, Glicerio.

MISIDE: Per mia fè, Lesbia, che la cosa va come tu hai detto: e' non si truova quasi mai veruno uomo che sia fedele ad una donna.

SIMO: Questa fantesca è da Andro: che dice ella?

DAVO: Così è.

MISIDE: Ma questo Panfilo . . .

SIMO: Che dice ella?

MISIDE: . . . l'ha dato la fede . . .

SIMO: Heimè!

DAVO: Dio volessi che o costui diventassi sordo o colei mutola!

MISIDE: . . . perché gli ha comandato che quel che la farà s'allievi.

SIMO: O Giove, che odo io? La cosa è spacciata, se costei dice il vero!

LESBIA: Tu mi narri una buona natura di giovane.

MISIDE: Ottima; ma vienmi dreto, acciò che tu sia a tempo, se l'avessi bisogno di te.

LESBIA: Io vengo.

DAVO: Che remedio troverrò io ora ad questo male?

SIMO: Che cosa è questa? è egli sì pazzo che d'una forestiera . . . già io so . . . ha! sciocco! io me ne sono avveduto!

DAVO: Di che dice costui essersi aveduto?

SIMO: Questo è il primo inganno che costui mi fa: ei fanno vista che colei partorisca per sbigottire Cremete.

ACT THREE
SCENE ONE

Miside, Simo, Lesbia, Davo, Glicerio.

MISIDE: Upon my word, Lesbia, things are going just as you said they would; you can hardly find any man who is faithful to a woman.

SIMO: This is the servant girl of the woman from Andros. What is she saying?

DAVO: Yes, she is.

MISIDE: But this Panfilo . . .

SIMO: What is she saying?

MISIDE: . . . has promised . . .

SIMO: Ah ha!

DAVO: (Would to God either he'd become deaf or she'd shut up!)

MISIDE: . . . for Panfilo has ordered that her child be brought up.

SIMO: Oh, heavens, what's this I'm hearing? If she's telling the truth, things are done for.

LESBIA: From what you say, he's a good-natured young man.

MISIDE: The best. But come on inside so that we'll be on time if she needs you.

LESBIA: I'm coming.

DAVO: (How can I find a way out of this mess?)

SIMO: What is this? Is he so insane that with a foreign woman . . . Now I see. Ah, what an idiot! I'm beginning to get the picture.

DAVO: (What did this guy say he's "beginning to get"?)

SIMO: This is the first scheme this Davo is setting me up for; they're making believe this woman is in labor to scare off Cremete.

GLICERIO: O Giunone, aiutami, io mi ti raccomando!

SIMO: Bembè, sì presto? Cosa da ridere. Poi che la mi ha veduto stare innanzi all'uscio, ella sollecita. O Davo, tu non hai bene compartiti questi tempi!

DAVO: Io?

SIMO: Tu ti ricordi del tuo discepolo.

DAVO: Io non so quello che tu di'.

SIMO: Come mi uccellerebbe costui, se queste nozze fussino vere e avessimi trovato impreparato! Ma ora ogni cosa si fa con periculo suo: io sono al sicuro.

SCENA SECONDA

Lesbia, Simo, Davo.

LESBIA: Infino a qui, o Archile, in costei si veggono tutti buoni segni. Fa' lavare queste cose, dipoi gli date bere quanto vi ordinai e non più punto che io vi dissi. E io di qui ad un poco darò volta di qua. Per mia fè, che gli è nato a Panfilo uno gentil figliuolo! Dio lo facci sano, sendo egli di sì buona natura che si vergogni di abbandonare questa fanciulla.

SIMO: E chi non crederrebbe chi ti conoscessi, che ancor questo fussi ordinato da te?

DAVO: Che cosa è?

SIMO: Perché non ordinava ella in casa quello che era di bisogno alla donna di parto? Ma, poi che la è uscita fuora, la grida della via a quegli che sono drento! O Davo, tieni tu sì poco conto di me, o paioti io atto ad essere ingannato sì apertamente? Fa' le cose almeno in modo che paia che tu abbia paura di me, quando io lo risapessi!

GLICERIO: (Oh, Juno, help me; I commend my soul to you!)

SIMO: Well, well, so soon? What a joke! As soon as she saw me at the front door, she sped things up. Oh Davo, you haven't worked out your timing very well.

DAVO: *Mine?*

SIMO: You're thinking about your crew. [13]

DAVO: I don't know what you're talking about.

SIMO: (What an ass he'd have made of me if the wedding were real and he had caught me with my pants down. But now everything is done at *his* risk—I'm safe.)

SCENE TWO

Lesbia, Simo, Davo.

LESBIA: So far, Archile, she is giving all the proper signs. Make sure she's washed, then give her the right amount of what I ordered for her to drink—and not any more than what I said. I'll be back here soon. (Upon my word, what a fine baby boy was born to Panfilo! God grant it health because his father's character is so good that he was reluctant to abandon this unmarried woman.)

SIMO: How could anybody who knew you not realize that even this was one of your put-up jobs?

DAVO: What do you mean?

SIMO: Why didn't that woman tell those women inside what a woman in labor needed? No, she comes right outside and shouts it back from the street to whoever's in there. Oh, Davo, do you think so little of me, do I appear to be such a proper fool as to be duped so obviously? You might at least act as if you were afraid of me if I ever got wind of it!

DAVO: Veramente costui s'inganna da sè, non lo inganno io.

SIMO: Non te lo ho io detto? Non ti ho minacciato che tu non lo faccia? Che giova? Credi tu ch'io ti creda che costei abbi portorito di Panfilo?

DAVO: Io so dove ei s'inganna; e so quel ch'io ho a fare.

SIMO: Perché non rispondi?

DAVO: Che vuoi tu credere? Come se non ti fussi stato ridetto ogni cosa.

SIMO: A me?

DAVO: He! ho! Ha' ti tu inteso da te che questa è una finzione?

SIMO: Io sono uccellato!

DAVO: E' ti è stato ridetto: come ti sarebbe entrato questo sospetto?

SIMO: Perch'io ti conoscevo.

DAVO: Quasi che tu dica che questo è fatto per mio consiglio.

SIMO: Io ne sono certo.

DAVO: O Simone, tu non conosci bene chi io sono.

SIMO: Io non ti conosco?

DAVO: Ma come io ti comincio a parlare, tu credi che io t'inganni . . .

SIMO: Bugie.

DAVO: . . . in modo che io non ho più ardire d'aprire la bocca.

SIMO: Io so una volta questo, che qui non ha partorito persona.

DAVO: Tu la intendi; ma di qui a poco questo fanciullo ti sarà portato innanzi all'uscio; io te ne avvertisco, acciò che tu lo sappia e che tu non dica poi che sia fatto per consiglio di Davo, perché io vorrei che si rimovessi da te questa opinione che tu hai di me.

DAVO: (This guy is really deceiving himself; I'm not the one doing it to him.)

SIMO: Didn't I tell you—didn't I warn you—not to do it? What's the use? Do you really think I believe you about this woman having had Panfilo's child?

DAVO: (I see where he's making his mistake—and I know what I can do about it.)

SIMO: Why don't you answer me?

DAVO: What do you want me to believe? As if you hadn't been told about everything before.

SIMO: Told?

DAVO: Ha, ha! Do you mean you realized all by yourself that this was a setup?

SIMO: I'm being mocked!

DAVO: You were told—or why else did you become suspicious?

SIMO: Because I know you.

DAVO: It's almost as if you're saying that this is my idea.

SIMO: I'm sure of it.

DAVO: Oh, Simo, you don't really know me well.

SIMO: I don't?

DAVO: Just as I start to speak, you think I'm tricking you . . .

SIMO: Lies!

DAVO: . . . so that I don't dare open my mouth.

SIMO: Once and for all, I know this much: nobody here has given birth.

DAVO: You're right. But in a little while a baby boy will be brought to you from out of that door. I'm reminding you of it now so that you'll know about it and won't say later on that it was done on Davo's say-so, because I'd like you to get the idea that you have about me out of your head.

SIMO: Donde sai tu questo?

DAVO: Io l'ho udito e credolo.

SIMO: Molte cose concorrono per le quali io fo questa coniettura: in prima, costei disse essere gravida di Panfilo, e non fu vero; ora poi che la vede aparecchiarsi le nozze, ella mandò per la levatrice, che venissi ad lei e portassi seco uno fanciullo.

DAVO: Se non accadeva che tu vedessi il fanciullo, queste nozze di Panfilo non si sarebbono sturbate.

SIMO: Che di' tu? Quando tu intendesti che si aveva ad pigliare questo partito, perché non me lo dicesti tu?

DAVO: Chi l'ha rimosso da lei, se non io? Perché, non sa ognuno quanto grandemente colui l'amava? Ora egli è bene che tolga moglie: però mi darai questa faccenda e tu nondimeno sèguita di fare le nozze. E io ci ho buona speranza, mediante la grazia di Dio.

SIMO: Vanne in casa, e quivi mi aspetta e ordina quello che fa bisogno. Costui non mi ha al tutto costretto a credergli, e non so s'egli è vero ciò che mi dice: ma lo stimo poco, perché questa è la importanza, che 'l mio figliuolo me lo ha promesso. Ora io troverrò Cremete e lo pregherrò che gliene dia: se io lo impetro, che voglio io altro, se non che oggi si faccino queste nozze? Perché, a quello che 'l mio figliuolo mi ha promesso, e' non è dubbio ch'io lo potrò forzare, quando ei non volessi. E apunto a tempo ecco Cremete.

SIMO: How do you know this?

DAVO: I heard about it and I believe it.

SIMO:[14] A lot of things are coming together and leading me to this conclusion. First, this woman said that Panfilo had gotten her pregnant and it wasn't true. Now that she realizes that people are making wedding preparations, she sends for the midwife to come—carrying a baby boy with her.

DAVO: If you hadn't chanced to have seen the baby, then Panfilo's wedding plans wouldn't have been upset.

SIMO: What do you mean? When you realized that they had reached this decision, why didn't you tell me about it?

DAVO: Who was it that got him away from her if I didn't? Everybody knows how tremendously in love with her he was. Now it is a good thing for him to get married, so leave this matter to me. You, however, go right on with the wedding plans. And, with God's help, I have high hopes for them.

SIMO: Go on in the house; wait for me there and see to it that what needs to be done gets done. That guy hasn't quite gotten me to believe him; I don't know whether he's telling me the truth or not. but I don't really care, because this is what's important: my son has made me a promise. Now I'll find Cremete and ask him for his daughter. If I get what I'm asking for, what more could I want—unless it's that the wedding be today? Given what my son has promised, there's no doubt—should he renege—that I can force him. And here's Cremete, just in the nick of time.

SCENA TERZA

Simo, Cremete.

SIMO: A! quel Cremete!

CREMETE: O! io ti cercavo.

SIMO: E io te.

CREMETE: Io ti desideravo perché molti mi hanno trovato e detto avere inteso da più persone come oggi io do la mia figliuola al tuo figliuolo: io vengo per sapere se tu o loro impazzano.

SIMO: Odi un poco e saprai per quel che io ti voglio e quello che tu cerchi.

CREMETE: Di' ciò che tu vuoi.

SIMO: Per Dio io ti prego, o Cremete, e per la nostra amicizia, la quale, cominciata de piccoli, insieme con la età crebbe; per la unica tua figliuola e mio figliuolo, la salute del quale è nella tua potestà; che tu mi aiuti in questa cosa e che quelle nozze, che si dovevono fare, si faccino.

CREMETE: Ha! non mi pregare, come se ti bisogni prieghi quando tu vogli da me alcun piacere. Credi tu che io sia d'altra fatta che io mi sia stato per lo adietro, quando io te la davo? S'egli è bene per l'una parte e per l'altra, facciamole; ma se di questa cosa a l'uno e l'altro di noi ne nascessi più male che commodo, io ti priego che tu abbi riguardo al comune bene, come se quella fussi tua, e io padre di Panfilo.

SIMO: Io non voglio altrimenti, e così cerco che si facci, o Cremete; né te ne richiederei, se la cosa non fussi in termine da farlo.

CREMETE: Che è nato?

SIMO: Glicerio e Panfilo sono adirati insieme.

SCENE THREE

Simo, Cremete.

SIMO: Ah, my friend Cremete.

CREMETE: Oh, I've been looking for you.

SIMO: And I you.

CREMETE: I wanted you because lots of people have been coming up to me and saying that they had learned from several sources that my daughter is marrying your son today. I'm here to find out who is crazy—you or them?

SIMO: Listen to me for a moment and you'll learn why I want you, and what you want to know.

CREMETE: Tell me what it is you want.

SIMO: Oh, Cremete, in the name of heaven and our friendship—which began when we were boys and has grown deeper through the years—and in the name of your only daughter and my son—whose salvation is in your power—I implore you to help me in this matter: let this marriage that should have been, be.

CREMETE: Ha! Don't beg me, as if you need to entreat me whenever you want some favor from me. Do you think I'm any different from what I was when I promised her to you? If it is a good thing for both of them, let's do it; but if more harm than good is going to come to either of them from this affair, then I beg you to consider the common good—as if she were your daughter and Panfilo my son.

SIMO: I'd have it no other way; so, I'm attempting to carry out the common good, Cremete. I shouldn't be asking you about it if it weren't propitious for the wedding to be carried out.

CREMETE: What has happened?

SIMO: Glicerio and Panfilo have had a falling out.

CREMETE: Intendo.

SIMO: E di qualità che io credo che non se ne abbi a fare pace.

CREMETE: Favole!

SIMO: Certo la cosa è così.

CREMETE: E' fia come io ti dirò, che l'ire degli amanti sono una reintegrazione d'amore.

SIMO: De! io ti priego che noi avanziano tempo in dargli moglie mentre che ci è dato questo tempo, mentre che la sua libidine è ristucca da le iniurie, innanzi che le sceleratezze loro e le lacrime piene d'inganno riduchino l'animo infermo a misericordia; perché spero, come e' fia legato da la consuetudine e dal matrimonio, facilmente si libererà da tanti mali.

CREMETE: E' pare a te così, ma io credo che non potrà lungamente patire me né lei.

SIMO: Che ne sai tu, se tu non ne fai esperienza?

CREMETE: Farne esperienza in una sua figliuola, è pazzia.

SIMO: In fine tutto il male che ne può risultare è questo: se non si corregge, che Dio guardi!, che si facci il divorzio; ma, se si corregge, guarda quanti beni: in prima tu restituirai ad uno tuo amico uno figliuolo, tu arai uno genero fermo e la tua figliuola marito.

CREMETE: Che bisogna altro? Se tu ti se' persuaso che questo sia utile, io non voglio che per me si guasti alcuno tuo commodo.

SIMO: Io ti ho meritamente sempre amato assai.

CREMETE: Ma dimmi . . .

CREMETE: So I understand.

SIMO: It is so bad I believe that there will be no reconciliation.

CREMETE: Nonsense!

SIMO: It's a fact!

CREMETE: I'll tell you how it's going to turn out: lovers' quarrels restore love.[15]

SIMO: Alas, I beg you—before the women's wicked wiles and crocodile tears reduce Panfilo's lovesick mind to a state of pity—let's save time by marrying them while there is still time given us, while his passion is cooled by insult. I'm counting on its being easier for him, once he's restrained by ties of habit and marriage, to get himself out of so many predicaments.

CREMETE: So it seems to you, but I believe Panfilo will not be able to tolerate either her or me for very long.

SIMO: How can you know unless you make the experiment?

CREMETE: To experiment with your own daughter is folly.

SIMO: In the long run, the only problem that could result from all this is that, if Panfilo doesn't mend his ways, then—may God forbid—there will be a divorce. But, if he does mend them, consider how many advantages there are: first of all, you restore a son to your friend, you'll have a resolute son-in-law, and you'll have a husband for your daughter.

CREMETE: What else is needed? If you're convinced that this idea is advantageous, I don't want any of your interests to be hurt on my account.

SIMO: I have always been very fond of you—and I was right.

CREMETE: But tell me . . .

SIMO: Che?

CREMETE: Onde sai tu ch'egli è infra loro inimicizia?

SIMO: Davo me lo ha detto, che è il primo loro consigliere; ed egli mi persuade che io faccia queste nozze il più presto posso. Credi tu che lo facessi, se non sapessi che 'l mio figliuolo volessi? Io voglio che tu stessi oda le sua parole proprie. Olà, chiamate qua Davo! Ma eccolo che viene fuora.

SCENA QUARTA

Davo, Simo, Cremete.

DAVO: Io venivo a trovarti.

SIMO: Che cosa è?

DAVO: Perché non mandate per la sposa? E' si fa sera.

SIMO: Odi tu quel che dice? Per lo adietro io ho dubitato assai, o Davo, che tu non facessi quel medesimo che suole fare la maggiore parte de' servi, d'ingannarmi per cagione del mio figliuolo.

DAVO: Che io facessi cotesto?

SIMO: Io lo credetti, e in modo ne ebbi paura, che io vi ho tenuto segreto quello che ora vi dirò.

DAVO: Che cosa è?

SIMO: Tu lo saprai, perché io comincio a prestarti fede.

DAVO: Quanto tu hai penato a conoscere chi io sono!

SIMO: Queste nozze non erano da dovero . . .

DAVO: Perché no?

SIMO: Ma io le finsi per tentarvi.

SIMO: What?

CREMETE: How do you know that there is bad blood between them?

SIMO: Davo, who is foremost among their advisers, told me; he persuaded me to arrange the wedding as soon as possible. You don't think he would do that unless he knew my son wanted the marriage, do you? I'd like you to hear it from his own lips. You there, call Davo out here. Ah, here he is coming out.

SCENE FOUR

Davo, Simo, Cremete.

DAVO: I was looking for you.

SIMO: What is it?

DAVO: Why hasn't the bride been sent for; it's getting on toward evening.

SIMO: Do you hear what he's saying? I used to feel quite afraid, Davo, that you would do exactly what the majority of slaves are wont to do—trick me because of my son.

DAVO: That *I* would do *that*?

SIMO: I did think so; it was because of that fear that I withheld the secret that I am now going to divulge.

DAVO: What's that?

SIMO: You'll find out because I'm just beginning to trust you.

DAVO: At last, you've taken the trouble to discover who I am.

SIMO: This wedding was not in earnest . . .

DAVO: Why not?

SIMO: I pretended it was in order to sound you two out.

DAVO: Che di' tu?

SIMO: Così sta la cosa.

DAVO: Vedi tu! mai me ne arei saputo avedere. U! Ha!, che consiglio astuto!

SIMO: Odi questo: poi che io ti feci entrare in casa, io riscontrai a tempo costui.

DAVO: Heimè! noi siam morti.

SIMO: Di' a costui quello che tu dicesti a me.

DAVO: Che odo io?

SIMO: Io l'ho pregato che ci dia la sua figliuola e con fatica l'ho ottenuto.

DAVO: Io son morto.

SIMO: Hem? che hai tu detto?

DAVO: Ho detto ch'egli è molto bene fatto.

SIMO: Ora per costui non resta.

CREMETE: Io me n'andrò a casa e dirò che si preparino; e, se bisognerà cosa alcuna, lo farò intendere a costui.

SIMO: Ora io ti prego, Davo, perché tu solo mi hai fatte queste nozze . . .

DAVO: Io veramente solo.

SIMO: . . . sfòrzati di correggere questo mio figliuolo.

DAVO: Io lo farò sanza dubio alcuno.

SIMO: Tu puoi ora, mentre ch'egli è adirato.

DAVO: Sta' di buona voglia.

SIMO: Dimmi, dove è egli ora?

DAVO: Io mi maraviglio se non è in casa.

SIMO: Io l'andrò a trovare e dirò a lui quel medesimo che io ho detto a te.

DAVO: Io sono diventato pichino. Che cosa terrà che io non sia per la più corta mandato a zappare? Io non ho speranza che i prieghi mi vaglino: io ho mandato sottosopra ogni cosa; io ho ingannato il padrone e ho fatto che oggi

DAVO: What are you saying?

SIMO: That's it.

DAVO: What do you know? I never would have figured that out. Humph, what a clever plan!

SIMO: Now hear this: right after I made you go into the house, I luckily met this man.

DAVO: (Oh brother, now we've had it!)

SIMO: Tell him what you have just told me.

DAVO: (What am I hearing?)

SIMO: I begged him for his daughter's hand in marriage and got it—with some difficulty.

DAVO: (Now I'm done for.)

SIMO: Huh, what did you say?

DAVO: I said, "he has done a good deed."

SIMO: Now, as for him, there's nothing left to be done.

CREMETE: I'll run along home and tell them to get things ready; if anything is needed, I'll let you know.

SIMO: Now, Davo, I implore you, because you alone have made this marriage possible for me . . .

DAVO: (I alone, ah yes!)

SIMO: . . . make every effort to set that son of mine straight.

DAVO: I'll do that, no problem.

SIMO: You can do it now, while he's angry.

DAVO: Relax.

SIMO: Tell me, where is he now?

DAVO: I'd be surprised if he weren't at home.

SIMO: I'll go find him and tell him exactly what I've told you.

DAVO: I'm a goner. [16] What's to prevent me from being sent off to dig ditches the short way 'round? I've no hope that my prayers can be of any use. I've turned everything upside down: I've deceived my master and caused the wed-

queste nozze si faranno, voglia Panfilo o no. O astuzia! Che se io mi fussi stato da parte, non ne sarebbe risultato male alcuno. Ma ecco, io lo veggo. Io sono spacciato! Dio volessi che fussi qui qualche balza dove io a fiaccacollo mi potessi gittare!

SCENA QUINTA

Panfilo, Davo.

PANFILO: Dove è quello scelerato che mi ha morto?

DAVO: Io sto male.

PANFILO: Ma io confesso essermi questo intervenuto ragionevolmente, quando io sono sì pazzo e sì da poco che io commetto e casi mia in sì disutile servo! Io ne porto le pene giustamente; ma io ne lo pagherò in ogni modo.

DAVO: Se io fuggo ora questo male, io so che poi tu non me ne pagherai.

PANFILO: Che dirò io ora a mio padre? Negherogli io quello che io gli ho promesso? Con che confidenza ardirò io di farlo? Io non so io stesso quello che mi fare di me medesimo.

DAVO: Né anch'io di me; ma io penso di dire di avere trovato qualche bel tratto, per differire questo male.

PANFILO: Ohè!

DAVO: E' mi ha veduto.

PANFILO: Olà, uom da bene, che fai? Vedi tu come tu m'hai aviluppato co' tuoi consigli?

DAVO: Io ti svilupperò.

PANFILO: Sviluppera'mi?

DAVO: Sì veramente, Panfilo!

PANFILO: Come ora?

ding to take place today whether Panfilo wants it or not.[17]
Clever, aren't I. Had I stayed out of it, there wouldn't have
been any problem. There he is—I see Panfilo. I'm done
for. God grant me a cliff right here so I can plunge over it
headlong!

SCENE FIVE

Panfilo, Davo.

PANFILO: Where is that scoundrel who has ruined me?

DAVO: (I'm in for it.)

PANFILO: Still, I must admit that all this happened to
me with good reason, for I was foolish enough—and in-
ept enough—to entrust my needs to such a no-good slave.
It's my own fault; but, in any case, I'll make him pay.

DAVO: (If I get out of this mess now, I know that you
won't make me pay for it later.)

PANFILO: What am I going to say to my father now?
How can I renege on what I've already promised him?
Where shall I find the courage to do it? I don't know ex-
actly what I ought to do.

DAVO: (Neither do I, but I'm thinking of telling him
that I've come up with some clever idea[18] to get us out of
this mess.)

PANFILO: Ah ha!

DAVO: He's spotted me.

PANFILO: Hey there, my good man, what's up? See
how you and your schemes have gotten me all tangled up?

DAVO: I'll untangle you.

PANFILO: *You*'ll get me out?

DAVO: Of course, Panfilo.

PANFILO: As you did just now?

DAVO: Spero pure di fare meglio.

PANFILO: Vuoi tu che io ti creda, impiccato, che tu rassetti una cosa aviluppata e perduta? O! di chi mi sono io fidato, che d'uno stato tranquillo m'hai rovesciato adosso queste nozze. Ma non ti dissi io che m'interverrebbe questo?

DAVO: Sì, dicesti.

PANFILO: Che ti si verrebbe egli?

DAVO: Le forche! Ma lasciami un poco poco ritornare in me: io penserò a qualcosa.

PANFILO: Heimè! perché non ho io spazio a pigliare di te quel suplizio che io vorrei? Perché questo tempo richiede che io pensi a' casi mia e non a vendicarmi.

DAVO: I hope even better.

PANFILO: You want me to believe you, you crook! You're going to put in order what's all tangled up and ruined? Oh, to think that I relied on this guy who has destroyed my tranquility and dumped this wedding on top of me. But didn't I tell you that this would happen?

DAVO: Yes, you did.

PANFILO: What do you deserve?

DAVO: The gallows! But let me gather my wits for a moment; I'll think of something.

PANFILO: Well, if only I had the time to exact from you the punishment I should like to. But the time available requires me to think about my own need—not about revenge.

ATTO QUARTO
SCENA PRIMA

Carino, Panfilo, Davo.

CARINO: È ella cosa degna di memoria o credibile che sia tanta pazzia nata in alcuno che si rallegri del male d'altri e degli incommodi d'altri cerchi i commodi suoi? Ah! non è questo vero? E quella sorte d'huomini è pessima, che si vergognano negare una cosa quando sono richiesti; poi, quando ne viene il tempo, forzati da la necessità, si scuoprono e temono. E pure la cosa gli sforza a negare, et allora usano parole sfacciate:—Chi se' tu? Che hai tu a fare meco? Perché ti ho io a dare le mia cose? Odi tu: io ho a volere meglio a me!—E se tu gli domandi dove è la fede, e' non si vergognono di niente; e prima, quando non bisognava, si vergognorno. Ma che farò io? Androllo io a trovare per dolermi seco di questa ingiuria? Io gli dirò villania. E se un mi dicessi:—Tu non farai nulla!—io gli darò pure questa molestia e sfogherò l'animo mio.

PANFILO: Carino, io ho rovinato imprudentemente te e me, se Dio non ci provede.

CARINO: Così, «imprudentemente»? Egli ha trovata la scusa! Tu m'hai osservata la fede!

PANFILO: O perché?

CARINO: Credimi tu ancora ingannare con queste tua parole?

PANFILO: Che cosa è cotesta?

CARINO: Poi che io dissi d'amarla, ella ti è piaciuta. De! misero a me, che io ho misurato l'animo tuo con l'animo mio!

PANFILO: Tu t'inganni.

ACT FOUR
SCENE ONE

Carino, Panfilo, Davo.

CARINO:[19] Is it within the realm of possibility to believe in or conceive of anyone being so insane that he would take delight in someone's misfortunes and take comfort in someone's discomfort? Can this be true? The worst sort of man is someone who is ashamed to say "no" to something when he is asked, but later, when the time is up and he is forced by circumstances, he comes out into the open and becomes shameless. If the situation forces such a person to refuse, then he talks impudently: "Who are you? What are you to me? Why should I give up my girl to you? Listen, I look out for number one!" And if you ask, what about your promise, this kind of person isn't ashamed of anything; whereas before, when he didn't need to be ashamed, he was. What should I do? Shall I go hunt him out and complain about this outrage? I'll insult him. If someone were to say, "you'll get nowhere," at least I shall have annoyed him and let off steam.

PANFILO: Carino, I have carelessly ruined both you and me, unless the Lord helps us out.

CARINO: "Carelessly," he says. You've found an out! You've kept your promise to me!

PANFILO: Oh, why?

CARINO: Do you still expect to deceive me with those speeches of yours?

PANFILO: What's the matter?

CARINO: Once I said that I loved Filomena, she became charming for you. Alas, how unfortunate I am to have measured your nature by my own.

PANFILO: You're mistaken.

CARINO: Questa tua allegrezza non ti sarebbe paruta intera, se tu non mi avessi nutrito e lattato d'una falsa speranza: abbitela.

PANFILO: Che io l'abbia? Tu non sai in quanti mali io sia rinvolto e in quanti pensieri questo mio manigoldo m'abbi messo con i suoi consigli.

CARINO: Maraviglitene tu? Egli ha imparato da te.

PANFILO: Tu non diresti cotesto, se tu conoscessi me e lo amore mio.

CARINO: Io so che tu disputasti assai con tuo padre: e per questo ti accusa, che non ti ha potuto oggi disporre a menarla.

PANFILO: Anzi, vedi come tu sai i mali mia! Queste nozze non si facevano, e non era alcuno che mi volessi dare moglie.

CARINO: Io so che tu se' stato forzato da te stesso.

PANFILO: Sta' un poco saldo: tu non lo sai ancora.

CARINO: Io so che tu l'hai a menare.

PANFILO: Perché mi ammazzi tu? Intendi questo: costui non cessò mai di persuadere, di pregarmi, che io dicessi a mio padre di essere contento di menarla, tanto che mi condusse a dirlo.

CARINO: Chi fu cotesto uomo?

PANFILO: Davo.

CARINO: Davo?

PANFILO: Davo manda sozopra ogni cosa.

CARINO: Per che cagione?

PANFILO: Io non lo so, se non che io so bene che Dio è adirato meco, poi che io feci a suo modo.

CARINO: Would your joy have seemed complete only if you fed and nourished me on false hope? Keep her!

PANFILO: Keep her? You can't imagine how many problems I've become tangled up in and how much trouble my executioner here has gotten me into with his schemes.

CARINO: Why are you surprised at that? He learned it from you.

PANFILO: You wouldn't talk like that if you knew me and my love.

CARINO: I know that you had a big fight with your father and thus he blames you; and so, he was unable to persuade you to marry Filomena today.

PANFILO: On the contrary, see how little you know about my troubles. The wedding was not to have taken place and there was no one trying to give me a wife.

CARINO: I know, you were forced to—because you were forcing yourself.

PANFILO: Hold your horses; you don't get it yet.

CARINO: I get that you're going to marry her.

PANFILO: You'll be the death of me. *Listen.* He never stopped influencing me and badgering me into telling my father that I'd be content to marry her; so, I was driven to tell him so.

CARINO: Who was this guy?

PANFILO: Davo.

CARINO: Davo?

PANFILO: Davo throws a monkey wrench into everything.

CARINO: Why?

PANFILO: I don't know why, but I do know that God has been angry with me ever since I started doing what he wanted.

CARINO: È ita così la cosa, Davo?

DAVO: Sì, è.

CARINO: Che di' tu, scelerato? Idio ti dia quel fine che tu meriti! Dimmi un poco: se tutti i suoi nimici gli avessino voluto dare moglie, arebbongli dato altro consiglio?

DAVO: Io sono stracco, ma non lasso.

CARINO: Io lo so.

DAVO: E' non ci è riuscito per questa via, enterreno per una altra: se già tu non pensi che, poi che la prima non riuscì, questo male non si possa guarire.

PANFILO: Anzi, credo che, ogni poco che tu ci pensi, che d'un paio di nozze tu me ne farai dua.

DAVO: O Panfilo, io sono obligato in tuo servizio sforzarmi con le mani e co' piè, dì e notte, e mettermi a periculo della vita per giovarti. E' s'appartiene poi a te perdonarmi, se nasce alcuna cosa fuora di speranza, e s'egli occorre cosa poco prospera, perché io arò fatto il meglio che io ho saputo; o veramente tu ti truovi uno altro che ti serva meglio, e lascia andare me.

PANFILO: Io lo desidero; ma rimettimi nel luogo dove tu mi traesti.

DAVO: Io lo farò.

PANFILO: Ei bisogna ora.

DAVO: Hem! Ma sta' saldo, io sento l'uscio di Glicerio.

PANFILO: E' non importa a te.

DAVO: Io vo pensando.

PANFILO: Hem? or ci pensi?

DAVO: Io l'ho già trovato.

CARINO: Is that how it was, Davo?

DAVO: Yes, it is.

CARINO: What do you mean, you wretch? God's going to get you for that! Tell me: if all his enemies had wanted to marry their daughters to him, would they have given him any other advice?

DAVO: I'm down, but not out.

CARINO: I know.

DAVO: We've had no success with this route, let's try another; unless you think that, because our first try was unsuccessful, there is no way to solve this problem.

PANFILO: On the contrary, I believe that without giving it much thought, you can come up with two weddings for me instead of one.

DAVO: Oh, Panfilo, I'm bound to you as your slave to strive to do my darnedest[20] day and night and to risk my life to help you. It's your duty, then, if something unexpected turns up, to forgive me; should it turn out that my plan is not so lucky, at least I did the best I know how. In fact, if you can come up with a better plan, let me go.

PANFILO: I'd like to; but put me back where you found me.

DAVO: I shall.

PANFILO: It must be done now.

DAVO: Hmm. Hold it, I hear Glicerio's door opening.

PANFILO: That's none of your business.

DAVO: I'm thinking.[21]

PANFILO: Ha, at last!

DAVO: I've already figured it out.

SCENA SECONDA

Miside, Panfilo, Carino, Davo.

MISIDE: Come io l'arò trovato, io procurerò per te e ne merrò meco il tuo Panfilo; ma tu, anima mia, non ti voler macerare.

PANFILO: O Miside!

MISIDE: Che è? O Panfilo, io t'ho trovato appunto.

PANFILO: Che cosa è?

MISIDE: La mia padrona mi ha comandato che io ti prieghi che, se tu l'ami, che tu la vadia a vedere.

PANFILO: U! Ha! ch'io son morto. Questo male rinnuova. Tieni tu con la tua opera così sospeso me e lei? La manda per me, perché la sente che si fanno le nozze.

CARINO: Da le quali facilmente tu ti saresti potuto astenere, se costui se ne fussi astenuto.

DAVO: Se costui non è per sè medesimo adirato, aizzalo!

MISIDE: Per mia fè, cotesta è la cagione; e però è ella maninconosa.

PANFILO: Io ti giuro, o Miside, per tutti gl'Iddei, che io non la abandonerò mai, non se io credessi che tutti gli uomini mi avessino a diventare nimici. Io me la ho cerca, la mi è tocca; i costumi s'affanno: morir possa qualunque vuole che noi ci separiamo! Costei non mi fia tolta se non da la morte.

MISIDE: Io risucito.

PANFILO: L'oraculo d'Apolline non è più vero che questo. Se si potrà fare che mio padre creda che non sia mancato per me che queste nozze si faccino, io l'arò caro; quanto che no, io farò le cose alla abandonata e vorrò ch'egli intenda che manchi da me. Chi ti paio io?

SCENE TWO

Miside, Panfilo, Carino, Davo.

MISIDE: Wherever he is, I shall have him found; I'll get him for you and bring back your Panfilo with me. But you, my darling, don't brood about it.

PANFILO: Oh, Miside.

MISIDE: What? Oh, Panfilo, I've found you just in time.

PANFILO: Why's that?

MISIDE: My mistress ordered me to beg you to come and see her, if you love her.

PANFILO: Ah, I've had it! This problem keeps cropping up. See what your deeds have done to keep her and me up in the air? She is sending for me because she has heard that the wedding plans are made.

CARINO: How easy it would have been for you to hold off on them if only this guy had backed off.

DAVO: Goad him on—as if my master weren't flying into a rage on his own!

MISIDE: I bet that's the reason why she is gloomy.

PANFILO: I swear to you, Miside, by all the gods, that I shall never desert her, not even if I knew that every man alive would become my enemy. I sought her out and I got her; we suit one another. Death to anyone who wants to separate us. Only death shall take her from me!

MISIDE: I feel much better.

PANFILO: Apollo's oracle is not more true than my words. If it's at all possible to arrange things so that my father doesn't believe that it was I who got the wedding called off, I'd be grateful; if not, though, I'll let things go their own way—I intend for him to understand that I was the one who called things off. How does that seem to you?

CARINO: Infelice come me.

DAVO: Io cerco d'un partito.

CARINO: Tu se' valente huomo.

PANFILO: Io so quel che tu cerchi.

DAVO: Io te lo darò fatto in ogni modo.

PANFILO: E' bisogna ora.

DAVO: Io so già quello che io ho a fare.

CARINO: Che cosa è?

DAVO: Io l'ho trovato per costui, non per te, acciò che tu non ti inganni.

CARINO: E' mi basta.

PANFILO: Dimmi quello che tu farai.

DAVO: Io ho paura che questo dì non mi basti a farlo, non che mi avanzi tempo a dirlo. Orsù, andatevi con Dio: voi mi date noia.

PANFILO: Io andrò a vedere costei.

DAVO: Ma tu dove n'andrai?

CARINO: Vuoi tu ch'io ti dica il vero?

DAVO: Tu mi cominci una istoria da capo.

CARINO: Quel che sarà di me?

DAVO: Eh! o! imprudente! Non ti basta egli che, s'io differisco queste nozze uno dì, che io lo do a te?

CARINO: Nondimeno . . .

DAVO: Che sarà?

CARINO: Ch'io la meni.

DAVO: Uccellaccio!

CARINO: Se tu puoi fare nulla, fa' di venire qui.

DAVO: Che vuoi tu ch'io venga? Io non ho nulla . . .

CARINO: Pure, se tu avessi qualche cosa . . .

DAVO: Orsù, io verrò!

CARINO: Unfortunate—like me.

DAVO: I'm looking for an alternative . . .

CARINO: You're a skillful one.[22]

PANFILO: I know what you're looking for.

DAVO: I'll give you results, come what may!

PANFILO: We need them now!

DAVO: I already know what I've got to do.

CARINO: What's that?

DAVO: It's for Panfilo, not you, so you won't make a mistake.

CARINO: That's OK by me.

PANFILO: Tell me what you're going to do.

DAVO: I'm afraid this day isn't long enough to *do* it, so you know that there's not enough time to *tell* it. Come on, now; may God be with you both—you're in my way.

PANFILO: I'll go and see Glicerio.

DAVO: And where will you be going?

CARINO: Would you like me to tell you the truth?

DAVO: You're about to start a story from the top.

CARINO: What's going to become of me?

DAVO: What? Oh, you're so rash![23] Isn't it enough that, if I'm putting off this wedding for one day, I'm giving that one day to you?

CARINO: Nevertheless . . .

DAVO: What's up?

CARINO: I want to marry Filomena.

DAVO: You fool!

CARINO: If you can do anything, come here to my house.

DAVO: Why do you want me to come? I have nothing . . .

CARINO: Still, if you might have something . . .

DAVO: Go on, now, I'll come.

CARINO: . . . Io sarò in casa.

DAVO: Tu, Miside, aspettami un poco qui, tanto che io peni a uscire di casa.

MISIDE: Perché?

DAVO: Così bisogna fare.

MISIDE: Fa' presto!

DAVO: Io sarò qui ora.

SCENA TERZA

Miside, Davo.

MISIDE: Veramente e' non ci è boccone del netto. O Idii! io vi chiamo in testimonio che io mi pensavo che questo Panfilo fussi alla padrona mia un sommo bene, sendo amico, amante e uom parato a tutte le sua voglie: ma ella, misera, quanto dolore piglia per suo amore! In modo che io ci veggo dentro più male che bene. Ma Davo esce fuora. Oimè! Che cosa è questa? dove porti tu il fanciullo?

DAVO: O Miside, ora bisogna che la tua astuzia e audacia sia pronta.

MISIDE: Che vuoi tu fare?

DAVO: Piglia questo fanciullo, presto, e pôllo innanzi all'uscio nostro.

MISIDE: In terra?

DAVO: Raccogli paglia e vinciglie della via, e mettigliene sotto.

MISIDE: Perché non fai tu questo da te?

DAVO: Per potere giurare al padrone di non lo avere posto.

MISIDE: Intendo; ma dimmi: come se' tu diventato sì religioso?

CARINO: I'll be at home.

DAVO: Miside, wait here a minute until I come out of the house.

MISIDE: Why?

DAVO: Just do it.

MISIDE: Hurry!

DAVO: I'll be right out.

SCENE THREE

Miside, Davo.

MISIDE: (Everything really does come with strings attached. Ye Gods, I call upon you as witnesses that I used to consider Panfilo to be the greatest good my mistress could have—a friend, a lover, someone in tune with her every desire; but, poor dear, what sorrow she gets from her love. I see more bad than good in this affair. But Davo is coming.) Oh no, what's this? Where are you taking the baby?

DAVO: Oh, Miside, now your cunning and boldness must be at the ready.

MISIDE: What are you going to do?

DAVO: Take the baby, quickly, and put him on the threshold of our door.

MISIDE: On the ground?

DAVO: Gather up some straw and willow branches from the street[24] and put them underneath him.

MISIDE: Why don't you do it yourself?

DAVO: So that I'll be able to swear to my master that I didn't put him there.

MISIDE: I see; but, tell me, since when did you become so scrupulous?

DAVO: Muoviti presto, acciò che tu intenda dipoi quel ch'io voglio fare. O Giove!

MISIDE: Che cosa è?

DAVO: Ecco il padre della sposa: io voglio lasciare il primo partito.

MISIDE: Io non so che tu ti di'.

DAVO: Io fingerò di venire qua da man dritta: fa' d'andare secondando il parlare mio dovunque bisognerà.

MISIDE: Io non intendo cosa che tu ti dica; me io starò qui, acciò, se bisognassi l'opera mia, io non disturbi alcuno vostro commodo.

SCENA QUARTA

Cremete, Miside, Davo.

CREMETE: Io ritorno per comandare che mandino per lei, poi che io ho ordinato tutte le cose che bisognano per le nozze . . . Ma questo che è? Per mia fè, ch'egli è un fanciullo! O donna, ha'lo tu posto qui?

MISIDE: Ove è ito colui?

CREMETE: Tu non mi rispondi?

MISIDE: Hei, misera a me! ché non è in alcun luogo! Ei mi ha lasciata qui sola ed èssene ito.

DAVO: O Dii, io vi chiamo in testimonio: che romore è egli in mercato! Quanta gente vi piatisce! E anche la ricolta è cara. Io non so altro che mi dire.

MISIDE: Perché mi hai tu lasciata qui così sola?

DAVO: Hem? che favola è questa? O Miside, che fanciullo è questo? Chi l'ha recato qui?

MISIDE: Se' tu impazzato? Di che mi domandi tu?

DAVO: Get a move on so you'll be able to find out what I want you to do next. Oh my God!

MISIDE: What's the matter?

DAVO: Here comes the bride's father. I'm going to abandon my original plan.

MISIDE: I don't understand what you're talking about.

DAVO: I'll pretend to be arriving here from the right. Try to follow me and back up what I'm saying whenever it's necessary.

MISIDE: I don't understand a thing you're talking about, but I'll be here; so, if you need my services, I'll not stand in your way.

SCENE FOUR

Cremete, Miside, Davo.

CREMETE: I'm coming back in order to have my daughter sent for, because I have made all the necessary wedding arrangements. But what's this? Upon my word, it's a baby! Hey, young woman, did you put this baby here?

MISIDE: (Where did Davo go?)

CREMETE: Are you going to answer me?

MISIDE: (Oh dear, dear—he's nowhere around. He's gone off and left me here all alone.)

DAVO: Ye Gods, I call upon you as my witnesses— what a commotion there is in the market place. What a crowd of people squabbling there and how expensive food is. (I don't know what else to say.)

MISIDE: Why did you leave me here all alone?

DAVO: Huh? What kind of comedy is this?[25] Whose baby is this, Miside? Who brought it here?

MISIDE: Are you crazy? Why are you asking me this?

DAVO: Chi ne ho io a domandare, che non ci veggo altri?

CREMETE: Io mi maraviglio che fanciullo sia questo.

DAVO: Tu m'hai a rispondere ad quel ch'io ti domando. Tìrati in su la man ritta.

MISIDE: Tu impazzi: non ce lo portasti tu?

DAVO: Guarda di non mi dire una parola fuora di quello che io ti domando.

MISIDE: Tu bestemmi.

DAVO: Di chi è egli? Di', ch'ognuno oda.

MISIDE: De' vostri.

DAVO: Ha! ha! io non mi maraviglio se una meretrice non ha vergogna.

CREMETE: Questa fantesca è da Andro, come mi pare.

DAVO: Paiamovi noi però uomini da essere così uccellati?

CREMETE: Io sono venuto a tempo.

DAVO: Presto, leva questo fanciullo di qui! Sta' salda; guarda di non ti partire di qui!

MISIDE: Gl'Idii ti sprofondino, in modo mi spaventi!

DAVO: Dico io a te o no?

MISIDE: Che vuoi?

DAVO: Domandimene tu ancora? Dimmi: di chi è cotesto bambino?

MISIDE: Nol sai tu?

DAVO: Lascia ire quel ch'io so: rispondi a quello che io ti domando.

MISIDE: È de' vostri.

DAVO: Di chi nostri?

MISIDE: Di Panfilo.

DAVO: Come di Panfilo?

MISIDE: O perché no?

DAVO: Whom should I ask about it? I don't see anyone else here.

CREMETE: I wonder whose baby this could be?

DAVO: Answer my question. (Come off here to the right.)[26]

MISIDE: (You're out of your mind! Didn't you bring it yourself?)

DAVO: (Be careful to say nothing more than what I ask you for.)

MISIDE: (You're talking nonsense.)

DAVO: Whose is it? (Speak up so everyone can hear.)

MISIDE: Your people's!

DAVO: Ha! It doesn't surprise me that a whore has no shame.

CREMETE: (It would appear that it's the woman from Andros's servant.)

DAVO: Do we appear to be people who could be so easily fooled?

CREMETE: (I got here in the nick of time.)

DAVO: Hurry up, get that baby away from here! (Wait, don't you dare move away from here.)

MISIDE: (Go to Hell, you're scaring me to death!)

DAVO: Am I talking to you or not?

MISIDE: What *do* you want?

DAVO: Are you asking me again? Tell me, whose baby is this?

MISIDE: Don't you know?

DAVO: Never mind what I know. Answer my question!

MISIDE: It's your people's.

DAVO: Ours?

MISIDE: Panfilo's.

DAVO: What do you mean, Panfilo's?

MISIDE: Well, isn't it?

CREMETE: Io ho sempre ragionevolmente fuggite queste nozze.

DAVO: O sceleratezza notabile!

MISIDE: Perché gridi tu?

DAVO: Non vidi io che vi fu ieri recato in casa?

MISIDE: O audacia d'uomo!

DAVO: Non vidi io una donna con uno involgime sotto?

MISIDE: Io ringrazio Dio che, quando ella partorì, v'intervennono molte donne da bene.

DAVO: Non so io per che cagione si è fatto questo?—Se Cremete vedrà il fanciullo innanzi all'uscio, non gli darà la figliuola!—Tanto più gliene darà egli!

CREMETE: Non farà, per Dio!

DAVO: Se tu non lievi via cotesto fanciullo, io rinvolgerò te e lui nel fango.

MISIDE: Per Dio, che tu se' obliàco!

DAVO: L'una bugia nasce da l'altra. Io sento già susurrare che costei è cittadina ateniese . . .

CREMETE: Heimè!

DAVO: . . . e che, forzato da le leggi, la torrà per donna.

MISIDE: A! U! per tua fè, non è ella cittadina?

CREMETE: Io sono stato per incappare in uno male da farsi beffe di me.

DAVO: Chi parla qui? O Cremete, tu vieni a tempo. Odi!

CREMETE: Io ho udito ogni cosa.

DAVO: Hai udito ogni cosa?

CREMETE: Io ho udito certamente il tutto da principio.

CREMETE: (I was right all along to steer clear of this wedding.)

DAVO: What monstrous villainy!

MISIDE: Why are you shouting?

DAVO: Isn't this the baby I saw being carried into your house yesterday?

MISIDE: What nerve!

DAVO: Didn't I see a woman with a bundle rolled up under her arm?

MISIDE: Thank God there were some reliable women around when Glicerio gave birth.

DAVO: Don't I know why this was done? "If Cremete sees a baby on his threshold," she thinks, "he won't let his daughter get married." But he'll be for it all the more.

CREMETE: (Oh no he won't, by God!)

DAVO: If you don't take this baby away, I'll roll you both in the mud.

MISIDE: My God, you're drunk!

DAVO: One story leads to another: I've heard it bruited about that Glicerio is a citizen of Athens . . .

CREMETE: (Ah ha!)

DAVO: . . . and that Panfilo will be compelled by law to marry her.

MISIDE: Oh, for heaven's sake, *isn't* she a citizen?

CREMETE: (I almost stumbled into a bad situation and made a fool of myself.)

DAVO: Who's that talking? Oh, Cremete, you're just in time. Listen!

CREMETE: I heard everything.

DAVO: You heard it all?

CREMETE: I heard everything clearly right from the beginning.

DAVO: Hai udito, per tua fè? Ve' che sceleratezza! Egli è necessario mandare costei al bargello! Questo è quello. Non credi di uccellare Davo!

MISIDE: O miser' a me! O vecchio mio, io non ho detto bugia alcuna.

CREMETE: Io so ogni cosa. Ma Simone è drento?

DAVO: È.

MISIDE: Non mi toccare, ribaldo! io dirò bene a Glicerio ogni cosa.

DAVO: O pazzerella! tu non sai quello che si è fatto.

MISIDE: Che vuoi tu che io sappia?

DAVO: Costui è il suocero e in altro modo non si poteva fare che sapessi quello che noi volavamo.

MISIDE: Tu me lo dovevi dire innanzi.

DAVO: Credi tu che vi sia differenza, o parlare da cuore, secondo che ti detta la natura, o parlare con arte?

SCENA QUINTA

Crito, Miside, Davo.

CRITO: E' si dice che Criside abitava in su questa piazza, la quale ha voluto più tosto aricchire qui inonestamente, che vivere povera onestamente nella sua patria. Per la sua morte i suoi beni ricaggiono a me . . . Ma io veggo chi io ne potrò domandare. Dio vi salvi!

MISIDE: Chi veggo io? È questo Crito, consobrino di Criside? Egli è esso.

CRITO: O Miside, Dio ti salvi!

MISIDE: E Crito sia salvo!

CRITO: Così Criside, he?

MISIDE: Ella ci ha veramente rovinate.

CRITO: Voi che fate? In che modo state qui? Fate voi bene?

DAVO: Oh dear, everything? What an outrage! That woman ought to be sent to prison! This is the man. Don't think you can fool a Davo.

MISIDE: Oh dear, oh dear—sir, I wasn't telling a story.

CREMETE: I know it all. Is Simo inside?

DAVO: Yes.

MISIDE: Don't touch me, you scoundrel! I'm going to tell Glicerio everything.

DAVO: Oh, silly goose, don't you realize what's going on?

MISIDE: How should I?

DAVO: He's the father-in-law; there was no other way he could learn what it is we want him to.

MISIDE: You might have told me about it beforehand.

DAVO: Don't you think it makes a difference whether you speak from the heart, as nature tells you to, or whether you speak from the head?

SCENE FIVE

Crito, Miside, Davo.

CRITO: This is the square where Criside used to live. She preferred getting rich here dishonestly rather than living in her own country in honest poverty. At her death her property reverts to me. But I see some people whom I can ask about her. Greetings!

MISIDE: Who's this? Is it Criside's cousin, Crito? It is.

CRITO: Hello, Miside.

MISIDE: Why hello, Crito.

CRITO: So, Criside . . . Alas.

MISIDE: We were really broken up about it.

CRITO: What have you been doing? How are you? Are you all right?

MISIDE: Oimè! Noi? Come disse colui:—Come si può—poiché, come si vorrebbe, non possiamo.

CRITO: Glicerio che fa? Ha ella ancora trovato qui i suoi parenti?

MISIDE: Dio il volessi!

CRITO: O! non ancora? Io ci sono venuto in male punto, ché, per mia fè, se io lo avessi saputo, io non ci arei mai messo un piede. Costei è stata tenuta, sempre mai tenuta sorella di Criside, e possiede le cose sua; ora, sendo io forestiero, quanto mi sia utile muovere una lite, mi ammuniscono gli esempli degli altri. Credo ancora che costei arà qualche amico e difensore, perché la si partì di là grandicella, che grideranno che io sia uno spione e che io voglia con bugie aquistare questa eredità; oltra di questo non mi è lecito spogliarla.

MISIDE: Tu se' uno uom da bene, Crito, e ritieni il tuo costume antico.

CRITO: Menami a lei, ché io la voglio vedere, poiché io sono qui.

MISIDE: Volentieri.

DAVO: Io andrò drieto a costoro, perch'io non voglio che in questo tempo il vecchio mi vegga.

MISIDE: Oh, well . . . us? As they say, we're doing what we can since we can't do what we'd like.

CRITO: What's Glicerio doing? Has she found her relatives yet?

MISIDE: I wish to God that she had!

CRITO: What, not yet? I've arrived at a bad time because, I swear, had I known that, I'd never have set foot in this town. She was thought of, she was always thought of, as Criside's sister; she is still in possession of Criside's property. Now, the example of others acts as fair warning about how much good it would do for me, a foreigner, to file suit. I assume Glicerio will still have some friend and protector because she was fairly well grown up when she left. People will be screaming that I'm a fraud[27] and that I want to get at this inheritance deceitfully. Besides, I have no desire to strip the girl.

MISIDE: You're a good man, Crito; you've held on to your old character.

CRITO: Now that I'm here, take me to her so I can see her.

MISIDE: Of course.

DAVO: I'll go along with them; I don't want the old man to spot me just now.

ATTO QUINTO
SCENA PRIMA

Cremete, Simo.

CREMETE: Tu hai, o Simone, assai conosciuta l'amicitia mia verso di te; io ho corsi assai periculi: fa' fine di pregarmi. Mentre che io pensavo di compiacerti, io sono stato per affogare questa mia figliuola.

SIMO: Anzi, ora ti priego io e suplico, o Cremete, che appruovi coi fatti questo benefizio cominciato con le parole.

CREMETE: Guarda quanto tu sia, per questo tuo desiderio, ingiusto! E pure che tu faccia quello desideri, non osservi alcuno termine di benignità né pensi quello che tu prieghi: ché se tu lo pensassi, tu cesseresti di agravarmi con queste ingiurie.

SIMO: Con quali?

CREMETE: Ha! domandine tu? Non mi hai tu forzato che io dia per donna una mia figliuola ad uno giovane occupato nello amore d'altri e alieno al tutto dal tôrre moglie? E hai voluto con lo affanno e dolore della mia figliuola medicare il tuo figliuolo. Io volli, quando egli era bene; ora non è bene; abbi pazienza. Costoro dicono che colei è cittadina ateniese e ne ha auto uno figliuolo: lascia stare noi.

SIMO: Io ti priego, per lo amore di Dio, che tu non creda a costoro: tutte queste cose sono finte e trovate per amore di queste nozze. Come fia tolta la cagione per che fanno queste cose, e' non ci fia più scandolo alcuno.

CREMETE: Tu erri: io vidi una fantesca e Davo, che si dicevano villania.

SIMO: Io lo so.

ACT FIVE
SCENE ONE

Cremete, Simo.

CREMETE: You've had ample proof of my friendship for you, Simo; I've run quite enough risks. Stop your pleading. While I was making up my mind to fall in with your whims, I almost did my daughter in.

SIMO: But, now, I beg you, I beseech you, Cremete, that you ratify with deeds this favor you just granted with words.

CREMETE: See how unfair you're being with your unwarranted enthusiasm. As long as you can get what you want, you pay no attention to any limits on kindness or think about what it is you're asking. If you thought about it, you'd stop taking advantage of me.

SIMO: What advantage?

CREMETE: How can you ask? Haven't you forced me to marry my daughter to a young man distracted by another love affair, averse to any marriage? You sought to heal your son through my daughter's pain and suffering. I cooperated as long as it was still a good idea; now that it isn't, resign yourself. People say that she is a citizen of Athens and that she has had a child by him. Count us out!

SIMO: For the love of God, I beg you don't believe them. Every one of those things is a set up designed for the sake of this wedding. Once their reason for doing these things is taken away, there won't be any more gossip.

CREMETE: You're wrong. I saw Davo having it out with their servant girl.

SIMO: I know.

CREMETE: E da dovero, perché nessuno sapeva che io fussi presente.

SIMO: Io lo credo; ed è un pezzo che Davo mi disse che volevono fare questo, e oggi te lo volli dire, e dimentica'melo.

SCENA SECONDA

Davo, Cremete, Simo, Dromo.

DAVO: Ora voglio io stare con l'animo riposato . . .

CREMETE: Ecco Davo a te.

SIMO: Onde esce egli?

DAVO: . . . parte per mia cagione, parte per cagione di questo forestiero.

SIMO: Che ribalderia è questa?

DAVO: Io non vidi mai uomo venuto più a tempo di questo.

SIMO: Chi loda questo scelerato?

DAVO: Ogni cosa è a buon porto.

SIMO: Tardo io di parlargli?

DAVO: Egli è il padrone: che farò io?

SIMO: Dio ti salvi, uom da bene!

DAVO: O Simone, o Cremete nostro, ogni cosa è ad ordine.

SIMO: Tu hai fatto bene.

DAVO: Manda per lei a tua posta.

SIMO: Bene veramente! e' ci mancava questo! Ma rispondimi: che faccenda avevi tu quivi?

DAVO: Io?

SIMO: Sì.

DAVO: Di' tu a me?

SIMO: A te dich'io.

DAVO: Io v'entrai ora . . .

CREMETE: They were serious about it because neither one of them was aware that I was present.

SIMO: I believe it. Davo told me earlier that they wanted to pull off that number today. I meant to tell you, but I forgot to.

SCENE TWO

Davo, Cremete, Simo, Dromo.

DAVO: (Now, I want to take a load off my mind . . .)

CREMETE: There's your Davo.

SIMO: Why is he coming out of there?

DAVO: (. . . partly on my own account and partly on this foreigner's account.)

SIMO: What kind of mischief is this?

DAVO: (I've never seen a man arrive more when he was needed that this guy did.)

SIMO: Now who's this rascal praising?

DAVO: (Everything is safe now.)

SIMO: Why am I hesitating to speak to him?

DAVO: (It's the boss. What shall I do?)

SIMO: Hello, my good man.

DAVO: Simo, Cremete—everything is shipshape.

SIMO: You've done well.

DAVO: Send for her when you're ready.

SIMO: Oh, that's a good one; that's all we need. Answer me: what business did you have in there?

DAVO: Me?

SIMO: Yes.

DAVO: Are you talking to me?

SIMO: I am talking to you!

DAVO: I went in there just now . . .

SIMO: Come s'io domandassi quanto è ch'e' vi entrò!

DAVO: . . . col tuo figliuolo.

SIMO: Ho! Panfilo è dentro?

DAVO: Io sono in su la fune.

SIMO: Ho! non dicesti tu ch'egli avieno quistione insieme?

DAVO: E hanno.

SIMO: Come è egli così in casa?

CREMETE: Che pensi tu che faccino? E' si azzuffano.

DAVO: Anzi, voglio, o Cremete, che tu intenda da me una cosa indegna: egli è venuto ora uno certo vecchio, che pare uom cauto ed è di buona presenza, con uno volto grave da prestargli fede.

SIMO: Che di' tu di nuovo?

DAVO: Niente veramente, se non quello che io ho sentito dire da lui: che costei è cittadina ateniese.

SIMO: O! Dromo! Dromo!

DAVO: Che cosa è?

SIMO: Dromo!

DAVO: Odi un poco.

SIMO: Se tu mi di' più una parola . . . Dromo!

DAVO: Odi, io te ne priego.

DROMO: Che vuoi?

SIMO: Porta costui di peso in casa.

DROMO: Chi?

SIMO: Davo.

DROMO: Perché?

SIMO: Perché mi piace: portalo via!

DAVO: Che ho io fatto?

SIMO: Portalo via!

SIMO: As if I asked you how long ago you went in there!

DAVO: . . . with your son.

SIMO: What, Panfilo's in there?

DAVO: I'm at the end of my rope.

SIMO: Hey, didn't you say that those two were squabbling?

DAVO: They are.

SIMO: So, why is he in the house?

CREMETE: What do you suppose he's doing in there? They're fighting.

DAVO: No, Cremete, but I'd like you to listen to me tell you about something shocking: just now a man came in, some old man who seemed prudent and dignified, with an earnest expression that made you want to trust him.

SIMO: What news do you have to tell?

DAVO: Nothing, really, except what I heard him say— that she is a citizen of Athens.

SIMO: Dromo, Dromo!

DAVO: What's the matter?

SIMO: Dromo!

DAVO: Listen.

SIMO: If you say one more word to me . . . Dromo!

DAVO: Listen, I beg you!

DROMO: What do you want?

SIMO: Take this man bodily into the house.

DROMO: Who?

SIMO: Davo.

DROMO: Why?

SIMO: Because I say so—take him now.

DAVO: What have I done?

SIMO: Get him out of here, now!

DAVO: Se tu truovi che io ti abbia dette le bugie, ammazzami.

SIMO: Io non ti odo. Io ti farò diventare destro.

DAVO: Egli è pure vero.

SIMO: Tu lo legherai e guardera'lo. Odi qua, mettigli un paio di ferri: fallo ora e, se io vivo, io ti mosterrò, Davo, innanzi che sia sera, quello che importa, a te ingannare il padrone, e a colui il padre.

CREMETE: Ha! non essere sì crudele.

SIMO: O Cremete, non ti incresce egli di me per la ribalderia di costui, che ho tanto dispiacere per questo figliuolo? Orsù, Panfilo! Esci, Panfilo! Di che ti vergogni tu?

SCENA TERZA

Panfilo, Simo, Cremete.

PANFILO: Chi mi vuole? Oimè! egli è mio padre.

SIMO: Che di' tu, ribaldo?

CREMETE: Digli come sta la cosa, sanza villania.

SIMO: E' non se gli può dire cosa che non meriti. Dimmi un poco: Glicerio è cittadina?

PANFILO: Così dicono.

SIMO: O gran confidenza! Forse che pensa quel che risponde? Forse che si vergogna di quel ch'egli ha fatto? Guardalo in viso, e' non vi si vede alcun segno di vergogna. È egli possibile che sia di sì corrotto animo, che voglia costei fuora delle leggi e del costume de' cittadini, con tanto obbrobrio?

PANFILO: Misero a me!

DAVO: If you discover that what I've been telling you
are lies, kill me.

SIMO: I'm not listening to you. I'll have you on the
line.

DAVO: But it's the truth!

SIMO: Tie him up and watch him. Listen, put him in
chains. Do it now! As sure as I'm alive, Davo, I'll show
you before this day is out what it is to deceive your master
and I'll show him what it is to deceive a father.

CREMETE: Oh, don't be so cruel!

SIMO: Oh, Cremete, don't you think that you ought to
feel sorry for me because of his dastardly behavior, for all
the chagrin I've had from that son of mine? Come now,
Panfilo! Come out here, Panfilo! What are you ashamed of?

SCENE THREE

Panfilo, Simo, Cremete.

PANFILO: Who wants me; oh my God, it's my father!

SIMO: What do you have to say for yourself, you rascal?

CREMETE: Tell him how things are without being
unpleasant.

SIMO: As if I could say something to him that he didn't
deserve. Tell me, is Glicerio a citizen?

PANFILO: That's what they say.

SIMO: How free and easy he is! Do you think he gives
a thought to what he's saying? Perhaps he's ashamed of
what he's done? Look at his face—not a sign of shame.
Can his mind be so corrupted that he wants her in spite
of the laws and customs of Athens, no matter how much
disgrace is involved?

PANFILO: I'm miserable.

SIMO: Tu te ne se' aveduto ora? Cotesta parola dovevi tu dire già quando tu inducesti l'animo tuo a fare in qualunque modo quello che ti aggradava: pure alla fine ti è venuto detto quello che tu se'. Ma perché mi macero e perché mi crucio io? Perché affliggo io la mia vecchiaia per la pazzia di costui? Voglio io portare le pene de' peccati suoi? Abbisela, tengasela, viva con quella!

PANFILO: O padre mio!

SIMO: Che padre! Come che tu habbi bisogno di padre, che hai trovato, a dispetto di tuo padre, casa, moglie, figliuoli e chi dice ch'ella è cittadina ateniese. Abbi nome Vinciguerra.

PANFILO: Possoti io dire dua parole, padre?

SIMO: Che mi dirai tu?

CREMETE: Lascialo dire.

SIMO: Io lo lascio: dica!

PANFILO: Io confesso che io amo costei e, s'egli è male, io confesso fare male, e mi ti getto, o padre, nelle braccia; impommi che carico tu vuoi: se tu vuoi che io meni moglie e lasci costei, io lo sopporterò il meglio che io potrò. Solo ti priego di questo, che tu non creda che io ci abbi fatto venire questo vecchio, e sia contento ch'io mi iustifichi e che io lo meni qui alla tua presenza.

SIMO: Che tu lo meni?

PANFILO: Sia contento, padre.

CREMETE: Ei domanda il giusto: contentalo.

PANFILO: Compiacimi di questo.

SIMO: Io sono contento, pure che io non mi truovi ingannato da costui.

CREMETE: Per uno gran peccato ogni poco di suplicio basta ad uno padre.

SIMO: So, you're just realizing that now? You should
have said that a long time ago when you decided to do
what you pleased and damn the consequences—that's when
such words described you. But why on earth am I worrying and tormenting myself? Why should I trouble my
old age with his craziness? Why should I bear the punish-
ments for his sins? Take her, keep her, live with her!

PANFILO: Father!

SIMO: What do you mean, "father"![28] As if you needed
a father now that, by defying your father, you've found a
house, wife and children, and people to swear that she's
a citizen of Athens. Call yourself Conqueror!

PANFILO: Father, may I say something?

SIMO: What can you say to me?

CREMETE: Let him speak!

SIMO: I'll let him: Speak!

PANFILO: I confess that I love the woman. If that's
wrong, I confess to doing wrong; I put myself in your
hands, father. Impose any punishment on me that you
want. If you want me to marry and let her go, I'll endure
it as best I can. I beg only this: that you not think that
I've made this old man come here; please let me bring him
out here before you and clear myself.

SIMO: Bring him out here?

PANFILO: Please, father.

CREMETE: That's a fair request; let him.

PANFILO: Grant me this one request.

SIMO: Agreed, just so I don't find out that Panfilo has
been deceiving me.

CREMETE: Even for a major crime, a father can go
easy on the punishment.

SCENA QUARTA

Crito, Cremete, Simo, Panfilo.

CRITO: Non mi pregare; una di queste cagioni basta a farmi fare ciò che tu vuoi: tu, il vero e il bene che voglio a Glicerio.

CREMETE: Io veggo Critone Andrio? Certo egli è desso.

CRITO: Dio ti salvi, Cremete!

CREMETE: Che fai tu così oggi, fuora di tua consuetudine, in Atene?

CRITO: Io ci sono a caso. Ma è questo Simone?

CREMETE: Questo è.

SIMO: Domandi tu me? Dimmi un poco: di' tu che Glicerio è cittadina?

CRITO: Neghilo tu?

SIMO: Se' tu così qua venuto preparato?

CRITO: Perché?

SIMO: Domandine tu? Credi tu fare queste cose sanza esserne gastigato? Vieni tu qui ad ingannare i giovanetti imprudenti e bene allevati e andare con promesse pascendo l'animo loro?

CRITO: Se' tu in te?

SIMO: E vai raccozzando insieme amori di meretrici e nozze?

PANFILO: Heimè! io ho paura che questo forestiero non si pisci sotto.

CREMETE: Se tu conoscessi costui, o Simone, tu non penseresti cotesto; costui è uno buono huomo.

SIMO: Sia buono a suo modo: debbesegli credere ch'egli è appunto venuto oggi nel dì delle nozze e non è venuto prima mai?

SCENE FOUR

Crito, Cremete, Simo, Panfilo.

CRITO: Don't entreat me. Any one of these reasons is enough to make me do what you want me to: yourself, the truth, and the love that I bear Glicerio.

CREMETE: Is this Crito of Andros whom I see? It certainly is the very man.

CRITO: Greetings, Cremete.

CREMETE: What are you doing here in Athens today? It's not part of your routine.

CRITO: I'm here by chance, but isn't this Simo?

CREMETE: Yes.

SIMO: Are you looking for me? Tell me, are you the one who's saying that Glicerio is a citizen?

CRITO: Are you the one who's denying it?

SIMO: So, that's how it is, is it—all primed?

CRITO: What?

SIMO: How can you wonder? Do you think you can do this sort of thing with impunity? Coming here to trick inexperienced, well-brought-up young men; going about and exciting their hearts with idle promises?

CRITO: Are you in your right mind?

SIMO: And joining meretricious love affairs together in bonds of matrimony?

PANFILO: (Yipes, I'm afraid this stranger is going to piss in his pants.)[29]

CREMETE: If you knew this man, Simo, you wouldn't think that; he is a good man.

SIMO: Good in his own way. Why should I believe that, when he's arrived today, just in time—on the day of the wedding, and never before?

PANFILO: Se io non avessi paura di mio padre, io gl'insegnerei la risposta.

SIMO: Spione!

CRITO: Heimè!

CREMETE: Così è fatto costui, Crito; lascia ire.

CRITO: Sia fatto come e' vuole: se sèguita di dirmi ciò che vuole, egli udirà ciò che non vuole; io non prezzo e non curo coteste cose, imperò che si può intendere se quelle cose che io ho dette sono false o vere, perché uno ateniese, per lo adrieto, avendo rotto la sua nave, rimase con una sua figlioletta in casa il padre di Criside, povero e mendico.

SIMO: Egli ha ordito una favola da capo.

CREMETE: Lascialo dire.

CRITO: Impediscemi egli così?

CREMETE: Sèguita.

CRITO: Colui che lo ricevette era mio parente; quivi io udi' dire da lui come egli era cittadino ateniese; e quivi si morì.

CREMETE: Come aveva egli nome?

CRITO: Ch'io ti dica il nome sì presto? Fania.

CREMETE: O! Hu!

CRITO: Veramente io credo ch'egli avessi nome Fania: ma io so questo certo, ch'e' si faceva chiamare Ramnusio.

CREMETE: O Giove!

CRITO: Queste medesime cose, o Cremete, sono state udite da molti altri in Andro.

CREMETE: Dio voglia che sia quello che io credo! Dimmi un poco: diceva egli che quella fanciulla fussi sua?

CRITO: No.

PANFILO: (If I weren't afraid of my father, I could set him straight.)

SIMO: Swindler![30]

CRITO: Well!

CREMETE: That's just the way he is, Crito, never mind him.

CRITO: Let him be just the way he is. If he continues telling me whatever he wants to, he'll hear what he doesn't want to. I don't put any stock in these affairs or meddle in them. Nevertheless, you can find out later whether or not the things that I've said are true or false. Some time ago an Athenian was shipwrecked and, because he was needy—destitute—he stayed with his little girl in the house of Criside's father.

SIMO: He has composed a comedy from the ground up.[31]

CREMETE: Let him tell it.

CRITO: Is he going to keep on badgering me like this?

CREMETE: Go on.

CRITO: The man who took the Athenian in was a relative of mine. It was there that I heard from him that he was a citizen of Athens and there that he died.

CREMETE: What was his name?

CRITO: Must I tell it so soon—uh, Fania.[32]

CREMETE: Oh, no!

CRITO: I really do believe that his name was Fania, but I'm sure of this, he was called Ramnusio.

CREMETE: My God!

CRITO: This same story, Cremete, was known to many other people on Andros.

CREMETE: May heaven let it be as I think it is. Tell me, did he say that the little girl was his own?

CRITO: No.

CREMETE: Di chi dunque?

CRITO: Figliuola del fratello.

CREMETE: Certo, ella è mia.

CRITO: Che di' tu?

SIMO: Che di' tu?

PANFILO: Rizza gli orecchi, Panfilo!

SIMO: Che credi tu?

CREMETE: Quel Fania fu mio fratello.

SIMO: Io lo conobbi e sòllo.

CREMETE: Costui, fuggendo la guerra mi venne in Asia drieto, e, dubitando di lasciare qui la mia figliuola, la menò seco; dipoi non ne ho mai inteso nulla, se non ora.

PANFILO: L'animo mio è sì alterato che io non sono in me per la speranza, per il timore, per la allegrezza, veggendo uno bene sì repentino.

SIMO: Io mi rallegro in molti modi che questa tua si sia ritrovata.

PANFILO: Io lo credo, padre.

SIMO: Ma e' mi resta uno scrupolo che mi fa stare di mala voglia.

PANFILO: Tu meriti di essere odiato con questa tua religione.

CRITO: Tu cerchi cinque piè al montone!

CREMETE: Che cosa è?

SIMO: Il nome non mi riscontra.

CRITO: Veramente da piccola la si chiamò altrimenti.

CREMETE: Come, Crito? Ricorditene tu?

CRITO: Io ne cerco.

CREMETE: Whose, then?

CRITO: His brother's daughter.

CREMETE: Then she is certainly mine.

CRITO: What's that you're saying?

SIMO: What's that you're saying?

PANFILO: Prick up your ears, Panfilo.

SIMO: What makes you think so?

CREMETE: Fania was my brother.

SIMO: I knew him and I know the story.

CREMETE: He was a refugee from the war; he was coming to meet me in Asia. He was afraid to leave my daughter here at the time, so he took her with him. Since then I have heard nothing about him—until now.

PANFILO: My heart is so aflutter that I can hardly control myself—I'm in such a state of hope, fear, and joy at these unexpected good tidings.

SIMO: I'm delighted in more ways than one that this girl of yours has been found again.

PANFILO: I believe you father.

SIMO: But there is one remaining scruple that keeps bothering me.

PANFILO: (You deserve to be despised for your religion with its scruples.)

CRITO: You're splitting hairs![33]

CREMETE: What's the matter?

SIMO: The name doesn't ring a bell.

CRITO: As a little girl she was really called something else.

CREMETE: What, Crito? Can you remember what it was?

CRITO: I'm trying to.

PANFILO: Patirò io che la smemorataggine di costui me nuoca, potendo io per me medesimo giovarmi? O Cremete, che cerchi tu? La si chiamava Passibula.

CRITO: La è essa!

CREMETE: La è quella!

PANFILO: Io gliene ho sentito dire mille volte.

SIMO: Io credo che tu, o Cremete, creda che noi siamo tutti allegri.

CREMETE: Così mi aiuti Idio, come io lo credo.

PANFILO: Che manca, o padre?

SIMO: Già questa cosa mi ha fatto ritornare nella tua grazia.

PANFILO: O piacevole padre! Cremete vuole che la sia mia moglie, come la è!

CREMETE: Tu di' bene, se già tuo padre non vuole altro.

PANFILO: Certamente.

SIMO: Cotesto.

CREMETE: La dota di Panfilo voglio che sia dieci talenti.

PANFILO: Io l'accetto.

CREMETE: Io vo a trovare la figliuola. O Crito mio, vieni meco, perché io non credo che la mi riconosca.

SIMO: Perché non la fai tu venire qua?

PANFILO: Tu di' bene: io commetterò a Davo questa faccenda.

SIMO: Ei non può.

PANFILO: Perché non può?

SIMO: Egli ha uno male di più importanza.

PANFILO: Che cosa ha?

SIMO: Egli è legato.

PANFILO: O padre, ei non è legato a ragione.

PANFILO: Do I have to put up with this person's absent-mindedness and let it do me harm when I can clear up my situation on my own? Cremete, what are you looking for? Her name was Passibula.

CRITO: That's it!

CREMETE: Yes, that's it!

PANFILO: I've heard her say it thousands of times.

SIMO: I believe, Cremete, that you must believe that we are all delighted at this news.

CREMETE: God help me, I do believe it.

PANFILO: What's missing, father?

SIMO: This event has already put you back in my good graces.

PANFILO: Oh what a wonderful father. If Cremete wants her still to be my wife, so be it!

CREMETE: You're right, unless your father wants something else.

PANFILO: Agreed?

SIMO: Yes.

CREMETE: I want the dowry for Panfilo to be ten talents.

PANFILO: I accept.

CREMETE: I'm going to find my daughter. Oh, Crito, my friend, come with me, because I don't think she will recognize me.

SIMO: Why don't you have her come over here?

PANFILO: You're right; I'll entrust the task to Davo.

SIMO: He can't.

PANFILO: Why can't he?

SIMO: He has a weightier problem.

PANFILO: What's that?

SIMO: He's in chains.

PANFILO Oh, father, it's not proper to chain him.

SIMO: Io volli così.

PANFILO: Io ti priego che tu faccia che sia sciolto.

SIMO: Che si sciolga!

PANFILO: Fa' presto!

SIMO: Io vo in casa.

PANFILO: O allegro e felice questo dì!

SCENA QUINTA

Carino, Panfilo.

CARINO: Io torno a vedere quel che fa Panfilo . . . Ma eccolo!

PANFILO: Alcuno forse penserà che io pensi che questo non sia vero, ma e' mi pare pure che sia vero. Però credo io che la vita degli Iddei sia sempiterna, perché i piaceri loro non sono mai loro tolti: perché io sarei, sanza dubio, immortale, se cosa alcuna non sturbassi questa mia allegrezza. Ma chi vorrei sopra ogni altro riscontrare per narrargli questo?

CARINO: Che allegrezza è questa di costui?

PANFILO: Io veggo Davo; non è alcuno che io desideri vedere più di lui, perché io so che solo costui si ha a rallegrare da dovero della allegrezza mia.

SCENA SESTA

Davo, Panfilo, Carino.

DAVO: Panfilo dove è?

PANFILO: O Davo!

DAVO: Chi è?

PANFILO: Io sono.

SIMO: I ordered it done that way.
PANFILO: I beg you to have him released.
SIMO: Release him!
PANFILO: Do it quickly.
SIMO: I'm going into the house.
PANFILO: Oh what a happy day!

SCENE FIVE

Carino, Panfilo.

CARINO: I'm coming back to see what's up with Panfilo. Why, there he is!

PANFILO: Perhaps some people will think I can't believe that this is true, but still it seems true enough to me.[34] I believe the gods enjoy eternal life because they never have their pleasures taken away from them. Why, I'll be immortal myself if nothing disturbs this joy of mine—there's no doubt of that! But whom should I like to meet more than anyone else so that I could tell him this story of mine?

CARINO: (What's this guy so happy about?)

PANFILO: I see Davo; there's no one I'd rather see than him because I know that he's the only one who can be genuinely delighted at my happiness.

SCENE SIX

Davo, Panfilo, Carino.

DAVO: Where's Panfilo?
PANFILO: Oh, Davo!
DAVO: Who's that?
PANFILO: It's I.

DAVO: O Panfilo!

PANFILO: Ha! tu non sai quello mi è accaduto.

DAVO: Veramente no: ma io so bene quello che è accaduto a me.

PANFILO: Io lo so anch'io.

DAVO: Egli è usanza degli uomini che tu abbi prima saputo il male mio che io il tuo bene.

PANFILO: La mia Glicerio ha ritrovato suo padre.

DAVO: O! la va bene.

CARINO: Hem?

PANFILO: Il padre è grande amico nostro.

DAVO: Chi?

PANFILO: Cremete.

DAVO: Di' tu il vero?

PANFILO: Né ci è più dificultà di averla io per donna.

CARINO: Sogna costui quelle cose ch'egli ha vegghiando volute?

PANFILO: Ma del fanciullo, o Davo?

DAVO: Ha! sta' saldo: tu se' solo amato dagl'Idii.

CARINO: Io sono franco, se costui dice il vero. Io gli voglio parlare.

PANFILO: Chi è questo? O Carino! Tu ci se' arrivato a tempo.

CARINO: O! la va bene.

PANFILO: O! hai tu udito?

CARINO: Ogni cosa. Or fa' di ricordarti di me in queste tua prosperità. Cremete è ora tutto tuo, e so che farà quello che tu vorrai.

PANFILO: Io lo so; e perché sarebbe troppo aspettare ch'egli uscissi fuora, sèguitami, perch'egli è in casa con

DAVO: Oh, Panfilo.

PANFILO: Ha—you don't know what's happened
to me.

DAVO: No, I really don't, but I certainly know what's
happened to me.

PANFILO: I know about it too.

DAVO: That's the way of the world: you find out about
my bad luck before I find out about your good luck.

PANFILO: My Glicerio has found her father.

DAVO: Oh, fine!

CARINO: (Hmmm.)

PANFILO: Her father is a great friend of ours.

DAVO: Who?

PANFILO: Cremete!

DAVO: Are you telling the truth?

PANFILO: And there's no longer any difficulty about
marrying her.

CARINO: (Does this guy dream up all the things he'd
like to have if he were awake?)

PANFILO: And, Davo, about the baby . . .

DAVO: Stop. You alone are beloved of the gods!

CARINO: (I'm saved, if what he says is true. I'm going
to speak to him.)

PANFILO: Who's this? Oh, Carino, you're just in time.

CARINO: Congratulations!

PANFILO: Have you heard?

CARINO: Everything. Now be sure to remember me in
your hour of prosperity. Cremete is absolutely on your side
now; I know he'll do anything you want.

PANFILO: I know it. Because it would take too long
for him to come outside, follow me—for he's inside the
house with Glicerio. Davo, go on home; hurry and send

Glicerio. Tu, Davo, vanne in casa e sùbito manda qua chi
la meni via. Perché stai? perché non vai?

DAVO: O voi, non aspettate che costoro eschino fuora.
Drento si sposerà e drento si farà ogni altra cosa che mancassi. Andate, al nome di Dio, e godete!

some people to get her out here. What are you waiting for, why aren't you going?

DAVO: Don't you wait for them to come out. Carino will get engaged inside, and everything else that's wrong will get fixed up inside too. May God be with you; enjoy yourselves.[35]

MANDRAGOLA
THE MANDRAKE

TRANSLATED BY

DAVID SICES

CHARACTERS

CALLIMACO: a young Florentine merchant
SIRO: his servant
MESSER NICIA: A Florentine lawyer
LIGURIO: a parasite
SOSTRATA: mother of Lucrezia
FRATE TIMOTEO: a friar
A WOMAN
LUCREZIA: wife of Messer Nicia

CANZONE

da dirsi innanzi alla commedia, cantata da ninfe e pastori
insieme

> Perché la vita è brieve
> e molte son le pene
> che vivendo e stentando ognun sostiene;
>
> dietro alle nostre voglie,
> andiam passando e consumando gli anni,
> ché chi il piacer si toglie
> per viver con angosce e con affani,
> non conosce gli inganni
> del mondo; o da quai mali
> e da che strani casi
> oppressi quasi—sian tutti i mortali.
>
> Per fuggir questa noia,
> eletta solitaria vita abbiamo,
> e sempre in festa e in gioia
> giovin' leggiadri e liete Ninfe stiamo.
> Or qui venuti siamo
> con la nostra armonia,
> sol per onorar questa
> sì lieta festa—e dolce compagnia.
>
> Ancor ci ha qui condutti
> il nome di colui che vi governa,
> in cui si veggon tutti
> i beni accolti in la sembianza eterna.
> Per tal grazia superna,
> per sì felice stato,
> potete lieti stare,
> godere e ringraziare—chi ve lo ha dato.

OPENING CHORUS

Sung by nymphs and shepherds together[1]

> Since life on earth is fleeting
> And many are the sorrows
> That every man must bear from dawn to morrow,
>
> We do whate'er we will,
> We live from day to day in search of pleasure,
> For he who seeks out ill,
> And clings to fear and grief as to a treasure,
> Regrets it at his leisure
> In sadness, for his mind is
> Deceived by dark illusion
> And deep confusion—as to what mankind is.
>
> To flee from what annoys
> We've chosen to live out here in the country
> Pursuing mirth and joys,
> Young men and happy Nymphs, a rustic gentry.
> We greet you all and sundry
> With song and dance adorning;
> And we wish you all gladness
> Instead of sadness—on this bright spring morning.
>
> The name of him who reigns
> Here also draws us to this landscape vernal,
> A prince whose heart contains
> All gifts in Jove's bright countenance eternal.[2]
> And for this grace supernal,
> This blessed state enchanted,
> You all should feel elation,
> Congratulation—offer him who has it granted.

PROLOGO

Idio vi salvi, benigni auditori,
quando e' par che dependa
questa benignità da lo esser grato.
Se voi seguite di non far romori,
noi vogliàn che s'intenda
un nuovo caso in questa terra nato.
Vedete l'apparato,
qual or vi si dimostra:
quest' è Firenze vostra,
un'altra volta sarà Roma o Pisa,
cosa da smascellarsi delle risa.

Quello uscio, che mi è in sulla man ritta,
la casa è d'un dottore,
che imparò in sul Buezio legge assai;
quella via, che è colà in quel canto fitta,
è la via dello Amore,
dove chi casca non si rizza mai;
conoscer poi potrai
a l'abito d'un frate
qual priore o abate
abita el tempio che all' incontro è posto,
se di qui non ti parti troppo tosto.

Un giovane, Callimaco Guadagno,
venuto or da Parigi,
abita là, in quella sinistra porta.
Costui, fra tutti gli altri buon compagno,
a' segni ed a' vestigi
l'onor di gentilezza e pregio porta.
Una giovane accorta

PROLOGUE

God bless you, gracious audience,
Since we know that your graciousness
Depends upon our pleasing you.
May your silence let our troupe commence
To play for you, with some finesse,
A recent case that's something new.
The stage set we've convoked you to,
As you shall presently be shown,
Is that dear Florence which you call your own.
Tomorrow Rome or some other setting
Will tickle you till your sides are splitting.

This entrance, on my right-hand side,
Is the door to the house of a doctor of law
Who's learned from Boethius [3] what law he could.
And that street there, you've no doubt espied,
Is called Lovers' Lane, where, as you know,
He who stumbles falls for good.
You shortly will have understood,
When you have seen the cloak he flaunts, [4]
What sort of monk or abbot haunts
That church there in the other part,
If you don't leave too near the start.

Callimaco Guadagni, a youth
Arrived from Paris recently,
Resides there on the left extreme.
Of all our rich young bloods, in truth,
He bears himself most decently,
And merits honor and esteem.
A circumspect young wife by him

fu da lui molto amata,
e per questo ingannata
fu, come intenderete, ed io vorrei
che voi fussi ingannate come lei.

La favola *Mandragola* si chiama:
la cagion voi vedrete
nel recitarla, com' i' m'indovino.
Non è il componitor di molta fama;
pur, se vo' non ridete,
egli è contento di pagarvi il vino.
Un amante meschino,
un dottor poco astuto,
un frate mal vissuto,
un parassito, di malizia il cucco,
fie questo giorno el vostro badalucco.

E, se questa materia non è degna,
per esser pur leggieri,
d'un uom, che voglia parer saggio e grave,
Scusatelo con questo, che s'ingegna
con questi van' pensieri
fare il suo tristo tempo più suave,
perché altrove non have
dove voltare el viso,
ché gli è stato interciso
mostrar con altre imprese altra virtùe,
non sendo premio alle fatiche sue.

El premio che si spera è che ciascuno
si sta da canto e ghigna,
dicendo mal di ciò che vede o sente.
Di qui depende, sanza dubbio alcuno,

Was hotly and at length pursued;
And how the woman, falsely wooed,
At last was brought to bed, you'll hear,
Mesdames, and you'd be, too, I fear.

Our tale's named for the mandrake root.[5]
You'll see the reason as we play it
For you, dear public, I opine.
Its author has no great repute,
But if you don't laugh while we essay it,
He'll treat you to a flask of wine.
A wretched swain will weep and whine,
A doltish man of law will bumble,
A venal monk will help him stumble,
A most ingenious parasite
Will guide them all, for your delight.

If such material seems unsound
Argument, and far too spare
For a man of serious pretense,
Excuse him on the following ground:
The author, with pastimes debonair,
Has sought to mask his impotence,
Since he's reduced to indolence
And has no other way to turn,
Condemned to an enforced sojourn,
All worthwhile occupations barred
Or, at the least, denied reward.[6]

The sole reward he may hope to reap
Is for all to stand aside and snicker,
Decrying what they see and hear.
And that is why, if we look deep,

che per tutto traligna
da l'antica virtù el secol presente,
imperò che la gente,
vedendo ch' ognun biasma,
non s'affatica e spasma
per far con mille sua disagi un'opra,
che 'l vento guasti o la nebbia ricuopra.

Pur, se credessi alcun, dicendo male,
tenerlo pe' capegli,
e sbigottirlo o ritirarlo in parte,
io l'ammonisco, e dico a questo tale
che sa dir male anch' egli,
e come questa fu la sua prim' arte,
e come in ogni parte
del mondo, ove el "sì" sona,
non istima persona,
ancor che facci sergieri a colui,
che può portar miglior mantel che lui.

Ma lasciam pur dir male a chiunque vuole.
Torniamo al caso nostro,
acciò che non trapassi troppo l'ora.
Far conto non si de' delle parole,
né stimar qualche mostro,
che non sa forse s' e' s'è vivo ancora.
Callimaco esce fuora
e Siro con seco ha,
suo famiglio, e dirà
l'ordin di tutto. Stia ciascuno attento,
né per ora aspettate altro argumento.

Today the ancient virtues flicker,
And high endeavors disappear;
For who would dare to persevere
In undertakings long or short,
Which nagging censure will abort,
And works on which fond hopes are pinned
Are cloaked in fog, or gone with the wind.

But still, if any critics thought
Through blame to have him by the hair,
And frighten or intimidate,
I warn them it will come to naught,
For he can slander, too, I swear,
And he's no mere initiate;
In truth, he doesn't hesitate
With any man who speaks his tongue;
He can sting back when he is stung;
Our author doesn't give a fig
For lackeys of the biggest wig.

But let us let the blackguards carp,
And come back to the work at hand,
For as it is the hour grows late.
It isn't meet for us to harp
On critics' words, or be unmanned
By monsters our vain fears inflate.
Callimaco is at his gate
With Siro, his servant boy, in traction;
The two of them will start the action.
Dear public, adieu, you've heard our plot:
Now let our tangled thread unknot.

ATTO PRIMO
SCENA PRIMA

Callimaco, Siro.

CALLIMACO: Siro, non ti partire, io ti voglio un poco.

SIRO: Eccomi.

CALLIMACO: Io credo che tu ti maravigliassi assai della mia sùbita partita da Parigi; ed ora ti maraviglierai, sendo io stato qui già un mese sanza fare alcuna cosa.

SIRO: Voi dite el vero.

CALLIMACO: Se io non ti ho detto infino a qui quello che io ti dirò ora, non è stato per non mi fidare di te, ma per iudicare che le cose che l'uomo vuole non si sappino, sia bene non le dire, se non forzato. Pertanto, pensando io di potere avere bisogno della opera tua, ti voglio dire el tutto.

SIRO: Io vi sono servidore: e servi non debbono mai domandare el padrone d'alcuna cosa, né cercare alcuno loro fatto, ma quando per loro medesimi le dicano, debbono servirgli con fede; e così ho fatto e sono per fare io.

CALLIMACO: Già lo so. Io credo che tu mi abbi sentito dire mille volte, ma e' non importa che tu lo intenda mille una, come io avevo dieci anni quando da e mia tutori, sendo mio padre e mia madre morti, io fui mandato a Parigi, dove io sono stato venti anni. E perché in capo de' dieci cominciorono, per la passata del re Carlo, le guerre in Italia, le quali ruinorono quella provincia, delibera' mi di vivermi a Parigi e non mi ripatriare mai, giudicando potere in quel luogo vivere più sicuro che qui.

SIRO: Egli è così.

ACT ONE
SCENE ONE

Callimaco, Siro.

CALLIMACO: Siro, don't go away. I need you for a
moment.

SIRO: At your service.

CALLIMACO: I imagine you must have wondered why
I left Paris so suddenly, and you must be wondering now
why I have stayed in Florence for a month already, without
doing a thing.

SIRO: I am indeed.

CALLIMACO: If I haven't told you up to now what I am
about to reveal, it's not because I don't trust you. I always
feel it is better not to talk about private matters unless one
is forced to. However, since I think I can use your help
now, I am going to let you in on the secret.

SIRO: I am your servant, and servants should never
ask questions or pry into their master's personal affairs.
But when we are told about them, we must serve you
faithfully. That is what I have always done and always
will do.

CALLIMACO: I know that. I imagine you must have
heard me say a thousand times, so it doesn't matter if you
hear it for the thousand and first, how, when I was a lad
of ten, my mother and father died, and my guardians sent
me to Paris, where I lived for twenty years. What with
King Charles's campaign in Italy,[7] which stirred up the
wars and ruined our country, I decided after ten years to
stay in France and never return home, judging I could live
more safely there than here.

SIRO: That is so.

CALLIMACO: E commesso di qua che fussino venduti tutti e mia beni, fuora che la casa, mi ridussi a vivere quivi, dove sono stato dieci altri anni con una felicità grandissima . . .

SIRO: Io lo so.

CALLIMACO: . . . avendo compartito el tempo parte alli studii, parte a' piaceri, e parte alle faccende; ed in modo mi travagliavo in ciascuna di queste cose, che l'una non mi impediva la via dell'altra. E per questo, come tu sai, vivevo quietissimamente, giovando a ciascuno, ed ingegnandomi di non offendere persona: talché mi pareva essere grato a' borghesi, a' gentiluomini, al forestiero, al terrazzano, al povero ed al ricco.

SIRO: Egli è la verità.

CALLIMACO: Ma, parendo alla Fortuna che io avessi troppo bel tempo, fece che e' capitò a Parigi uno Cammillo Calfucci.

SIRO: Io comincio a 'ndovinarmi del male vostro.

CALLIMACO: Costui, come li altri fiorentini, era spesso convitato da me; e, nel ragionare insieme, accadde un giorno che noi venimo in disputa dove erano più belle donne, o in Italia o in Francia. E perché io non potevo ragionare delle italiane, sendo sì piccolo quando mi parti', alcuno altro fiorentino, che era presente, prese la parte franzese, e Cammillo la italiana; e, dopo molte ragione assegnate da ogni parte, disse Cammillo, quasi che irato, che, se tutte le donne italiane fussino monstri, che una sua parente era per riavere l'onore loro.

SIRO: Io sono or chiaro di quello che voi volete dire.

CALLIMACO: E nominò madonna Lucrezia, moglie di messer Nicia Calfucci: alla quale e' dètte tante laude e di bellezza e di costumi, che fece restare stupidi qualunque di noi, ed in me destò tanto desiderio di vederla, che io, la-

CALLIMACO: And having commissioned someone
here to sell off all my belongings except for the house, I
settled down and lived most happily there for the next ten
years . . .

SIRO: I know.

CALLIMACO: . . . dividing my time between studies,
pleasure and business. And I arranged things so nicely that
none of these activities ever interfered with any of the others. In this fashion, as you well know, I lived tranquilly,
helping my fellow man and being sure never to offend anyone. So I felt accepted by merchant and nobleman, foreigner and countryman, rich and poor alike.

SIRO: That is quite true.

CALLIMACO: But fortune, deeming no doubt that
things were going too well for me, saw to it that a certain
Cammillo Calfucci came to Paris.

SIRO: I'm beginning to guess what your trouble is.

CALLIMACO: Like many other Florentines, he was
often a guest in my house, and talking together one day,
we happened to get into an argument as to whether the
women are more beautiful in France or in Italy. I couldn't
speak about Italian women, since I was so young when
I left, but another Florentine who was there took the part
of the French, and Cammillo that of the Italians. After a
great deal of discussion on both sides, Cammillo almost
flew into a rage, saying that, even if all the other women
in Italy were monsters, one of his relatives was enough by
herself to win back their honor.

SIRO: Now I see exactly what you're getting at.

CALLIMACO: He named Madonna Lucrezia, the wife
of Messer[8] Nicia Calfucci. He paid such homage to her
beauty and her grace that he silenced all the rest of us,
and he aroused in me so great a desire to see her for my-

sciato ogni altra deliberazione, né pensando più alle guerre o alle pace d'Italia, mi messi a venire qui. Dove arrivato, ho trovato la fama di Madonna Lucrezia essere minore assai che la verità, il che occorre rarissime volte, e sommi acceso in tanto desiderio d'esser seco, che io non truovo loco.

SIRO: Se voi me n'avessi parlato a Parigi, io saprei che consigliarvi; ma ora non so io che mi vi dire.

CALLIMACO: Io non ti ho detto questo per voler tua consigli, ma per sfogarmi in parte, e perché tu prepari l'animo adiutarmi, dove el bisogno lo richerchi.

SIRO: A cotesto son io paratissimo; ma che speranza ci avete voi?

CALLIMACO: Ehimè! nessuna.

SIRO: O perché?

CALLIMACO: Dirotti. In prima mi fa guerra la natura di lei, che è onestissima ed al tutto aliena dalle cose d'amore; l'avere el marito ricchissimo, e che al tutto si lascia governare da lei, e, se non è giovane, non è al tutto vecchio, come pare; non avere parenti o vicini, con chi ella convenga ad alcuna vegghia o festa o ad alcuno altro piacere, di che si sogliono dilettare le giovane. Delle persone meccaniche non gliene càpita a casa nessuna; non ha fante né famiglio, che non triemi di lei: in modo che non c'è luogo ad alcuna corruzione.

SIRO: Che pensate, adunque, di poter fare?

CALLIMACO: E' non è mai alcuna cosa sì disperata, che non vi sia qualche via da poterne sperare; e benché la fussi debole e vana, e la voglia e 'l desiderio, che l'uomo ha di condurre la cosa, non la fa parere così.

SIRO: Infine, e che vi fa sperare?

self that, without stopping to consider anything else, or whether there was war or peace in Italy, I set out for Florence. Upon my arrival, I found Madonna Lucrezia's reputation to be nothing, compared to the truth, which you will admit is rare indeed. I have been inflamed with such burning desire to be with her, that I cannot bear it.

SIRO: If you had spoken to me in Paris, I would have known how to advise you, but now I really don't know what to say.

CALLIMACO: I haven't told you all this to get your advice, but just to find a little relief, and get you ready to help me if I should need it.

SIRO: I am quite ready to do that, but what hopes do you have?

CALLIMACO: I don't have any.

SIRO: Oh, why?

CALLIMACO: I'll tell you. In the first place, I have to overcome Madonna Lucrezia's own nature, since she is completely virtuous and not interested in affairs of the heart. Secondly, she has a husband who is very rich, who lets her have her way in all things and, although he isn't young, doesn't appear to be all that old. Third, she doesn't have relatives or neighbors whom she meets at parties, dances, or other kinds of entertainment where young women generally go to have fun. No workmen frequent her house, she has no maids or servants who are not afraid of her, so there is no chance of bribery.

SIRO: What do you think you can do, then?

CALLIMACO: Nothing is ever so desperate that there is no ground for hope. Even if the hope is vain and foolish, a man's will and desire to achieve what he wants will make it seem not to be.

SIRO: Well, then, what gives you hope?

CALLIMACO: Dua cose: l'una, la semplicità di messer Nicia, che, benché sia dottore, egli è el più semplice ed el più sciocco uomo di Firenze; l'altra, la voglia che lui e lei hanno di avere figliuoli, che, sendo stata sei anni a marito e non avendo ancora fatti, ne hanno, sendo ricchissimi, un desiderio che muoiono. Una terza ci è, che la sua madre è suta buona compagna, ma la è ricca, tale che io non so come governarmene.

SIRO: Avete voi per questo tentato per ancora cosa alcuna?

CALLIMACO: Sì ho, ma piccola cosa.

SIRO: Come?

CALLIMACO: Tu conosci Ligurio, che viene continuamente a mangiar meco. Costui fu già sensale di matrimoni, dipoi s'è dato a mendicare cene e desinari; e perché gli è piacevole uomo, messer Nicia tiene con lui una stretta dimestichezza, e Ligurio l'uccella; e benché non lo meni a mangiare seco, li presta alle volte danari. Io me l'ho fatto amico, e gli ho comunicato el mio amore: lui m'ha promesso d'aiutarmi con le mani e co' piè.

SIRO: Guardate e' non v'inganni: questi pappatori non sogliono avere molta fede.

CALLIMACO: Egli è el vero. Nondimeno, quando una cosa fa per uno, si ha a credere, quando tu gliene communichi, che ti serva con fede. Io gli ho promesso quando e' riesca, donarli buona somma di danari; quando e' non riesca, ne spicca un desinare ed una cena, ché ad ogni modo i' non mangerei solo.

SIRO: Che ha egli promesso, insino a qui, di fare?

CALLIMACO: Ha promesso di persuadere a messer Nicia che vada con la sua donna al bagno in questo maggio.

SIRO: Che è a voi cotesto?

CALLIMACO: Two things: first, the stupidity of her husband, Messer Nicia who, although he is a Doctor of Laws, is the simplest and most foolish man in all Florence. Second, the desire of both of them for children; they have been married for six years now without having any, and since they are rich, they are dying to have an heir. There is a third reason, too: her mother; she used to play around a bit when she was younger. But now she is well-to-do, so I don't know how to take advantage of that.

SIRO: Have you attempted anything at all yet?

CALLIMACO: Yes, but nothing much.

SIRO: What?

CALLIMACO: You know Ligurio, who is always showing up to eat at my house. He used to make his living as a marriage-broker, but then he took up mooching lunches and dinners. Since he is an agreeable fellow, Messer Nicia has grown quite inseparable from him, and Ligurio strings him along. Nicia hasn't asked him home to dinner yet, but sometimes he lends him money. I have made friends with Ligurio and told him about my love. He has promised to help me in any way he can.

SIRO: Watch out that he doesn't trick you. Those moochers can never be trusted.

CALLIMACO: That is true. However, when there is nothing else to lose, if you take someone into your confidence, you have to believe he will serve you faithfully. I have promised to give him a goodly sum of money if he succeeds; if he doesn't, all he gets out of it is a lunch and dinner, and I wouldn't eat alone anyway.

SIRO: What has he promised to do so far?

CALLIMACO: He promised to persuade Messer Nicia to take his wife to the baths[9] this coming May.

SIRO: What good will that do you?

CALLIMACO: Che è a me! Potrebbe quel luogo farla diventare d'un'altra natura, perché in simili lati non si fa se non festeggiare; ed io me n'andrei là, e vi condurrei di tutte quelle ragion' piaceri che io potessi, né lascerei indrieto alcuna parte di magnificenzia; fare'mi familiar suo, del marito . . . che so io? Di cosa nasce cosa, e 'l tempo la governa.

SIRO: E' non mi dispiace.

CALLIMACO: Ligurio si partì questa mattina da me, e disse che sarebbe con messer Nicia sopra questa cosa, e me ne risponderebbe.

SIRO: Eccogli di qua insieme.

CALLIMACO: Io mi vo' tirare da parte, per essere a tempo a parlare con Ligurio, quando si spicca dal dottore. Tu, intanto ne va' in casa alle tue faccende; e, se io vorrò che tu faccia cosa alcuna, io tel dirò.

SIRO: Io vo.

SCENA SECONDA

Messer Nicia, Ligurio.

NICIA: Io credo ch' e tua consigli sien buoni, e parla'ne iersera alla donna: disse che mi risponderebbe oggi; ma, a dirti el vero, io non ci vo di buone gambe.

LIGURIO: Perché?

NICIA: Perché io mi spicco mal volentieri da bomba; dipoi, ad avere a travasare moglie, fante, masserizie, ella non mi quadra. Oltr' a questo, io parlai iersera a parecchi medici: l'uno dice che io vadia a San Filippo, l'altro alla Porretta, e l'altro alla Villa; e' mi parvono parecchi uc-

CALLIMACO: Well, who knows? A place like that could change her mind, since people have nothing to do there but have fun. I would go along and seize every opportunity for pleasure, and I wouldn't neglect any chance to show off my wealth. I would get on good terms with her and her husband. Who can say? One thing leads to another, and only time will tell.

SIRO: That sounds all right to me.

CALLIMACO: Ligurio went off this morning to sound out Messer Nicia on the subject, and he promised to let me know what he said.

SIRO: Ssh . . . There they are together now.

CALLIMACO: I think I'll move off a little way, so that I can speak to Ligurio as soon as he has got rid of Nicia. Meanwhile, you go on with your business back at the house. If I want you for anything, I'll call you.

SIRO: I'm off.

SCENE TWO

Messer Nicia, Ligurio.

NICIA: I'm sure your advice is sound, and I spoke of it with the missus last night. She said she would give me an answer today; but to tell you the truth, I'm not so keen on going.

LIGURIO: Why not?

NICIA: Because I have a hard time dragging myself away from home base. And then to have to pack up the wife, the servants, all our household stuff—it just doesn't sit right with me. Aside from that, I spoke with a couple of doctors yesterday, and one says go to San Filippo, the next one says Porretta, and the third says Villa [10]—they all

cellacci; e a dirti el vero, questi dottori di medicina non sanno quello che si pescano.

LIGURIO: E' vi debbe dar briga, quello che voi dicesti prima, perché voi non sete uso a perdere la Cupola di veduta.

NICIA: Tu erri. Quando io ero più giovane, io sono stato molto randagio: e' non si fece mai la fiera a Prato, che io non vi andassi; e' non c'è castel veruno all'intorno, dove io non sia stato; e ti vo' dir più là: io sono stato a Pisa ed a Livorno, o va'!

LIGURIO: Voi dovete avere veduta la carrucola di Pisa.

NICIA: Tu vuo' dire la Verucola.

LIGURIO: Ah! sì, la Verucola. A Livorno, vedesti voi el mare?

NICIA: Ben sai che io il vidi!

LIGURIO: Quanto è egli maggior che Arno?

NICIA: Che Arno? Egli è per quattro volte, per più di sei, per più di sette, mi farai dire: e' non si vede se non acqua, acqua, acqua.

LIGURIO: Io mi maraviglio, adunque, avendo voi pisciato in tante neve, che voi facciate tanta difficultà d'andare ad uno bagno.

NICIA: Tu hai la bocca piena di latte. E' ti pare a te una favola avendo a sgominare tutta la casa? Pure, io ho tanta voglia d'avere figliuoli, che io son per fare ogni cosa. Ma parlane un po' tu con questi maestri, vedi dove e' mi consigliassino che io andassi; ed io sarò intanto con la donna, e ritroverrenci.

LIGURIO: Voi dite bene.

seem like a bunch of quacks to me. To be frank, I don't
think those doctors know their ass from their elbows.

LIGURIO: What is really bothering you is what you
were talking about before. You're just not used to getting
out of sight of the Cupola. [11]

NICIA: There's where you're all wrong! When I was
younger, I was a real vagabond. There was never a fair over
in Prato that I didn't go to, and there isn't a castle around
Florence I haven't visited. And what is even more, I've
been to Pisa and Leghorn, [12] what do think of that?

LIGURIO: Then you must have seen the Leaking Tower
of Pisa. [13]

NICIA: You mean the Leaning Tower?

LIGURIO: Oh yes! The Leaning Tower. Did you see the
sea at Leghorn?

NICIA: What do you mean? Of course I saw it!

LIGURIO: How much bigger is it than the Arno?

NICIA: Than the Arno? It's at least four times—more
than six times; I'd go so far as to say even seven times
bigger, and all you can see is water, water, and more
water!

LIGURIO: I'm really amazed, then, that such a man
of the world, who had ants in his pants once upon a time,
should make such a fuss about going off to the baths.

NICIA: You're talking drivel, man! Do you think it's a
trifle to have to turn the whole household upside down?
Still, I'm so anxious to have children that I'm ready to do
just about anything. You go and talk to those doctors, find
out where they advise me to go. I'll be with the missus
meanwhile, and we'll see each other later.

LIGURIO: That's a good idea.

SCENA TERZA

Ligurio, Callimaco.

LIGURIO: Io non credo che sia nel mondo el più sciocco
uomo di costui; e quanto la Fortuna lo ha favorito! Lui
ricco, lui bella donna, savia, costumata, ed atta a governare un regno. E parmi che rare volte si verifichi quel
proverbio ne' matrimoni, che dice: "Dio fa gli uomini, e'
s'appaiano"; perché spesso si vede uno uomo ben qualifi-
cato sortire una bestia, e, per avverso, una prudente donna
avere un pazzo. Ma della pazzia di costui se ne cava questo
bene, che Callimaco ha che sperare.—Ma eccolo. Che vai
tu appostando, Callimaco?

CALLIMACO: Io t'avevo veduto col dottore, ed aspettavo che tu ti spicassi da lui, per intendere quello avevi
fatto.

LIGURIO: Egli è uno uomo della qualità che tu sai,
di poco prudenzia, di meno animo, e partesi mal volentieri
da Firenze; pure, io ce l'ho riscaldato: e' mi ha detto infine
che farà ogni cosa; e credo che, quando e' ti piaccia questo
partito, che noi ve lo condurreno; ma io non so se noi ci
fareno el bisogno nostro.

CALLIMACO: Perché?

LIGURIO: Che so io? Tu sai che a questi bagni va
d'ogni qualità gente, e potrebbe venirvi uomo a chi madonna Lucrezia piacessi come a te, che fussi ricco più di te,
che avessi più grazia di te: in modo che si porta pericolo di
non durare questa fatica per altri, e che c'intervenga che la
copia de' concorrenti la faccino più dura, o che, dimesti-
candosi, la si volga ad un altro e non a te.

SCENE THREE

Ligurio, Callimaco.

LIGURIO: (I don't believe there is a more stupid man in all the world, and look how Fortune has favored him! He is rich, and has a beautiful, virtuous wife with fine manners, fit to rule a kingdom. You know, it's seldom the case, as the old saying goes, that marriages are made in heaven. Often you see a fine, upstanding man paired off with a beast, and on the contrary, an intelligent woman married to a nit-wit. But there is one thing to be gained from Messer Nicia's foolishness: Callimaco has grounds for hope. Ah, there he is now.) What are you doing standing there, Callimaco?

CALLIMACO: I saw you with Messer Nicia, and I was waiting for you to get rid of him, to hear how you made out.

LIGURIO: You know what kind of man he is: little sense and less spirit. He is hard to pry away from Florence. But I have warmed him up to it, and he has told me that he will do everything I ask. So if we want to follow that plan, I think he will go along with us. Only I'm not sure we'll be able to accomplish what we want that way.

CALLIMACO: Why not?

LIGURIO: Who can tell? All kinds of people go to those baths, you know. Some fellow might come along who liked Madonna Lucrezia as much as you do, one who is richer or more attractive than you. In that case, there is a risk of your going to all that trouble for someone else. Or it might happen that all the competition would make her harder to get, or that when her resistance was worn down, she would land in someone else's arms.

CALLIMACO: Io conosco che tu di' el vero. Ma come ho a fare? Che partito ho a pigliare? Dove mi ho a volgere? A me bisogna tentare qualche cosa, sia grande, sia periculosa, sia dannosa, sia infame. Meglio è morire che vivere così. Se io potessi dormire la notte, se io potessi mangiare, se io potessi conversare, se io potessi pigliare piacere di cosa veruna, io sarei più paziente ad aspettare el tempo; ma qui non c'è rimedio; e, se io non sono tenuto in speranza da qualche partito, i' mi morrò in ogni modo; e, veggendo d'avere a morire, non sono per temere cosa alcuna, ma per pigliare qualche partito bestiale, crudele, nefando.

LIGURIO: Non dire così, raffrena cotesto impeto dello animo.

CALLIMACO: Tu vedi bene che, per raffrenarlo, io mi pasco di simili pensieri. E però è necessario o che noi seguitiamo di mandare costui al bagno, o che noi entriano per qualche altra via, che mi pasca d'una speranza, se non vera, falsa almeno, per la quale io nutrisca un pensiero, che mitighi in parte tanti mia affani.

LIGURIO: Tu hai ragione, ed io sono per farlo.

CALLIMACO: Io lo credo, ancora che io sappia che e pari tuoi vivino di uccellare li uomini. Nondimanco, io non credo essere in quel numero, perché, quando tu el facessi ed io me ne avvedessi, cercherei valermene, ed perderesti per ora l'uso della casa mia, e la speranza di avere quello che per lo avvenire t'ho promesso.

LIGURIO: Non dubitare della fede mia, ché, quando e' non ci fussi l'utile che io sento e che io spero, e' c'è che 'l tuo sangue si confà col mio, e desidero che tu adempia questo tuo desiderio presso a quanto tu. Ma lasciamo ir questo. El dottore mi ha commesso che io truovi un medico, e intenda a quale bagno sia bene andare. Io voglio

CALLIMACO: I realize you're right. But what can I do? What plans can I make? Where can I turn? I absolutely have to try something, whether it is noble, dangerous, drastic or vile. It's better to die than to live like this. If I could only sleep at night, if I could eat, if I could talk with people, if I could enjoy anything at all any more, I would be patient and bide my time. But there is no cure; and if my hope isn't kept alive by some plan or other, I will surely die. So, seeing that I'll die anyway, I have to do something; and I won't stop at anything, no matter how brutal, cruel or foul.

LIGURIO: Don't say that, you must restrain these impulses!

CALLIMACO: To tell you the truth, I only indulge in thoughts like that in order to restrain them. So we either have to get this fellow to the baths or work out some other way, so I can nourish some hope, even a false one—just so I can ease my suffering.

LIGURIO: You're right, and I'm going to do something about it.

CALLIMACO: I believe you, though I know that people like you live by tricking others. Still I don't think you will try to dupe me, because if you did and I discovered it, I would be sure to get even. You would lose not only my hospitality, but all hopes of getting what I promised you for the future.

LIGURIO: Don't worry, you can trust me. Even if I didn't have a stake in this, the fact is I feel a kinship for you, and I want to satisfy your desires almost as much as you do. But let's get down to business. Messer Nicia has asked me to find a doctor and see which baths he should

che tu faccia a mio modo, e questo è che tu dica di avere
studiato in medicina, e che abbi fatto a Parigi qualche
sperienzia: lui è per crederlo facilmente per la semplicità
sua, e per essere tu litterato e poterli dire qualche cosa in
gramatica.

CALLIMACO: A che ci ha a servire cotesto?

LIGURIO: Serviracci a mandarlo a qual bagno noi vor-
reno, ed a pigliare qualche altro partito che io ho pensato,
che sarà più corto, più certo, più riuscibile che 'l bagno.

CALLIMACO: Che di' tu?

LIGURIO: Dico che, se tu arai animo e se tu confiderai
in me, io ti do questa cosa fatta, innanzi che sia domani
questa otta. E, quando e' fussi uomo che non è, da ricer-
care se tu se' o non se' medico, la brevità del tempo, la
cosa in sé farà o che non ne ragionerà o che non sarà a
tempo a guastarci el disegno, quando bene e' ne ragionassi.

CALLIMACO: Tu mi risuciti. Questa è troppa gran
promessa, e pascimi di troppa gran speranza. Come farai?

LIGURIO: Tu el saprai, quando e' fia tempo; per ora
non occore che io te lo dica, perché el tempo ci mancherà a
fare, nonché dire. Tu, vanne in casa, e quivi m'aspetta, ed
io andrò a trovare el dottore, e, se io lo conduco a te andrai
seguitando el mio parlare ed accomodandoti a quello.

CALLIMACO: Così farò, ancora che tu mi riempia
d'una speranza, che io temo non se ne vadia in fumo.

go to. Here is what you'll do: tell him you have studied medicine and had a practice in Paris. He is bound to fall for it, given his stupidity and your learning, and your ability to say a few words in Latin.

CALLIMACO: What good will that do us?

LIGURIO: It will let us send him to the baths we choose, and follow up on another idea I have just thought of which will be quicker, surer, and more practical than the baths.

CALLIMACO: What do you mean?

LIGURIO: Let me just say that if you have courage, and trust me, I will swing this deal for you by this time tomorrow. Then even if he had enough brains, which he doesn't, to verify whether you are a doctor or not, either he won't think about it, or he won't have time to spoil our plan, even if he does think about it.

CALLIMACO: You're giving me a new lease on life! That is too much to promise, and I don't know whether I can bear such great hope. How will you do it?

LIGURIO: You'll find out when the time comes. For now I had better not tell you, because there is scarcely enough time to act, much less to talk about it. Go back home and wait for me, and I will go get Messer Nicia. When I bring him to you, just listen to what I say and follow my lead.

CALLIMACO: I'll do it, though you are filling me with such hope that I'm afraid it will all go up in smoke.

CANZONE

Chi non fa prova, Amore,
della tua gran possanza, indarno spera
di far mai fede vera
qual sia del cielo il più alto valore;
né sa come si vive, insieme, e muore,
come si segue il danno e'l ben si fugge,
come s'ama se stesso
men d'altrui, come spesso
timore e speme i cori adiaccia e strugge;
né sa come ugualmente uomini e dèi
paventan l'arme di che armato sei.

SONG

No man can, without trying
The sweetness of thy power, Love, imagine
In any rightful fashion
High heaven's greatest virtue, love undying;
Nor can he know mix'd death and life, while
    sighing,
Or how we flee our welfare as from error,
And think more of our lover
Than self; over and over
Our hearts are racked with hope and then with
    terror;
For thou strik'st fear into the very marrow
Of gods and mortals with thy bow and arrow.

ATTO SECONDO
SCENA PRIMA

Ligurio, Messer Nicia, Siro.

LIGURIO: Come io vi ho detto, io credo che Iddio ci abbia mandato costui, perché voi adempiate el desiderio vostro. Egli ha fatto a Parigi esperienzie grandissime; e non vi maravigliate se a Firenze e' non ha fatto professione dell'arte, che n'è suto cagione, prima, per essere ricco, secondo, perché egli è ad ogni ora per tornarsi a Parigi.

NICIA: Ormai, frate sì, cotesto bene importa; perché io non vorrei che mi mettessi in qualche lecceto, e poi mi lasciassi in sulle secche.

LIGURIO: Non dubitate di cotesto; abbiate solo paura che non voglia pigliare questa cura; ma, se la piglia, e' non e' per lasciarvi infino che non ne veda el fine.

NICIA: Di cotesta parte io mi vo' fidare di te, ma della scienzia io ti dirò bene io, come io gli parlo, s' egli è uomo di dottrina, perché a me non venderà egli vesciche.

LIGURIO: E perché io vi conosco, vi meno io a lui, acciò li parliate. E se, parlato li avete, e' non vi pare per presenzia, per dottrina, per lingua uno uomo da metterli il capo in grembo, dite che io non sia desso.

NICIA: Or sia, al nome dell'Agnol santo! Andiamo. Ma dove sta egli?

LIGURIO: Sta in su questa piazza, in quello uscio che voi vedete al dirimpetto a noi.

NICIA: Sia con buona ora. Picchia.

LIGURIO: Ecco fatto.

SIRO: Chi è?

ACT TWO
SCENE ONE

Ligurio, Messer Nicia, Siro.

LIGURIO: As I told you, I think the good Lord has sent us this doctor for the fulfillment of your desire. He has an enormous practice in Paris, but don't be surprised that he hasn't opened an office in Florence. The reasons are, first, that he is very rich, and second, that he is due to return to Paris at any moment.

NICIA: Well now, brother, that's an important consideration. I wouldn't want him to get me into deep water and then leave me high and dry.

LIGURIO: Don't worry about that. Let's just hope that he'll be willing to take your case. If he does accept, I know he is going to see it through right to the end.

NICIA: As far as that's concerned, I'll take your word for it. But when it comes to medical knowledge, I'll tell you after I've talked with him whether he is a man of learning. He won't be able to pull the wool over my eyes!

LIGURIO: I know you only too well. That is why I am taking you to meet him. And when you have talked with him, if he doesn't seem to you, by his character, his learning, and his speech, to be someone in whose hands you can put your wife, then I'm not the man you think I am.

NICIA: All right, by Jesus! Let's go! But where does he live?

LIGURIO: Right in this square, at the door you see in front of you.

NICIA: That's just fine. You knock.

LIGURIO: Here we go.

SIRO: Who is it?

LIGURIO: E'vi Callimaco?

SIRO: Sì, è.

NICIA: Che non di' tu "maestro Callimaco"?

LIGURIO: E' non si cura di simil' baie.

NICIA: Non dir così, fa' 'l tuo debito, e, s' e' l'ha per male, scingasi!

SCENA SECONDA

Callimaco, Messer Nicia, Ligurio.

CALLIMACO: Chi è quel che mi vuole?

NICIA: *Bona dies, domine magister.*

CALLIMACO: *Et vobis bona, domine doctor.*

LIGURIO: Che vi pare?

NICIA: Bene, alle guagnele!

LIGURIO: Se voi volete che io stia qui con voi, voi parlerete in modo che io v'intenda, altrimenti noi fareno duo fuochi.

CALLIMACO: Che buone faccende?

NICIA: Che so io? Vo cercando duo cose, ch' un altro per avventura fuggirebbe: questo è di dare briga a me e ad altri. Io non ho figliuoli, e vorre'ne, e, per avere questa briga, vengo a dare impaccio a voi.

CALLIMACO: A me non fia mai discaro fare piacere a voi ed a tutti li uomini virtuosi e da bene come voi; e non mi sono a Parigi affaticato tanti anni per imparare per altro, se non per potere servire a' pari vostri.

NICIA: Gran mercè; e, quando voi avessi bisogno dell'arte mia, io vi servirei volentieri. Ma torniamo *ad rem nostram.* Avete voi pensato che bagno fussi buono a disporre

LIGURIO: Is Callimaco there?

SIRO: Yes, he is.

NICIA: Why don't you call him Doctor Callimaco?

LIGURIO: He doesn't care about such trifles.

NICIA: Well, never mind him. You do what's right, and if he doesn't like it, he can screw it.

SCENE TWO

Callimaco, Messer Nicia, Ligurio.

CALLIMACO: Who wishes to speak to me?

NICIA: *Bona dies, domine magister.*[14]

CALLIMACO: *Et vobis bona, domine doctor.*[15]

LIGURIO: What do you think?

NICIA: Fine, by the Holy Gospel!

LIGURIO: Well, if you want me to stick around, you had better talk so that I understand you; otherwise we'll be at cross-purposes.

CALLIMACO: What can I do for you?

NICIA: I wish I knew. Here I am looking for two things that anybody else would probably fly from: I want to make trouble for myself, and for others, too. I have no children and I want to get some, and in order to have this trouble, I've come to make a nuisance for you.

CALLIMACO: Never let it be said that I refused my services to you, or to any other good, deserving man like you. I haven't exhausted myself in Paris all these years, studying, for any other reason than to serve people of your kind.

NICIA: Thank you, thank you! And any time you need my professional talents, doctor, I'll be delighted to return the favor. But let's get back *ad rem nostram.*[16] Have you

la donna mia ad impregnare? Ché io so che qui Ligurio vi ha detto quel che vi s'abbi detto.

CALLIMACO: Egli è la verità; ma, a volere adempiere el desiderio vostro, è necessario sapere la cagione della sterilità della donna vostra, perché le possono essere più cagione; *nam causae sterilitatis sunt: aut in semine, aut in matrice, aut in instrumentis seminariis, aut in virga, aut in causa extrinseca.*

NICIA: Costui è il più degno uomo che si possa trovare!

CALLIMACO: Potrebbe, oltr' a di questo, causarsi questa sterilità da voi, per impotenzia; che quando questo fussi, non ci sarebbe rimedio alcuno.

NICIA: Impotente io? Oh! voi mi farete ridere! Io non credo che sia el più ferrigno ed il più rubizzo uomo in Firenze di me.

CALLIMACO: Se cotesto non è, state di buona voglia, che noi vi troverremo qualche remedio.

NICIA: Sarebbeci egli altro remedio che bagni? Perché io non vorrei quel disagio, e la donna uscirebbe di Firenze mal volentieri.

LIGURIO: Sì, sarà! Io vo' rispondere io: Callimaco è tanto respettivo, che è troppo. Non m'avete voi detto di sapere ordinare certe pozione, che indubitatamente fanno ingravidare?

CALLIMACO: Sì, ho; ma io vo rattenuto con gli uomini che io non conosco, perché io non vorrei mi tenessino un cerretano.

NICIA: Non dubitate di me, perché voi mi avete fatto maravigliare di qualità, che non è cosa io non credessi o facessi per le vostre mani.

LIGURIO: Io credo che bisogni che voi veggiate el segno.

decided which baths would be best for getting my wife pregnant? I know Ligurio here has told you what there is to tell you.

CALLIMACO: That is true, but in order to gratify your desire, I have to know the cause of your wife's sterility. There are several possible causes. *Nam causae sterilitatis sunt: aut in semine, aut in matrice, aut in instrumentis seminariis, aut in virga, aut in causa extrinseca.*[17]

NICIA: (This is the most worthy man I have ever met!)

CALLIMACO: Aside from these causes, this sterility might be occasioned by your impotence. If that were the case, I have no remedy for you.

NICIA: Me impotent!? Why, you're making me laugh! I'm as tough as nails, and I don't believe there is a more virile man in all of Florence.

CALLIMACO: If that is so, then you can rest assured that we will find a cure for your problem.

NICIA: Mightn't there be some other remedy than the baths? Because I'd rather not go to all that trouble, and the missus isn't anxious to leave Florence.

LIGURIO: Yes, there is! Excuse me for interrupting, but Dr. Callimaco is far too modest. Didn't you tell me that you could concoct a certain potion that is absolutely guaranteed to result in pregnancy?

CALLIMACO: Yes, I did. But I have to be cautious with people I don't know. I wouldn't want them to take me for a charlatan.

NICIA: You don't have to worry about me. You have impressed me so deeply that there is nothing I wouldn't believe or do in your hands.

LIGURIO: I imagine that you will have to see a specimen.

CALLIMACO: Sanza dubbio, e' non si può fare di meno.

LIGURIO: Chiama Siro, che vadia con el dottore a casa per esso, e torni qui; e noi l'aspetteremo in casa.

CALLIMACO: Siro! Va' con lui. E, se vi pare, messere, tornate qui sùbito, e pensereno a qualche cosa di buono.

NICIA: Come, se mi pare? Io tornerò qui in uno stante, che ho più fede in voi che gli Ungheri nelle spade.

SCENA TERZA

Messer Nicia, Siro.

NICIA: Questo tuo padrone è un gran valente uomo.

SIRO: Più che voi non dite.

NICIA: El re di Francia ne de' far conto.

SIRO: Assai.

NICIA: E per questa ragione e' debbe stare volentieri in Francia.

SIRO: Così credo.

NICIA: E' fa molto bene: in questa terra non ci è se non cacastecchi, non ci si apprezza virtù alcuna. S' egli stessi qua, non ci sarebbe uomo che lo guardassi in viso. Io ne so ragionare, che ho cacato le curatelle per imparare dua *hac*, e se io ne avessi a vivere, io starei fresco, ti so dire!

SIRO: Guadagnate voi l'anno cento ducati?

NICIA: Non cento lire, non cento grossi, o va'! E questo è che, chi non ha lo stato in questa terra, de' nostri pari,

CALLIMACO: Of course, we can't do without it.

LIGURIO: Call Siro, and let him go home with Messer Nicia here to get one. We will wait in your house for him to bring it back.

CALLIMACO: Siro, you go with him. And if you will, sir, come back here right away, and we will find something good for you.

NICIA: What do you mean, if I will? I'll be back in a second. I have more faith in you than an Arab in his stallion.[18]

SCENE THREE

Messer Nicia, Siro.

NICIA: That master of yours is a very capable man.

SIRO: More than you can imagine.

NICIA: The King of France must have a high regard for him.

SIRO: Exceptional.

NICIA: That is probably why he prefers to remain in France.

SIRO: Evidently.

NICIA: He's got the right idea. In this town there's nothing but a bunch of shit-asses; nobody has an appreciation for class. If he stuck around here, there isn't a man who could look him in the eye. I know what I'm talking about, because I had to work my butt off just to learn *amo, amas, amat*. If I didn't have money of my own, I'd be up the creek, let me tell you!

SIRO: What do you make, a hundred ducats a year?

NICIA: Not a hundred lire, not even a hundred centimes, what do you think of that? And the reason is that

non truova can che gli abbai; e non siàn buoni ad altro che andare a' mortori o alle ragunate d'un mogliazzo, o a starci tuttodì in sulla panca del Proconsolo a donzellarci. Ma io ne li disgrazio, io non ho bisogno di persona: così stessi chi sta peggio di me! Ma non vorrei però ch' elle fussino mia parole, ché io arei di fatto qualche balzello o qualche porro di drieto, che mi fare' sudare.

SIRO: Non dubitate.

NICIA: Noi siamo a casa. Aspettami qui: io tornerò ora.

SIRO: Andate.

SCENA QUARTA

Siro solo.

SIRO: Se gli altri dottori fussin fatti come costui, noi faremo a' sassi pe' forni: che sì, che questo tristo di Ligurio e questo impazzato di questo mio padrone lo conducono in qualche loco, che gli faranno vergogna! E veramente io lo desiderrei, quando io credessi che non si risapessi, perché, risapendosi, io porto pericolo della vita, el padrone della vita e della roba. Egli è già diventato medico: non so io che disegno si sia el loro, e dove si tenda questo loro inganno . . .—Ma ecco el dottore, che ha uno orinale in mano: chi non riderebbe di questo uccellaccio?

SCENA QUINTA

Messer Nicia, Siro.

NICIA: Io ho fatto d'ogni cosa a tuo modo: di questo vo' io che tu facci a mio. Se io credevo non avere figliuoli, io arei preso più tosto per moglie una contadina che te. To'

anybody who doesn't have connections in this town is lucky if he can get the time of day. All we're good for is going to funerals or to wedding parties, or sitting on the Proconsul's bench all day long watching the people go by. But I don't give a damn, I don't need anyone. There are a lot worse off than I am, believe you me. All this is strictly off the record, of course, I don't want to have some tax or fine, or some other pain in the ass slapped on me.

SIRO: Don't worry.

NICIA: Here's my house. Wait for me, I'll be right out.

SIRO: Go ahead.

SCENE FOUR

Siro alone.

SIRO: If all men of learning were like this one, the rest of us would be hanging from the treetops. That rascal, Ligurio, and that crazy master of mine are leading him into something he'll be sorry for. To tell the truth, that doesn't bother me, as long as word doesn't get around. If it does, my life is in jeopardy, and so is my master's, and his property, too. He has already turned into a doctor; I don't know what their plans are and what this swindle is leading to. But here comes Messer Nicia with a chamber pot in his hands. How can you help laughing at the poor sucker?

SCENE FIVE

Messer Nicia, Siro.

NICIA: (I've always done everything your way, now I want you to do this my way, for once. If I had known I wasn't going to have children, I would have married some

costì, Siro; viemmi drieto. Quanta fatica ho io durata a
fare che questa mia mona sciocca mi dia questo segno! E
non è dire che la non abbi caro di fare figliuoli, ché la ne
ha più pensiero di me; ma, come io le vo' far fare nulla,
egli è una storia.

SIRO: Abbiate pazienza: le donne si sogliono con le
buone parole condurre dove altri vuole.

NICIA: Che buone parole! ché mi ha fracido. Va' ratto,
di' al maestro ed a Ligurio che io son qui.

SIRO: Eccogli che vengon fuori.

SCENA SESTA

Ligurio, Callimaco, Messer Nicia.

LIGURIO: El dottore fia facile a persuadere; la difficultà
fia la donna ed a questo non ci mancherà modi.

CALLIMACO: Avete voi el segno?

NICIA: E' l'ha Siro, sotto.

CALLIMACO: Dàllo qua. Oh! questo segno mostra de-
bilità di rene.

NICIA: E' mi par torbidiccio; eppur l'ha fatto ora ora.

CALLIMACO: Non ve ne maravigliate. *Nam mulieris
urinae sunt semper maioris grossitiei et albedinis et minoris
pulchritudinis quam virorum. Huius autem, inter caetera, causa
est amplitudo canalium, mixtio eorum quae ex matrice exeunt
cum urinis.*

NICIA: Oh! uh! potta di san Puccio! Costui mi
raffinisce in tralle mani; guarda come ragiona bene di
queste cose!

peasant girl rather than you.) Here, take this, Siro.[19] Come
along with me. What a hard time I had getting that silly
missus of mine to give me this specimen! It's not as if she
isn't anxious to have children, too; she's more concerned
than I am, but as soon as I try to get her to do something
about it, it's another story.

SIRO: Be patient. You always have to use sweet talk
with women to get your way.

NICIA: What do you mean, sweet talk! She got me
madder than a wet hen. Go quickly, tell the doctor and
Ligurio that I'm back.

SIRO: Here they are, coming out of the house.

SCENE SIX

Ligurio, Callimaco, Messer Nicia.

LIGURIO: Messer Nicia will be easy to convince. The
real problem will be his wife, but we'll find a way around
that.

CALLIMACO: Do you have the specimen?

NICIA: Siro has it there, covered up.

CALLIMACO: Hand it over. Aha! This specimen shows
signs of a weakness in the glands.

NICIA: It does look a little murky, and yet she just did
it a few moments ago.

CALLIMACO: Do not be surprised. *Nam mulieris urinae
sunt semper maioris grossitiei et albedinis et minoris pulchritudinis
quam virorum. Huius autem, inter caetera, causa est amplitudo
canalium, mixtio eorum quae ex matrice exeunt cum urinis.*[20]

NICIA: (Wow! By Saint Christopher's cock! This fellow
gets more subtle by the minute! Listen to how well he
speaks of these things!)

CALLIMACO: Io ho paura che costei non sia la notte mal coperta, e per questo fa l'orina cruda.

NICIA: Ella tien pure adosso un buon coltrone; ma la sta quattro ore ginocchioni ad infilzar paternostri, innanzi che la se ne venghi al letto, ed è una bestia a patir freddo.

CALLIMACO: Infine, dottore, o voi avete fede in me, o no; o io vi ho ad insegnare un rimedio certo, o no. Io, per me, el rimedio vi darò. Se voi arete fede in me, voi la piglierete; e se, oggi ad uno anno, la vostra donna non ha un suo figliuolo in braccio, io voglio avervi a donare dumilia ducati.

NICIA: Dite pure, ché io son per farvi onore di tutto, e per credervi più che al mio confessoro.

CALLIMACO: Voi avete ad intender questo, che non è cosa più certa ad ingravidare una donna che dargli bere una pozione fatta di mandragola. Questa è una cosa esperimentata de me dua paia di volte, e trovata sempre vera; e, se non era questo, la reina di Francia sarebbe sterile, ed infinite altre principesse de quello stato.

NICIA: È egli possibile?

CALLIMACO: Egli è come io vi dico. E la Fortuna vi ha in tanto voluto bene, che io ho condutto qui meco tutte quelle cose che in quella pozione si mettono, e potete averla a vostra posta.

NICIA: Quando l'arebbe ella a pigliare?

CALLIMACO: Questa sera dopo cena, perché la luna è ben disposta, ed el tempo non può essere più appropriato.

NICIA: Cotesto non fia molto gran cosa. Ordinatela in ogni modo: io gliene farò pigliare.

CALLIMACO: I am afraid that the reason why this woman passes such raw water is that she has been badly covered at night.

NICIA: I have a nice, thick comforter; but she insists on stringing out prayers for hours on end, down on her knees, before she'll get into bed. She's a real horse when it comes to standing the cold.

CALLIMACO: All right, Messer Nicia: either you have confidence in me or you don't. Either I have a sure cure to prescribe for your wife or I don't. For my part, I'll give it to you straight: if you trust in me, you'll let your wife have it, and if within a year she doesn't have a baby in her arms, I am willing to give you two thousand ducats.

NICIA: Go on. I'm ready to take your word without question, and I trust you more than my father-confessor.

CALLIMACO: You must understand this: there is nothing more certain to make a woman conceive than to give her a potion made with mandrake root. That is something I have tested half a dozen times, and always found true. If it were not for that, the Queen of France and countless other Princesses of that realm would be barren.

NICIA: You don't say!

CALLIMACO: It is exactly as I have told you. And it just so happens, by a stroke of good fortune, that I have brought with me all the ingredients which go into this potion, so now you can have it, too.

NICIA: When would she have to take it?

CALLIMACO: This evening, after supper. According to the moon, this is just the right time of month. We couldn't choose a better moment.

NICIA: There won't be any big problem, then. You just go ahead and mix it up, and I'll get her to swallow it.

CALLIMACO: E' bisogna ora pensare a questo: che quello uomo che ha prima a fare seco, presa che l'ha, cotesta pozione, muore infra otto giorni, e non lo camperebbe el mondo.

NICIA: Cacasangue! Io non voglio cotesta suzzacchera! A me non l'apiccherai tu! Voi mi avete concio bene!

CALLIMACO: State saldo, e' ci è rimedio.

NICIA: Quale?

CALLIMACO: Fare dormire sùbito con lei un altro che tiri, standosi seco una notte, a sè tutta quella infezione della mandragola: dipoi iacerete voi sanza periculo.

NICIA: Io non vo' fare cotesto.

CALLIMACO: Perché?

NICIA: Perché io non vo' fare la mia donna femmina e me becco.

CALLIMACO: Che dite voi, dottore? Oh! io non vi ho per savio come io credetti. Sì che voi dubitate di fare quello che ha fatto el re di Francia e tanti signori quanti sono là?

NICIA: Chi volete voi che io truovi che facci cotesta pazzia? Se io gliene dico, e' non vorrà; se io non gliene dico, io lo tradisco, ed è caso da Otto: io non ci vo' capitare sotto male.

CALLIMACO: Se non vi dà briga altro che cotesto, lasciatene la cura a me.

NICIA: Come si farà?

CALLIMACO: Dirovelo: io vi darò la pozione questa sera dopo cena; voi gliene darete bere e, subito, la metterete nel letto, che fieno circa a quattro ore di notte. Dipoi ci travestiremo, voi, Ligurio, Siro ed io, e andrencene cercando in Mercato Nuovo, in Mercato Vecchio, per

CALLIMACO: There is just one thing you ought to
know: the first man who has relations with her, after she
has taken the potion, will die within a week, and nothing
in the world can save him.

NICIA: Holy shit! I don't want your filthy brew! You
won't stick me with it! What a fine mess you've got me in!

CALLIMACO: Steady now, steady. There is an antidote.

NICIA: What is it?

CALLIMACO: You just have someone else sleep with her
right away, and he will draw off all the poison of the mandrake after one night. Then you can have her without any
risk.

NICIA: I don't want to do that.

CALLIMACO: Why not?

NICIA: Because I don't want to play the pimp to my
own wife's whoring!

CALLIMACO: Messer Nicia, what are you saying? I
thought you were more astute than that. Are you really
worried about doing what the King of France and all those
other nobleman up there have done?

NICIA: Who do you think I can get to do this crazy
nonsense? If I tell him, he won't want to; if I don't tell
him, it's a breach of confidence, and that's a case for the
High Court.[21] I don't want to put my head in a noose.

CALLIMACO: If that is all that is bothering you, leave
it to me.

NICIA: What will you do?

CALLIMACO: I'll tell you what. I will give you the
potion tonight after supper; you get your wife to swallow
it, and then put her to bed. That will be around ten
o'clock. Then you, Ligurio, Siro and I will disguise ourselves, and go looking around in the New Market and the
Old Market, and thereabouts. The first young scamp we

questi canti; ed el primo garzonaccio che noi troverremo
scioperato, lo imbavaglieremo, ed a suon di mazzate lo condurreno in casa ed in camera vostra al buio. Quivi lo met-
tereno nel letto, direngli quel che gli abbia a fare, non ci
fia difficultà veruna. Dipoi, la mattina, ne manderete colui
innanzi dì, farete lavare la vostra donna, starete con lei a
vostro piacere e sanza periculo.

NICIA: Io sono contento, poiché tu di' che e re e prin-
cipi e signori hanno tenuto questo modo. Ma sopratutto,
che non si sappia, per amore degli Otto!

CALLIMACO: Chi volete voi che lo dica?

NICIA: Una fatica ci resta, e d'importanza.

CALLIMACO: Quale?

NICIA: Farne contenta mogliama, a che io non credo
ch' ella si disponga mai.

CALLIMACO: Voi dite el vero. Ma io non vorrei innanzi
essere marito, se io non la disponessi a fare a mio modo.

LIGURIO: Io ho pensato el rimedio.

NICIA: Come?

LIGURIO: Per via del confessoro.

CALLIMACO: Chi disporrà el confessoro, tu?

LIGURIO: Io, e danari, la cattività nostra, loro.

NICIA: Io dubito, non che altro, che per mio detto la
non voglia ire a parlare al confessoro.

LIGURIO: Ed anche a cotesto è rimedio.

CALLIMACO: Dimmi.

LIGURIO: Farvela condurre alla madre.

NICIA: La le presta fede.

LIGURIO: Ed io so che la madre è della opinione nostra.—Orsù! avanziam tempo, ché si fa sera. Vatti, Callimaco, a spasso, e fa' che alle ventitrè ore ti ritroviamo in

find strolling about, we'll gag him and march him back to your house. We'll take him up the stairs in the dark, then put him in bed, tell him what he has to do, and he won't make any trouble, I'm sure. Tomorrow morning, you throw him out before daybreak, get your wife cleaned up, and you can stay with her at your leisure and without any danger.

NICIA: It's all right with me, as long as you say that kings and princes and noblemen have done it that way. But above all, it better not be found out, for love of the High Court!

CALLIMACO: Who do you think would tell?

NICIA: Well, there's one problem left, and a big one.

CALLIMACO: What?

NICIA: Getting the little woman to accept. I don't think she'll like the idea at all.

CALLIMACO: That's true. But I would never want to take a wife if I couldn't get her to do things my way.

LIGURIO: I've thought of a remedy.

NICIA: How?

LIGURIO: Through her confessor.

CALLIMACO: But who will persuade her confessor—you?

LIGURIO: Me, money, our villainy and theirs.

NICIA: I'm afraid, along with all the rest, that she won't go and speak to the priest just on my say-so.

LIGURIO: There's a remedy for that, too.

CALLIMACO: Tell me!

LIGURIO: Get her mother to take her.

NICIA: Yes, she trusts her.

LIGURIO: And I know her mother agrees with us. Come on, it's almost evening; we are wasting time. Callimaco, you go take a walk, and make sure we find you

casa con la pozione ad ordine. Noi n' andreno a casa la madre, el dottore ed io, a disporla, perché è mia nota. Poi ne
andreno al frate, e vi raguaglieren di quello che noi areno
fatto.

CALLIMACO: Deh! non mi lasciar solo.

LIGURIO: Tu mi par' cotto.

CALLIMACO: Dove vuoi tu ch' io vadia ora?

LIGURIO: Di là, di qua, per questa via, per quell' altra: egli è sì grande Firenze!

CALLIMACO: Io son morto.

CANZONE

Quanto felice sia ciascun sel vede,
chi nasce sciocco ed ogni cosa crede!
Ambizione nol preme,
non lo muove il timore,
che sogliono esser seme
di noia e di dolore.
Questo vostro dottore,
bramando aver figlioli,
credria ch'un asin voli;
e qualunque altro ben posto ha in oblìo,
e solo in questo ha posto il suo disìo.

at five o'clock with the potion all made up. Messer Nicia and I will go off to the mother's house and get her all set. I know her well. Then we'll go see the friar and we will let you know what we have accomplished.

CALLIMACO: Hey! Don't leave me all alone!

LIGURIO: You look in bad shape!

CALLIMACO: Where do you want me to go?

LIGURIO: Here, there, up this street, down that one. Florence is such a big city!

CALLIMACO: I think I'll die!

SONG

That ignorance is bliss is widely known;
How bless'd the imbecile is, with head of bone!
He thirsts not after gold, nor aches for pow'r,
Believes what he is told, hour after hour;
He is not dogg'd by fear, which haunts the wise
    man,
Of pain or troubles drear that may arise, man.
Our lawyer's such a guy, mad for begattin';
He'd think an ass can fly, if told in Latin.
No other riches count, despite the bother:
He'll gladly trade his mount, to be a father.

ATTO TERZO
SCENA PRIMA

Sostrata, Messer Nicia, Ligurio.

SOSTRATA: Io ho sempremai sentito dire che gli è ufizio d'un prudente pigliare de' cattivi partiti el migliore: se, ad avere figliuoli, voi non avete altro rimedio che questo, si vuole pigliarlo, quando e' non si gravi la coscienzia.

NICIA: Egli è così.

LIGURIO: Voi ve ne andrete a trovare la vostra figliuola, e messere ed io andreno a trovare fra' Timoteo, suo confessoro, e narrerègli el caso, acciò che non abbiate a dirlo voi: vedrete quello che vi dirà.

SOSTRATA: Così sarà fatto. La via vostra è di costà; ed io vo a trovare la Lucrezia, e la merrò a parlare al frate, in ogni modo.

SCENA SECONDA

Messer Nicia, Ligurio.

NICIA: Tu ti maravigli forse, Ligurio, che bisogni fare tante storie a disporre mogliama; ma, se tu sapessi ogni cosa, tu non te ne maraviglieresti.

LIGURIO: Io credo che sia, perché tutte le donne sono sospettose.

NICIA: Non è cotesto. Ella era la più dolce persona del mondo e la più facile; ma, sendole detto da una sua vicina che, s' ella si botava d'udire quaranta mattine la prima messa de' Servi, ch' ella impregnerebbe, la si botò, ed andòvi forse venti mattine. Ben sapete che un di que' fratacchioni le cominciò andare da torno, in modo che la non vi

ACT THREE
SCENE ONE

Sostrata, Messer Nicia, Ligurio.

SOSTRATA: I have always heard it said that the wise person chooses the lesser of two evils. If you have no other prescription than this for having a child, you should grab it, as long as it doesn't weigh on your conscience.

NICIA: That's the way it is.

LIGURIO: You go and get your daughter, and Messer Nicia and I will go see her confessor, Friar Timoteo. We'll discuss the case with him, so you won't have to waste time telling him about it. Then you'll see what he has to say.

SOSTRATA: Let's do that. Your way lies down that street, and I'll go get Lucrezia and bring her to talk to the friar, one way or another.

SCENE TWO

Messer Nicia, Ligurio.

NICIA: Perhaps you're wondering, Ligurio, why we should have such a time persuading the little woman. But if you knew the whole story, you wouldn't be so surprised.

LIGURIO: I suppose it's because all women are suspicious.

NICIA: That's not it. She was the sweetest, most easygoing creature in the world. But one day, a woman in our neighborhood told her that, if she vowed to hear the first Mass at Santa Annunziata[22] forty mornings in a row, she would get pregnant. She made the vow, and went there twenty mornings or so. Of course, wouldn't you know that one of those dirty friars started sniffing around her, so she

volle più tornare. Egli è pur male però che quegli che ci arebbono a dare buoni essempli sien fatti così. Non dich' io el vero?

LIGURIO: Come diavol, s'egli è vero!

NICIA: Da quel tempo in qua ella sta in orecchi come la lepre; e, come se le dice nulla, ella vi fa dentro mille difficultà.

LIGURIO: Io non mi maraviglio più. Ma, quel boto, come si adempiè?

NICIA: Fecesi dispensare.

LIGURIO: Sta bene. Ma datemi, se voi avete, venticinque ducati, ché bisogna, in questi casi, spendere, e farsi amico el frate presto, e darli speranza di meglio.

NICIA: Pigliagli pure; questo non mi dà briga, io farò masserizia altrove.

LIGURIO: Questi frati sono trincati, astuti; ed è ragionevole, perché sanno e peccati nostri, e loro, e chi non è pratico con essi potrebbe ingannarsi e non li sapere condurre a suo proposito. Pertanto io non vorrei che voi nel parlare guastassi ogni cosa, perché un vostro pari, che sta tuttodì nello studio, s'intende di que' libri, e delle cose del mondo non sa ragionare. Costui è sì sciocco, che io ho paura non guasti ogni cosa.

NICIA: Dimmi quel che tu vuoi ch' io faccia.

LIGURIO: Che voi lasciate parlare a me, e non parliate mai, s' io non vi accenno.

NICIA: Io sono contento. Che cenno farai tu?

LIGURIO: Chiuderò un occhio; morderommi el labro . . . Deh! no, facciàno altrimenti. Quanto è egli che voi non parlasti al frate?

NICIA: È più di dieci anni.

refused to go back any more. It's just a shame, though, that the very ones who ought to be setting a good example should act that way. Don't you think so?

LIGURIO: I sure as hell do!

NICIA: Since that time she has been as jumpy as a rabbit. No matter what you ask of her, she thinks up a hundred difficulties.

LIGURIO: I'm not surprised any more. What did you do about her vow?

NICIA: She bought a dispensation.

LIGURIO: That's good. Now, I want you to give me twenty-five ducats. In cases like this you have to spend a little to get in the friar's good graces right away, and make him think there's more where that came from.

NICIA: Well, here you are. It doesn't matter to me, I can make it up somewhere else.

LIGURIO: These friars are shrewd and cunning. They have to be, because they know all about our sins as well as their own. Anyone who isn't used to dealing with them could be fooled, and not get what he wants from them. I wouldn't want you to butt in and spoil the whole deal. A man like you, who spends all day in his study, knows a lot about books, but he doesn't know how to talk about worldly things. (This fellow is such an imbecile, I'm afraid he'll ruin everything.)

NICIA: Tell me what you want me to do.

LIGURIO: Let me do the talking, and don't you say a thing unless I give you the sign.

NICIA: I'll be delighted. What sign will you give?

LIGURIO: I'll close one eye. I'll bite my lip. No, wait! Let's do it another way. How long has it been since you last talked with this friar?

NICIA: More than ten years.

LIGURIO: Sta bene. Io gli dirò che voi sete assordato, e voi non risponderete e non direte mai cosa alcuna, se noi non parliamo forte.

NICIA: Così farò.

LIGURIO: Oltre a questo, non vi dia briga che io dica qualche cosa che e' vi paia disforme a quel che noi vogliamo, perché tutto tornerà a proposito.

NICIA: In buon' ora.

LIGURIO: Ma io veggo el frate che parla con una donna. Aspettian che l'abbi spacciata.

SCENA TERZA

Fra' Timoteo, una Donna.

FRATE: Se voi vi volessi confessare, io farò ciò che voi volete.

DONNA: Non, per oggi; io sono aspettata: e' mi basta essermi sfogata un poco, così ritta ritta. Avete voi dette quelle messe della Nostra Donna?

FRATE: Madonna sì.

DONNA: Togliete ora questo fiorino, e direte dua mesi ogni lunedì la messa de' morti per l'anima del mio marito. Ed ancora che fussi un omaccio, pure le carne tirono: io non posso fare non mi risenta, quando io me ne ricordo. Ma credete voi che sia in purgatorio?

FRATE: Sanza dubio.

DONNA: Io non so già cotesto. Voi sapete pure quel che mi faceva qualche volta. Oh, quanto me ne dolsi io con esso voi! Io me ne discostavo quanto io potevo; ma egli era sì importuno! Uh, nostro Signore!

FRATE: Non dubitate, la clemenzia di Dio è grande: se non manca a l'uomo la voglia, non gli manca mai el tempo a pentersi.

LIGURIO: That's fine. I'll tell him that you've gone deaf, and you won't answer or say anything at all, unless we speak very loud.

NICIA: I'll do that.

LIGURIO: In addition, don't be upset if I say some things that sound a bit twisted from what we're really after; everything will turn out right in the end.

NICIA: Go right ahead.

LIGURIO: Oh, I see the friar talking with a lady. Let's wait until he's gotten rid of her.

SCENE THREE

Friar Timoteo, a Woman.

TIMOTEO: If you feel like confessing, I'm ready and willing to serve you.

WOMAN: Not today, thank you. Someone is expecting me. All I wanted was to get a few things off my chest on the run. Have you said those masses for Our Lady?

TIMOTEO: Yes, my lady.

WOMAN: Take this florin, then, and you're to say the requiem mass every Monday for two months, for the soul of my late husband. Even though he was a terrible man, still, flesh is flesh; I can't help feeling that whenever I remember him. But do you think he is really in Purgatory?

TIMOTEO: Absolutely!

WOMAN: I just don't know about that. You remember what he used to do to me sometimes. Oh, how I complained to you about it! I tried to stay away from him as much as I could, but he was so insistent! Ugh! Good Lord!

TIMOTEO: Don't worry, God's mercy is great. If a man doesn't lack the will, he never lacks time to repent.

DONNA: Credete voi che 'l Turco passi questo anno in Italia?

FRATE: Se voi non fate orazione, sì.

DONNA: Naffe! Dio ci aiuti, con queste diavolerie! Io ho una gran paura di quello impalare.—Ma io veggo qua in chiesa una donna che ha certa accia di mio: io vo' ire a trovarla. Fate col buon dì.

FRATE: Andate sana.

SCENA QUARTA

Fra' Timoteo, Ligurio, Messer Nicia.

FRATE: Le più caritative persone che sieno sono le donne, e le più fastidiose. Chi le scaccia, fugge e fastidii e l'utile; chi le intrattiene, ha l'utile ed e fastidii insieme. Ed è 'l vero che non è el mele sanza le mosche. Che andate voi facendo, uomini da bene? Non riconosco io messer Nicia?

LIGURIO: Dite forte, ché gli è in modo assordato, che non ode quasi nulla.

FRATE: Voi sete el ben venuto, messere!

LIGURIO: Più forte!

FRATE: El ben venuto!

NICIA: El ben trovato, padre!

FRATE: Che andate voi faccendo?

NICIA: Tutto bene.

LIGURIO: Volgete el parlare a me, padre, perché voi, a volere che v' intendessi, aresti a mettere a romore questa piazza.

FRATE: Che volete voi da me?

WOMAN: Do you think the Turks will penetrate into Italy this year?[23]

TIMOTEO: They will if you don't offer prayers.

WOMAN: Heavens! God help us, with those devilish brutes! I'm so terrified of that impalement business. But I see there is a woman in church who has a skein of yarn of mine. I'm going to go and speak with her. Good day to you!

TIMOTEO: I wish you good health!

SCENE FOUR

Friar Timoteo, Ligurio, Messer Nicia.

TIMOTEO: (Women are the most charitable creatures in the world, and also the most tiresome. If you shoo them off, you avoid the nuisance and the benefit; if you pay attention to them, you have the benefit and the nuisance at the same time. But it has always been true that you can't have honey without the bees.) What are you doing here, my good gentlemen? Isn't that Messer Nicia I see?

LIGURIO: Speak louder. He's grown so deaf he can hardly hear a thing.

TIMOTEO: I bid you welcome, Messer Nicia!

LIGURIO: Louder!

TIMOTEO: Welcome!

NICIA: Same to you padre.

TIMOTEO: What are you doing here?

NICIA: Very fine, thank you.

LIGURIO: Just direct your talk to me, father. Otherwise, if you want him to hear, you'll end up with the whole square listening.

TIMOTEO: Now, what can I do for you?

LIGURIO: Qui messer Nicia ed un altro uomo da bene, che voi intenderete poi, hanno a fare distribuire in limosine parecchi centinaia di ducati.

NICIA: Cacasangue!

LIGURIO: Tacete, in malora, e' non fien molti! Non vi maravigliate, padre, di cosa che dica, ché non ode, e pargli qualche volta udire, e non risponde a proposito.

FRATE: Sèguita pure, e lasciagli dire ciò che vuole.

LIGURIO: De' quali danari io ne ho una parte meco; ed hanno disegnato che voi siate quello che li distribuiate.

FRATE: Molto volentieri.

LIGURIO: Ma egli è necessario, prima che questa limosina si faccia, che voi ci aiutiate d'un caso strano intervenuto a messere, che solo voi ci potete aiutare, dove ne va al tutto l'onore di casa sua.

FRATE: Che cosa è?

LIGURIO: Io non so se voi conoscesti Cammillo Calfucci, nipote qui di messere.

FRATE: Sì, conosco.

LIGURIO: Costui n'andò per certe sua faccende, uno anno fa, in Francia; e, non avendo donna, che era morta, lasciò una sua figliuola da marito in serbanza in uno monistero, del quale non accade dirvi ora el nome.

FRATE: Che è seguìto?

LIGURIO: È seguìto che, o per straccurataggine delle monache o per cervellinaggine della fanciulla, la si truova gravida di quattro mesi; di modo che, se non ci si ripara con prudenzia, el dottore, le monache, la fanciulla, Cammillo, la casa de' Calfucci è vituperata; ed il dottore stima tanto questa vergogna che s'è botato, quando la non si palesi, dare trecento ducati per l'amore di Dio.

LIGURIO: Messer Nicia here, and another worthy gentleman you will hear from later, have several hundred ducats to distribute to charity.

NICIA: Holy shit!

LIGURIO: (Shut the hell up, it won't take that many.) Don't be surprised, father, at whatever he says. He doesn't hear things, but sometimes he imagines he does, and talks nonsense.

TIMOTEO: Go on, and let him say what he wants.

LIGURIO: I have part of the money here with me, and they have chosen you to distribute it.

TIMOTEO: Most willingly.

LIGURIO: But before giving this charity, it will be necessary for you to help us in a strange case that has arisen with Messer Nicia here. Only you can help us; it is a matter where the honor of his entire house is at stake.

TIMOTEO: Whatever can that be?

LIGURIO: I don't know if you knew Cammillo Calfucci, the nephew of Messer Nicia?

TIMOTEO: Why yes, I do.

LIGURIO: He went on a business trip to France a year ago, and since his wife had died, he left one of his marriageable daughters in the custody of a convent, whose name we don't need to mention.

TIMOTEO: What happened?

LIGURIO: What happened is that, either through the nuns' inattention or through the girl's silliness, she finds herself four months pregnant. And so, if we don't take care of this discreetly, Messer Nicia, the nuns, the girl, Cammillo, and the entire house of Calfucci will be disgraced. Messer Nicia is so concerned about this scandal that he has vowed, if it doesn't leak out, to give three hundred ducats for the love of God.

NICIA: Che chiacchiera!

LIGURIO: State cheto! E daragli per le vostre mani; e voi solo e la badessa ci potete rimediare.

FRATE: Come?

LIGURIO: Persuadere alla badessa che dia una pozione alla fanciulla per farla sconciare.

FRATE: Cotesta è cosa da pensarla.

LIGURIO: Come, cosa da pensarla? Guardate, nel far questo, quanti beni ne resulta: voi mantenete l'onore al munistero, alla fanciulla, a' parenti; rendete al padre una figliuola; satisfate qui a messere, a tanti sua parenti; fate tante elemosine, quante con questi trecento ducati potete fare; e, dall'altro canto, voi non offendete altro che un pezzo di carne non nata, sanza senso, che in mille modi si può sperdere; ed io credo che quel sia bene, che facci bene a' più, e che e più se ne contentino.

FRATE: Sia, col nome di Dio! Faccisi ciò che voi volete, e, per Dio e per carità, sia fatto ogni cosa. Ditemi el munistero, datemi la pozione, e, se vi pare, cotesti danari, da potere cominciare a fare qualche bene.

LIGURIO: Or mi parete voi quel religioso, che io credevo che voi fussi. Togliete questa parte de' danari. El munistero è . . . Ma aspettate, egli è qui in chiesa una donna che mi accenna: io torno ora ora; non vi partite da messer Nicia; io le vo' dire dua parole.

NICIA: (Horse shit!)

LIGURIO: (Shut up!) And he will give them through your hands. You alone, and the mother superior can take care of this.

TIMOTEO: How?

LIGURIO: By persuading the mother superior to give a potion to the girl that will cause an abortion.

TIMOTEO: This is something I will have to think about.

LIGURIO: What? Something you'll have to think about? Look at how many benefits result from your doing it: you uphold the honor of the convent, the girl, and the relatives; you restore a daughter to her father, you satisfy Messer Nicia here, and all his family; you distribute all the alms you can with these three hundred ducats; and on the other hand, you harm nothing but a bit of unborn, unconscious flesh, that might have disappeared in a thousand ways, in any case. I believe that to be good which does the most good to the most people, and makes the most people happy.

TIMOTEO: Amen, in the name of the Lord. Let it be as you will, and may everything be done for God and for divine Charity. Tell me the name of the convent, give me the potion, and, if you like, the money, too, and then we can begin to do some good.

LIGURIO: Now you sound like the friar I thought you were. Take this portion of the money. The convent is . . . But wait a moment. I see a lady there in church who is waving at me. I'll be right back, don't leave Messer Nicia here alone. I want to say a few words to her.

SCENA QUINTA

Fra' Timoteo, Messer Nicia.

FRATE: Questa fanciulla, che tempo ha?

NICIA: Io strabilio.

FRATE: Dico, quanto tempo ha questa fanciulla?

NICIA: Mal che Dio gli dia!

FRATE: Perché?

NICIA: Perché se lo abbia!

FRATE: E' mi pare essere nel gagno. Io ho a fare con uno pazzo e con un sordo: l'un si fugge, l'altro non ode. Ma se questi non sono quarteruoli, io ne farò meglio di loro!—Ecco Ligurio, che torna in qua.

SCENA SESTA

Ligurio, Fra' Timoteo, Messer Nicia.

LIGURIO: State cheto, messere. Oh! io ho la gran nuova, padre.

FRATE: Quale?

LIGURIO: Quella donna con chi io ho parlato, mi ha detto che quella fanciulla si è sconcia per se stessa.

FRATE: Bene! questa limosina andrà alla Grascia.

LIGURIO: Che dite voi?

FRATE: Dico che voi tanto più doverete fare questa limosina.

LIGURIO: La limosina si farà, quando voi vogliate: ma e' bisogna che voi facciate un'altra cosa in benefizio qui del dottore.

FRATE: Che cosa è?

SCENE FIVE

Friar Timoteo, Messer Nicia.

TIMOTEO: How old is this girl?

NICIA: (I'm flabbergasted.)

TIMOTEO: I said, how old is this girl?

NICIA: God send him the plague!

TIMOTEO: Why?

NICIA: So he'll get it!

TIMOTEO: (I think I'm getting into an awful mess. I'm dealing with a crazy man on one side and a deaf man on the other. One runs away, and the other doesn't hear. But unless these coins are counterfeit, I can use them better than they can!) Here is Ligurio coming back.

SCENE SIX

Ligurio, Friar Timoteo, Messer Nicia.

LIGURIO: (Keep still, Messer Nicia.) Ah, I have important news, father.

TIMOTEO: What?

LIGURIO: That woman I just spoke with told me that the girl has had a miscarriage.

TIMOTEO: Fine; this money will go to the building fund.[24]

LIGURIO: What did you say?

TIMOTEO: I said you ought to be all the more willing, son, to give this to charity.

LIGURIO: You can have the rest of the money if you really want it, but first you will have to do something else for the benefit of Messer Nicia.

TIMOTEO: What might that be?

LIGURIO: Cosa di minor carico, di minor scandolo, più accetta a noi, e più utile a voi.

FRATE: Che è? Io sono in termine con voi, e parmi avere contratta tale dimestichezza, che non è cosa che io non facessi.

LIGURIO: Io ve lo vo' dire in chiesa, da me e voi, ed el dottore fia contento d'aspettare qui e prestarmi dua parole. Aspettate qui; noi torniamo ora.

NICIA: Come disse la botta a l'erpice!

FRATE: Andiamo.

SCENA SETTIMA

Messer Nicia solo.

NICIA: È egli di dì o di notte? Sono io desto o sogno? Sono io obliàco, e non ho beuto ancora oggi, per ire drieto a queste chiacchiere? Noi rimagnàn di dire al frate una cosa, e' ne dice un'altra; poi volle che io facessi el sordo, e bisognava io m'impeciassi gli orecchi come el Danese, a volere che io non avessi udite le pazzie, che gli ha dette, e Dio il sa con che proposito! Io mi truovo meno venticinque ducati, e del fatto mio non si è ancora ragionato; ed ora m'hanno qui posto, come un zugo, a piuolo.—Ma eccogli che tornano: in mala ora per loro, se non hanno ragionato del fatto mio!

LIGURIO: Something much easier, with less scandal involved, more agreeable to us, and more useful to you.

TIMOTEO: What is it? I am in total harmony with you, and I feel as if we've come to such good terms that there is nothing I wouldn't do.

LIGURIO: I'll tell you about it in the church, between the two of us. Messer Nicia here will be delighted to wait outside and let me have a couple of words with you. We'll be right back.

NICIA: (As the meat cleaver said to the sausage.)[25]

TIMOTEO: Come on.

SCENE SEVEN

Messer Nicia alone.

NICIA: Is it night or day? Am I awake or dreaming? I haven't had a drop today, and yet I must be drunk, to go along with all this horseshit! We stop to talk about one thing with the friar, and he says something completely different. Then he wants me to play deaf, and I really should have plugged up my ears, like what's-his-name with the Sirens,[26] so I wouldn't have to listen to the crazy stuff he said, God knows for what purpose! Here I am, out twenty-five ducats already, and nobody has talked about my real business yet. Now they've left me hanging around here like a doughnut on a stick. Here they come again; they're going to be in real trouble if they haven't discussed my business.

SCENA OTTAVA

Fra' Timoteo, Ligurio, Messer Nicia.

FRATE: Fate che le donne venghino. Io so quello ch' i' ho a fare; e, se l'autorità mia varrà, noi concluderemo questo parentado questa sera.

LIGURIO: Messer Nicia, fra' Timoteo è per fare ogni cosa. Bisogna vedere che le donne venghino.

NICIA: Tu mi ricrii tutto quanto. Fia egli maschio?

LIGURIO: Maschio.

NICIA: Io lacrimo per la tenerezza.

FRATE: Andatevene in chiesa, io aspetterò qui le donne. State in lato che le non vi vegghino; e, partite che le fieno, vi dirò quello che l'hanno detto.

SCENA NONA

Fra' Timoteo solo.

FRATE: Io non so chi si abbi giuntato l'uno l'altro. Questo tristo di Ligurio ne venne a me con quella prima novella, per tentarmi, acciò, se io li consentivo quella, m'inducessi più facilmente a questa; se io non gliene consentivo, non mi arebbe detta questa, per non palesare e disegni loro sanza utile, e di quella che era falsa non si curavano. Egli è vero che io ci sono suto giuntato; nondimeno, questo giunto è con mio utile. Messer Nicia e Callimaco sono ricchi, e da ciascuno, per diversi rispetti, sono per trarre assai; la cosa convien stia secreta, perché l'importa così a loro, a dirla, come a me. Sia come si voglia,

SCENE EIGHT

Friar Timoteo, Ligurio, Messer Nicia.

TIMOTEO: Have the women come and see me. I know what I have to do, and if my authority has any weight, we will settle this engagement by tonight.

LIGURIO: Messer Nicia, Friar Timoteo has agreed to do everything we want. We just have to see to it that the women come and talk to him.

NICIA: You've made me feel like a new man. Will it be a boy?

LIGURIO: A boy.

NICIA: I'm crying for joy.

TIMOTEO: You two go into the church, and I will wait for the women here. Keep to the side so they don't see you, and as soon as they've gone, I'll tell you what they have said.

SCENE NINE

Friar Timoteo alone.

TIMOTEO: I really don't know who has tricked whom. That scoundrel Ligurio came up to me with that first story just to test me out, so that if I agreed to that, he would have persuaded me more easily to do this; and if I didn't agree to that, he wouldn't have told me about this, so as not to reveal their plans unnecessarily; and they didn't care at all about the fake story. It's true that I've been tricked; nevertheless, this trick is to my benefit. Messer Nicia and Callimaco are both well off, and I stand to gain quite a bit from each of them, for different reasons. This business is bound to remain a secret, because that is just as impor-

io non me ne pento. È ben vero che io dubito non ci avere
dificultà, perché madonna Lucrezia è savia e buona: ma io
la giugnerò in sulla bontà. E tutte le donne hanno alla fine
poco cervello; e come ne è una sappi dire dua parole, e' se
ne predica, perché in terra di ciechi chi vi ha un occhio è
signore. Ed eccola con la madre, la quale è bene una bestia,
e sarammi uno grande adiuto a condurla alle mia voglie.

SCENA DECIMA

Sostrata, Lucrezia.

SOSTRATA: Io credo che tu creda, figliuola mia, che io
stimi l'onore ed el bene tuo quanto persona del mondo, e
che io non ti consiglierei di cosa che non stessi bene. Io ti
ho detto e ridicoti, che se fra' Timoteo ti dice che non ti
sia carico di coscienzia, che tu lo faccia sanza pensarvi.

LUCREZIA: Io ho sempremai dubitato che la voglia,
che messer Nicia ha d'avere figliuoli, non ci facci fare
qualche errore; e per questo, sempre che lui mi ha parlato
di alcuna cosa, io ne sono stata in gelosia e sospesa, mas-
sime poi che m'intervenne quello che vi sapete, per andare
a' Servi. Ma di tutte le cose, che si son tentate, questa mi
pare la più strana, di avere a sottomettere el corpo mio a
questo vituperio, ad esser cagione che uno uomo muoia per
vituperarmi: perché io non crederrei, se io fussi sola rimasa
nel mondo e da me avessi a risurgere l'umana natura, che
mi fussi simile partito concesso.

SOSTRATA: Io non ti so dire tante cose, figliuola mia.
Tu parlerai al frate, vedrai quello che ti dirà, e farai quello

tant to them as it is to me. Whatever happens, I have
no regrets. It is true, of course, that I may still have some
trouble because, unfortunately, Madonna Lucrezia is a good
and virtuous woman; but I think I can get at her through
her goodness. After all, women are all short on brains:
whenever one of them can put a couple of words together,
suddenly she is a prophet; it is a case of the one-eyed leading the blind. Here she comes now, with her mother, who
is a real fool. She will be very useful in getting her daughter to do what I want.

SCENE TEN

Sostrata, Lucrezia.

SOSTRATA: You must believe, my dear, that I prize
your honor and your welfare as much as anyone in the
world, and I would never advise you to do anything that
wasn't right. I have already told you, and I'll say it again:
if Friar Timoteo tells you there will be no burden on your
conscience, then you can do it without any qualms.

LUCREZIA: I have always been afraid that Messer
Nicia's desire to have children would lead us to do something wrong. That is why, whenever he suggested anything to me, I always felt suspicious and apprehensive,
especially since that experience at Santa Annunziata: you
remember. But of all the things that we have tried, this
one is the most appalling! To have to submit my body to
this abomination, and to make a man die for my dishonor!
I wouldn't have thought, if I were the last woman left in
the world and the human race depended on me for sur-
vival, that I would have to undergo such a thing.

SOSTRATA: I can't explain all this to you, my dear.
Speak to the friar, you will see what he tells you, and then

che tu dipoi sarai consigliata da lui, da noi, da chi ti vuole bene.

LUCREZIA: Io sudo per la passione.

SCENA UNDECIMA

Fra' Timoteo, Lucrezia, Sostrata.

FRATE: Voi siate le ben venute. Io so quello che voi volete intendere da me, perché messer Nicia m'ha parlato. Veramente, io sono stato in su' libri più di dua ore a studiare questo caso; e, dopo molte essamine, io truovo di molte cose che, ed in particulare ed in generale, fanno per noi.

LUCREZIA: Parlate voi da vero o motteggiate?

FRATE: Ah, madonna Lucrezia! Sono, queste, cose da motteggiare? Avetemi voi a conoscere ora?

LUCREZIA: Padre, no; ma questa mi pare la più strana cosa che mai si udissi.

FRATE: Madonna, io ve lo credo, ma io non voglio che voi diciate più così. E' sono molte cose che discosto paiano terribili, insopportabili, strane, che, quando tu ti appressi loro, le riescono umane, sopportabili, dimestiche; e però si dice che sono maggiori li spaventi che e mali: e questa è una di quelle.

LUCREZIA: Dio el voglia!

FRATE: Io voglio tornare a quello, ch' io dicevo prima. Voi avete, quanto alla coscienzia, a pigliare questa generalità, che, dove è un bene certo ed un male incerto, non si debbe mai lasciare quel bene per paura di quel male. Qui è un bene certo, che voi ingraviderete, acquisterete una

you will do as you have been advised by him, by us, and by everyone who loves you.

LUCREZIA: I'm so distraught, I'm breaking out in a sweat.

SCENE ELEVEN

Friar Timoteo, Lucrezia, Sostrata.

TIMOTEO: Welcome, ladies! I know what you have come to see me about, because Messer Nicia has spoken to me. To tell the truth, I have spent two whole hours poring over my books about this case, and after much examination I find many things going for us, both in general and in particular.

LUCREZIA: Are you serious, father, or are you joking?

TIMOTEO: Ah, Madonna Lucrezia! Is this a matter to joke about? Don't you know me better than that?

LUCREZIA: I know, father, but this seems to me the strangest business I ever heard of.

TIMOTEO: My lady, I believe you. But I don't want you to talk that way any more. There are many things that, seen from afar, seem awful, strange, unbearable; and then when you get up close to them, they turn out to be ordinary, familiar, bearable.—That is why it is often said that their bark is worse than their bite.—This is one of those things.

LUCREZIA: The Lord only knows!

TIMOTEO: I would like to return to what I was saying before. As far as conscience is concerned, one must make the following generalization: where there is a certain good and an uncertain evil, one must never abandon that good for fear of the evil. Here we have a certain good: you will get pregnant, you will provide another soul for the good

anima a messer Domenedio; el male incerto è che colui che
iacerà, dopo la pozione, con voi, si muoia; ma e' si truova
anche di quelli che non muoiono. Ma perché la cosa è du-
bia, però è bene che messer Nicia non corra quel periculo.
Quanto allo atto, che sia peccato, questo è una favola,
perché la volontà è quella che pecca, non el corpo; e la
cagione del peccato è dispiacere al marito, e voi li com-
piacete; pigliarne piacere, e voi ne avete dispiacere. Oltr' a
di questo, el fine si ha a riguardare in tutte le cose: el fine
vostro si è di riempiere una sedia in paradiso, e contentare
el marito vostro. Dice la Bibia che le figliuole di Lotto,
credendosi essere rimase sole nel mondo, usorono con el
padre; e, perché la loro intenzione fu buona, non peccorono.

LUCREZIA: Che cosa mi persuadete voi?

SOSTRATA: Làsciati persuadere, figliuola mia. Non
vedi tu che una donna, che non ha figliuoli, non ha casa?
Muorsi el marito, resta come una bestia, abandonata da
ognuno.

FRATE: Io vi giuro, madonna, per questo petto sacrato,
che tanta conscienzia vi è ottemperare in questo caso al
marito vostro, quanto vi è mangiare carne el mercoledì,
che è un peccato che se ne va con l'acqua benedetta.

LUCREZIA: A che mi conducete voi, padre?

FRATE: Conducovi a cose, che voi sempre arete cagione
di pregare Dio per me; e più vi satisfarà questo altro anno
che ora.

SOSTRATA: Ella farà ciò che voi volete. Io la voglio
mettere stasera al letto io. Di che hai tu paura, moccicona?
E' ci è cinquanta donne, in questa terra, che alzerebbono
le mani al cielo.

Lord up there. The uncertain evil is that the man who sleeps with you after the potion may die; but there are always those who don't die. However, since there is some question, it is better for Messer Nicia not to run that risk. As for the act itself, it is only an old wives' tale that it is a sin, for the will is what commits sin, not the body. The real sin is going against a husband's wishes, and here you are following his wishes; or taking pleasure in it, and here you are filled with displeasure. Besides that, we must always consider whether the end justifies the means. Your end is to fill a seat in Heaven and to make your husband happy. The Bible tells us that the daughters of Lot, thinking they were the last women on earth, consorted with their father; and because their intentions were pure, they did not commit a sin.

LUCREZIA: What are you telling me to do?

SOSTRATA: Listen to him, my dear. Don't you see that a woman without children is a woman without a home? If her husband dies, she is left like an animal, abandoned by everybody.

TIMOTEO: I swear to you, my lady, by this consecrated breast, that there is no more sin in obeying your husband in this case than there is in eating meat on Wednesday, and that is a sin that a little holy water can wash away.

LUCREZIA: What are you getting me into, father?

TIMOTEO: Something you will always have cause to thank God for, and I know you will be more satisfied a year from now than you are at the present.

SOSTRATA: She will do as you say. I will put her to bed this evening myself. What are you afraid of, you silly girl? There are fifty women in this town who would thank Heaven for this opportunity.

LUCREZIA: Io sono contenta: ma io non credo mai essere viva domattina.

FRATE: Non dubitar, figliuola mia: io pregherrò Iddio per te, io dirò l'orazione dell'Angiolo Raffaello, che ti accompagni. Andate, in buona ora, e preparatevi a questo misterio, ché si fa sera.

SOSTRATA: Rimanete in pace, padre.

LUCREZIA: Dio m'aiuti e la Nostra Donna, che io non càpiti male.

SCENA DUODECIMA

Fra' Timoteo, Ligurio, Messer Nicia.

FRATE: O Ligurio, uscite qua!

LIGURIO: Come va?

FRATE: Bene. Le ne sono ite a casa disposte a fare ogni cosa, e non ci fia difficultà, perché la madre s'andrà a stare seco, e vuolla mettere al letto lei.

NICIA: Dite voi el vero?

FRATE: Bembè, voi sete guarito del sordo?

LIGURIO: Santo Chimenti gli ha fatto grazia.

FRATE: E' si vuol porvi una immagine, per rizzarci un poco di baccanella, acciò che io abbia fatto quest'altro guadagno con voi.

NICIA: Non entriano in cetere. Farà la donna difficultà di fare quel ch' io voglio?

FRATE: Non, vi dico.

NICIA: Io sono el più contento uomo del mondo.

FRATE: Credolo. Voi vi beccherete un fanciul mastio; e chi non ha non abbia.

LUCREZIA: All right, I'll do it. But I don't think I will live to see tomorrow morning.

TIMOTEO: Do not worry, my dear. I will pray to the Lord for you. I will recite the prayer to the Archangel Raphael, so that he will be by your side. Go along, now, and prepare yourself for this mystery, for it is getting dark already.

SOSTRATA: Peace be with you, father.

LUCREZIA: May God and Our Lady help me, and keep me from harm!

SCENE TWELVE

Friar Timoteo, Ligurio, Messer Nicia.

TIMOTEO: Oh, Ligurio, come on out!

LIGURIO: How did it go?

TIMOTEO: Fine. They have gone back home, ready to do everything. There won't be any problem. Her mother is going to stay with her, and will put her to bed herself.

NICIA: Is that the truth?

TIMOTEO: Well, well! You have been cured of your deafness!

LIGURIO: Another miracle of San Clemente!

TIMOTEO: We ought to erect a plaque, to stir up a little publicity, so I can share even further in your good fortune.

NICIA: Let's not lose track of matters. Will the missus make any fuss about doing what I want?

TIMOTEO: No, I can assure you.

NICIA: I'm the happiest man in the world!

TIMOTEO: I'm sure you are. If I'm not deceived, the doctor is going to give you a fine young son.

LIGURIO: Andate, frate, a le vostre orazioni, e, se bisognerà altro, vi verreno a trovare. Voi messere, andate a lei, per tenerla ferma in questa opinione, ed io andrò a trovare maestro Callimaco, che vi mandi la pozione; ed a l'un' ora fate che io vi rivegga, per ordinare quello che si de' fare alle quattro.

NICIA: Tu di' bene. Addio!

FRATE: Andate sani.

CANZONE

Sì suave è l'inganno
al fin condotto imaginato e caro,
ch' altrui spoglia d'affanno,
e dolce face ogni gustato amaro.
O rimedio alto e raro,
tu mostri il dritto calle all'alme erranti;
tu, col tuo gran valore,
nel far beato altrui, fai ricco Amore;
tu vinci, sol co' tuoi consigli santi,
pietre, veneni e incanti.

LIGURIO: Friar, you go back to your prayers, and if we need anything else, we'll come and find you. Messer Nicia, you go make sure your wife doesn't change her mind, and I'll go and get Callimaco to send you the potion. Be sure I can find you at seven o'clock, to plan what has to be done at ten.[27]

NICIA: You're right. So long.

TIMOTEO: I wish you good health!

SONG

How gentle is deception
When carried to fruition as intended,
For it defies perception
And soothes the blissful dupes we have befriended.
Oh draught by heaven blended,
You show the quickest way to true contentment,
And with your magic power
You comfort those whose wealth we would devour:
And vanquish, by your devious presentment,
Stone walls, and arm'd resentment.

ATTO QUARTO
SCENA PRIMA

Callimaco solo.

CALLIMACO: Io vorrei pure intendere quello che costoro hanno fatto. Può egli essere che io non rivegga Ligurio? E, nonchè le ventitrè, le sono le ventiquattro ore! In quanta angustia d'animo sono io stato e sto! Ed è vero che la Fortuna e la Natura tiene el conto per bilancio: la non ti fa mai un bene, che, a l'incontro, non surga un male. Quanto più mi è cresciuta la speranza, tanto mi è cresciuto el timore. Misero a me! Sarà egli mai possibile che io viva in tanti affanni e perturbato da questi timori e queste speranze? Io sono una nave vessata da dua diversi venti, che tanto più teme, quanto ella è più presso al porto. La semplicità di messer Nicia mi fa sperare, la prudenzia e durezza di Lucrezia mi fa temere. Ohimè, che io non truovo requie in alcuno loco! Talvolta io cerco di vincere me stesso, riprendomi di questo mio furore, e dico meco:—Che fai tu? Se' tu impazzato? Quando tu l'ottenga, che fia? Conoscerai el tuo errore, pentira'ti delle fatiche e de' pensieri che hai aùti. Non sai tu quanto poco bene si truova nelle cose che l'uomo desidera, rispetto a quello che l'uomo ha presupposto trovarvi? Da l'altro canto, el peggio che te ne va è morire ed andarne in inferno: e' son morti tanti degli altri! e' sono in inferno tanti uomini da bene! Ha'ti tu a vergognare d'andarvi tu? Volgi el viso alla sorte; fuggi el male, o, non lo potendo fuggire, sopportalo come uomo; non ti prosternere, non ti invilire come una donna.—E così mi fo di buon cuore; ma io ci sto poco sù, perché da ogni parte mi assalta tanto desìo d'essere una volta con costei, che io mi sento, dalle piante de' piè al capo, tutto

ACT FOUR
SCENE ONE

Callimaco alone.

CALLIMACO: I wish I could find out what they have
done. Why doesn't Ligurio show up? He is already an hour
late! What torment my mind has been going through
all this time. It is true that Nature and Fortune hold all
accounts in the balance. You never receive anything
good without some evil springing up on the other side.
The more my hopes have risen, the greater my fears have
grown. Wretched me! How will I ever be able to sur-
vive amid so many troubles, and assailed by such hopes
and doubts? I am a vessel tossed by two conflicting
winds, fearing all the more the closer it gets to port. Messer Nicia's stupidity makes my hopes rise, but then Lucrezia's prudence and virtue make them fall. Alas! I find no
respite anywhere! At times I try to get a grip on myself, I
curse my passion, and I say to myself: What are you doing? Have you gone mad? Even if you do possess her, what
then? You will realize your error, you will regret the anx-
ieties and the efforts you have gone through. Don't you
know how little pleasure men find in the things they desire, compared to what they expected? But then on the
other hand, the worst that can happen to you is to die
and go off to Hell. How many others have died! And how
many excellent men have gone to Hell! Why should you
be ashamed to go there, too? Face up to your destiny. Flee
from evil, but if you can't, bear it like a man. Don't bend
your knee, don't be cowardly, like a woman.—And so I
screw my courage up; but it doesn't stay up for long, since
I am buffeted on all sides by such desire to be with her,
just once, that I feel as if I were being turned inside out:

alterare: le gambe triemano, le viscere si commuovono, el cuore mi si sbarba del petto, le braccia s'abandonono, la lingua diventa muta, gli occhi abarbagliano, el cervello mi gira. Pure, se io trovassi Ligurio, io arei con chi sfogarmi.—Ma ecco che ne viene verso me ratto: el rapporto di costui mi farà o vivere allegro qualche poco, o morire affatto.

SCENA SECONDA

Ligurio, Callimaco.

LIGURIO: Io non desiderai mai più tanto di trovare Callimaco, e non penai mai più tanto a trovarlo. Se io li portassi triste nuove, io l'arei riscontro al primo. Io sono stato a casa, in Piazza, in Mercato, al Pancone delli Spini, alla Loggia de' Tornaquinci, e non l'ho trovato. Questi innamorati hanno l'ariento vivo sotto e piedi, e non si possono fermare.

CALLIMACO: Che sto io ch' io non lo chiamo? E' mi par pure allegro! Oh, Ligurio! Ligurio!

LIGURIO: Oh, Callimaco! dove se' tu stato?

CALLIMACO: Che novelle?

LIGURIO: Buone.

CALLIMACO: Buone in verità?

LIGURIO: Ottime.

CALLIMACO: È Lucrezia contenta?

LIGURIO: Sì.

CALLIMACO: El frate fece el bisogno?

LIGURIO: Fece.

CALLIMACO: Oh, benedetto frate! Io pregherrò sempre Dio per lui.

my legs tremble, my bowels quake, my heart threatens
to fly through my ribs, my arms grow weak, my tongue
grows mute, my eyes grow dim, my brain begins to whirl.
If only I could find Ligurio, I would have someone to let
off steam to. Ah, there he is, running toward me. His
news will either give me a new lease on life, or kill me
altogether.

SCENE TWO

Ligurio, Callimaco.

LIGURIO: (I have never wanted so much to find Callimaco, and I never had such a hard time doing it. If I had
bad news, I would run into him right away. I have been to
his house, to the square, the Market, the counter of the
Spini, the Tornaquinci arcade, and I couldn't find him anywhere. These lovers must have quicksilver under their feet,
they can't stand still.)

CALLIMACO: (I don't know what is keeping me from
calling him. He does look happy.) Hey! Ligurio! Ligurio!

LIGURIO: Oh, Callimaco, where have you been?

CALLIMACO: What news do you have?

LIGURIO: Good news!

CALLIMACO: Really good?

LIGURIO: Excellent!

CALLIMACO: Is Lucrezia willing?

LIGURIO: Yes.

CALLIMACO: The friar did what was needed?

LIGURIO: He did.

CALLIMACO: Oh, blessed friar! I will pray to God for
him forever.

LIGURIO: Oh, buono! Come se Idio facessi le grazie del male, come del bene! El frate vorrà altro che prieghi!

CALLIMACO: Che vorrà?

LIGURIO: Danari.

CALLIMACO: Darègliene. Quanti ne gli hai tu promessi?

LIGURIO: Trecento ducati.

CALLIMACO: Hai fatto bene.

LIGURIO: El dottore ne ha sborsati venticinque.

CALLIMACO: Come?

LIGURIO: Bastiti che gli ha sborsati.

CALLIMACO: La madre di Lucrezia, che ha fatto?

LIGURIO: Quasi el tutto. Come la 'ntese che la sua figliuola aveva avere questa buona notte sanza peccato, la non restò mai di pregare, comandare, confortare la Lucrezia, tanto che ella la condusse al frate, e quivi operò in modo, che la li consentì.

CALLIMACO: Oh, Iddio! Per quali mia meriti debbo io avere tanti beni? Io ho a morire per l'alegrezza!

LIGURIO: Che gente è questa? Ora per l'alegrezza, ora pel dolore, costui vuole morire in ogni modo. Hai tu ad ordine la pozione?

CALLIMACO: Sì, ho.

LIGURIO: Che li manderai?

CALLIMACO: Un bicchiere d'ipocrasso, che è a proposito a racconciare lo stomaco, rallegra el cervello . . . — Ohimè, ohimè, ohimè, i' sono spacciato!

LIGURIO: Che è? Che sarà?

CALLIMACO: E' non ci è rimedio.

LIGURIO: Che diavol fia?

LIGURIO: That's a good one! Do you think God gives his grace for evil as well as good? The friar will want more than just prayers!

CALLIMACO: What will he want?

LIGURIO: Money!

CALLIMACO: We'll give it to him. How much did you promise?

LIGURIO: Three hundred ducats.

CALLIMACO: You did very well.

LIGURIO: Messer Nicia has shelled out twenty-five of them.

CALLIMACO: What?

LIGURIO: Don't ask questions. He did it.

CALLIMACO: What did Lucrezia's mother do?

LIGURIO: Practically the whole thing. When she heard that her daughter could have such a good night of it without any sin, she never left off begging, bullying and reassuring Lucrezia until she had gotten her to see the friar, and then she managed things so that her daughter gave in.

CALLIMACO: Oh God! What have I done to deserve such a reward? I'm ready to die for joy.

LIGURIO: (What kind of people are these? For joy or for sorrow, one way or another he wants to die!) Do you have the potion ready?

CALLIMACO: Yes, I have.

LIGURIO: What are you going to send him?

CALLIMACO: A glass of vermouth,[28] which is excellent for settling the stomach and stimulating the brain. Ay! yay, yay! I'm done for!

LIGURIO: What is it? What's the matter?

CALLIMACO: There is no cure for this.

LIGURIO: What the hell is wrong?

CALLIMACO: E' non si è fatto nulla, i' mi son murato in un forno.

LIGURIO: Perché? Ché non lo di'? Lèvati le mani dal viso.

CALLIMACO: O non sai tu che io ho detto a messer Nicia che tu, lui, Siro ed io piglieremo uno per metterlo a lato a la moglie?

LIGURIO: Che importa?

CALLIMACO: Come, che importa? Se io sono con voi, non potrò essere quel che sia preso; s' io non sono, e' s'avvedrà dello inganno.

LIGURIO: Tu di' el vero. Ma non c'è egli rimedio?

CALLIMACO: Non, credo io.

LIGURIO: Sì, sarà bene.

CALLIMACO: Quale?

LIGURIO: Io voglio un poco pensallo.

CALLIMACO: Tu m'ha' chiaro: io sto fresco, se tu l'hai a pensare ora!

LIGURIO: Io l'ho trovato.

CALLIMACO: Che cosa?

LIGURIO: Farò che 'l frate, che ci ha aiutato infino a qui, farà questo resto.

CALLIMACO: In che modo?

LIGURIO: Noi abbiamo tutti a travestirci. Io farò travestire el frate: contrafarà la voce, el viso, l'abito; e dirò al dottore che tu sia quello; e' se 'l crederrà.

CALLIMACO: Piacemi; ma io che farò?

LIGURIO: Fo conto che tu ti metta un pitocchino adosso, e con un liuto in mano te ne venga costì, dal canto della sua casa, cantando un canzoncino.

CALLIMACO: A viso scoperto?

CALLIMACO: There's nothing wrong, nothing at all. I've just painted myself into a corner!

LIGURIO: Why? Why don't you tell me? Take your hands away from your face.

CALLIMACO: Don't you remember that I told Messer Nicia that you, he, Siro and I would grab somebody to put in bed with his wife?

LIGURIO: So what?

CALLIMACO: What do you mean, so what? If I'm with you, I can't be the one you grab! And if I'm not, he'll see through our trick.

LIGURIO: That's true. But isn't there some way out?

CALLIMACO: Not that I can see.

LIGURIO: Yes, there must be.

CALLIMACO: What?

LIGURIO: Let me think about it a little.

CALLIMACO: That's just great. I'm in real trouble if you have to start thinking about it now!

LIGURIO: I've got it!

CALLIMACO: What?

LIGURIO: I'll get the friar, who has been willing to help us out up to now, to do a little bit more.

CALLIMACO: In what way?

LIGURIO: We all have to disguise ourselves. I'll have the friar put on a disguise, too. He'll change his voice, his face, and his robes, and I'll tell Messer Nicia that it's you. He'll believe it.

CALLIMACO: I like that, but what will I do?

LIGURIO: I picture you wearing a short cape, and coming up around the corner of his house there, with a guitar in your hands and singing a little song.

CALLIMACO: Without a mask?

LIGURIO: Sì, ché se tu portassi una maschera, e' gli enterrebbe sospetto.

CALLIMACO: E' mi conoscerà.

LIGURIO: Non farà, perché io voglio che tu ti storca el viso, che tu apra, aguzzi o digrigni la bocca, chiugga un occhio. Pruova un poco.

CALLIMACO: Fo io così?

LIGURIO: No.

CALLIMACO: Così?

LIGURIO: Non basta.

CALLIMACO: A questo modo?

LIGURIO: Sì, sì, tieni a mente cotesto. Io ho un naso in casa: i' voglio che tu te l'appichi.

CALLIMACO: Orbè, che sarà poi?

LIGURIO: Come tu sarai comparso in sul canto, noi saren quivi, torrènti el liuto, piglierenti, aggirerenti, condurrenti in casa, metterenti al letto. El resto doverrai tu fare da te!

CALLIMACO: Fatto sta condursi costì.

LIGURIO: Qui ti condurrai tu. Ma a fare che tu vi possa ritornare, sta a te, e non a noi.

CALLIMACO: Come?

LIGURIO: Che tu te la guadagni in questa notte, e che, innanzi che tu ti parta, te le dia a conoscere, scuoprale lo 'nganno, mostrile l'amore li porti, dicale el bene le vuoi, e come sanza sua infamia la può esser tua amica, e con sua grande infamia tua nimica. È impossibile che la non convenga teco, e che la voglia che questa notte sia sola.

CALLIMACO: Credi tu cotesto?

LIGURIO: Yes, because if you were wearing a mask, he might get suspicious.

CALLIMACO: He'll recognize me.

LIGURIO: No, he won't because I want you to twist your face up. Keep your mouth open, or pulled tight, or screwed up. Close one eye. Give it a try.

CALLIMACO: Like this?

LIGURIO: No.

CALLIMACO: Like this?

LIGURIO: That still won't do.

CALLIMACO: What about this way?

LIGURIO: Yes! Yes! Try to remember that. I have a false nose at home. I want you stick it on.

CALLIMACO: Fine. What happens then?

LIGURIO: When you come around the corner, we'll be here; we'll snatch your guitar, grab hold of you, twirl you around, rush you into the house, and throw you into bed. The rest you'll have to do yourself!

CALLIMACO: Lead me to it!

LIGURIO: I think you can be led that far. But it's up to you, and not us, to manage it so you can go back again.

CALLIMACO: How?

LIGURIO: You will have to win her over tonight. Then, before you leave her, you will have to let her know who you are, reveal the trick, tell her how much you love her and how much you have wanted her. Mention, too, how easy it will be for her to be your friend, without any scandal, and how much scandal she risks if she wants to be your enemy. I can't imagine that she won't come to terms with you, or that she would really want this night to be the only one.

CALLIMACO: Do you really think so?

LIGURIO: Io ne son certo. Ma non perdiàn più tempo: e' son già dua ore. Chiama Siro, manda la pozione a messer Nicia, e me aspetta in casa. Io andrò per il frate: farollo travestire, e condurrollo qui, e troverreno el dottore, e fareno quello manca.

CALLIMACO: Tu di' bene. Va' via.

SCENA TERZA

Callimaco, Siro.

CALLIMACO: O Siro!

SIRO: Messere!

CALLIMACO: Fàtti costì.

SIRO: Eccomi.

CALLIMACO: Piglia quel bicchiere d'argento, che è drento allo armario di camera, e, coperto con un poco di drappo, portamelo, e guarda a non lo versare per la via.

SIRO: Sarà fatto.

CALLIMACO: Costui è stato dieci anni meco, e sempre m'ha servito fedelmente. Io credo trovare, anche in questo caso, fede in lui; e, benché io non gli abbi comunicato questo inganno, e' se lo indovina, ché gli è cattivo bene, e veggo che si va accomodando.

SIRO: Eccolo.

CALLIMACO: Sta bene. Tira, va' a casa messer Nicia, e digli che questa è la medicina, che ha a pigliare la donna dipo' cena sùbito; e quanto prima cena, tanto sarà meglio; e, come noi sareno in sul canto ad ordine, al tempo, ch' e' facci d'esservi. Va' ratto.

SIRO: Io vo.

LIGURIO: I'm positive. But let's not lose any more time: it is already eight o'clock. Call Siro, send him with the potion to Messer Nicia, and wait for me at home. I'll go get the friar, and have him put on a disguise. Then I'll bring him back here, we'll pick up Messer Nicia, and we'll take care of the rest.

CALLIMACO: That sounds fine! Go ahead!

SCENE THREE

Callimaco, Siro.

CALLIMACO: Hey, Siro!

SIRO: Sir!

CALLIMACO: Come over here.

SIRO: Here I am.

CALLIMACO: Go get that silver goblet that is in my bedroom cupboard, cover it with a napkin, bring it to me, and make sure you don't spill it on the way.

SIRO: It's as good as done.

CALLIMACO: That fellow has been with me for ten years now, and he has always served me faithfully. I think I can trust him in this case, too. Though I haven't let him in on the trick, he has figured it out. He is a pretty shrewd character, and I can see that he is catching on as we go along.

SIRO: Here it is.

CALLIMACO: That's fine. Quick now, go to Messer Nicia's house and tell him this is the medicine his wife has to take right after supper. And the earlier she eats, the better. We will be around the corner waiting, so tell him to be there on time. Go quickly!

SIRO: I'm going.

CALLIMACO: Odi qua. Se vuole che tu l'aspetti, aspettalo, e vientene qui con lui; se non vuole, torna qui da me, dato che tu glien' hai, e fatto che tu gli arai l'ambasciata. Intendi?

SIRO: Messer, sì.

SCENA QUARTA

Callimaco solo.

CALLIMACO: Io aspetto che Ligurio torni col frate; e chi dice che gli è dura cosa l'aspettare, dice el vero. Io scemo ad ogni ora dieci libre, pensando dove io sono ora, dove io potrei essere di qui a dua ore, temendo che non nasca qualche caso, che interrompa el mio disegno. Che se fussi, e' fia l'ultima notte della vita mia, perché o io mi gitterò in Arno, o io m'impiccherò, o io me gitterò da quelle finestre, o io mi darò d'un coltello in sull'uscio suo. Qualche cosa farò io, perché io non viva più. Ma veggo io Ligurio? Egli è desso. Egli ha seco uno che pare scrignuto, zoppo: e' fia certo el frate travestito. Oh, frati! Conoscine uno, e conoscigli tutti! Chi è quell'altro, che si è accostato a loro? E' mi pare Siro, che arà digià fatto l'ambiasciata al dottore. Egli è esso. Io gli voglio aspettare qui, per convenire con loro.

SCENA QUINTA

Siro, Ligurio, Callimaco, Fra' Timoteo travestito.

SIRO: Chi è teco, Ligurio?

CALLIMACO: Listen here. If he wants you to wait for him, wait and then return here with him; if he doesn't, come back to me here as soon as you've handed it to him and given him the message. Do you understand?

SIRO: Yes, sir.

SCENE FOUR

Callimaco alone.

CALLIMACO: Here I stand, waiting for Ligurio to return with the friar, and whoever said waiting is the hardest part knew what he was talking about. I must be losing ten pounds an hour, just thinking about where I am now and where I might be in two hours, and worrying whether something may come up that will spoil my plans. If that should happen, this will be the last night of my life, because I'll throw myself into the Arno, or hang myself, or jump out of that window up there, or plunge a dagger into my breast right on her doorstep. Well, I'll do something or other, rather than go on living like this. But is that Ligurio I see? It is, and he has someone with him who is limping and hunchbacked. That must be the friar in disguise. Oh, these friars! One is worse than the other! Who is that other fellow who has joined them? It looks to me like Siro; he must have brought the message to Messer Nicia. Yes, that's him. I'll wait for them here, so we can make our final plans.

SCENE FIVE

Siro, Ligurio, Friar in disguise, Callimaco.

SIRO: Who is that with you, Ligurio?

LIGURIO: Un uom da bene.

SIRO: È egli zoppo, o fa le vista?

LIGURIO: Bada ad altro.

SIRO: Oh! gli ha el viso del gran ribaldo!

LIGURIO: Deh! sta' cheto, che ci hai fracido! Ove è Callimaco?

CALLIMACO: Io son qui. Voi sete e ben venuti!

LIGURIO: O Callimaco! avvertisci questo pazzerello di Siro: egli ha detto già mille pazzie.

CALLIMACO: Siro, odi qua: tu hai questa sera a fare tutto quello che ti dirà Ligurio; e fa' conto, quando e' ti comanda, ch' e' sia io; e ciò che tu vedi, senti o odi, hai a tenere segretissimo, per quanto tu stimi la roba, l'onore, la vita mia ed il bene tuo.

SIRO: Così si farà.

CALLIMACO: Desti tu el bicchiere al dottore?

SIRO: Messer, sì.

CALLIMACO: Che disse?

SIRO: Che sarà ora ad ordine di tutto.

FRATE: È questo Callimaco?

CALLIMACO: Sono a' comandi vostri. Le proferte tra noi sien fatte: voi avete a disporre di me e di tutte le fortune mia, come di voi.

FRATE: Io l'ho inteso, e credolo; e sommi messo a fare quel per te, che io non arei fatto per uomo del mondo.

CALLIMACO: Voi non perderete la fatica.

FRATE: E' basta che tu mi voglia bene.

LIGURIO: Lasciamo stare le cirimonie. Noi andreno a travestirci, Siro ed io. Tu, Callimaco, vien' con noi, per potere ire a fare e fatti tua. El frate ci aspetterà qui: noi torneren sùbito, ed andreno a trovare Messer Nicia.

LIGURIO: A most worthy gentleman.

SIRO: Is he a cripple, or just pretending?

LIGURIO: Never mind.

SIRO: Hey! He looks like old Nick[29] himself!

LIGURIO: Will you keep still? You're annoying us. Where is Callimaco?

CALLIMACO: Here I am. Welcome to you all!

LIGURIO: Oh, Callimaco, tell this dunce, Siro, not to shoot his mouth off so much.

CALLIMACO: Siro, listen here. Tonight you're to do everything that Ligurio tells you. Remember, when he commands, it's as if it were me. Whatever you see or hear is to be kept strictly secret, if you value my honor, my fortune, my life, and your own good.

SIRO: I'll do that.

CALLIMACO: Did you give the goblet to Messer Nicia?

SIRO: Yes, sir.

CALLIMACO: What did he say?

SIRO: He will do everything as directed.

TIMOTEO: Is this Callimaco?

CALLIMACO: Yes, at your orders. Let us settle the conditions of our collaboration. I put myself and my entire fortune at your disposal.

TIMOTEO: So I understand, and I take your word for it. I have already begun to do for you things that I would not have done for anybody else in the world.

CALLIMACO: Your efforts will not go unrewarded.

TIMOTEO: I seek nothing more than your love.

LIGURIO: Let's drop the ceremonies. Siro and I will go and put on our disguises. Callimaco, you come with us so that you can go and do your part. The friar will wait for us here, we'll be right back and then go get Messer Nicia.

CALLIMACO: Tu di' bene. Andiamo.
FRATE: Io vi aspetto.

SCENA SESTA

Fra' Timoteo solo.

FRATE: E' dicono el vero quelli che dicono che le cattive compagnie conducono li uomini alle forche. E molte volte uno càpita male così per essere troppo facile e troppo buono, come per essere troppo tristo. Dio sa che io non pensavo ad iniuriare persona, stavomi nella mia cella, dicevo el mio ufizio, intrattenevo e mia devoti: capitommi innanzi questo diavol di Ligurio, che mi fece intignere el dito in uno errore, donde io vi ho messo el braccio, e tutta la persona, e non so ancora dove io mi abbia a capitare. Pure mi conforto che, quando una cosa importa a molti, molti ne hanno aver cura.—Ma ecco Ligurio e quel servo che tornano.

SCENA SETTIMA

Fra' Timoteo, Ligurio, Siro travestiti.

FRATE: Voi sete e ben tornati.
LIGURIO: Stiàn noi bene?
FRATE: Benissimo.
LIGURIO: E' ci manca el dottore. Andian verso casa sua: e' son più di tre ore, andian via!
SIRO: Chi apre l'uscio suo? E' egli el famiglio?
LIGURIO: No: gli è lui. Ah, ah, ah, uh!
SIRO: Tu ridi?

CALLIMACO: That's a good idea. Let's go.
TIMOTEO: I will wait for you here.

SCENE SIX

Friar alone, in disguise.

TIMOTEO: Whoever said that bad company can lead a man to the gallows was no fool. Many times a man falls into evil ways, not from being too bad, but from being too good and easygoing. God knows I never intended to harm anybody. I kept to my cell, I said the holy services, and I looked after my parishioners. Suddenly that devil Ligurio appears before me, and he gets me to dip my hands so deep into mischief that now I'm in it up to my neck, and I don't yet know how far I'll have to go before I'm finished. Still, I can console myself with the thought that when a thing concerns many people, many people have to take care of it. But here comes Ligurio with that servant.

SCENE SEVEN

Friar Timoteo, Ligurio, Siro, in disguise.

TIMOTEO: Welcome back!

LIGURIO: How do we look?

TIMOTEO: Perfect.

LIGURIO: All we need now is Messer Nicia. Let's head toward his house, it's past nine o'clock already. Come on!

SIRO: Who's that coming out of his door? Is it his servant?

LIGURIO: No, it's him. Ha, ha, ha, ha!

SIRO: Why are you laughing?

LIGURIO: Chi non riderebbe? Egli ha un guarnacchino indosso, che non gli cuopre el culo. Che diavolo ha egli in capo? E' mi pare un di questi gufi de' canonici, ed uno spadaccin sotto: ah, ah! e' borbotta non so che. Tirianci da parte, ed udireno qualche sciagura della moglie.

SCENA OTTAVA

Messer Nicia travestito.

NICIA: Quanti lezzi ha fatto questa mia pazza! Ella ha mandato le fante a casa la madre, e 'l famiglio in villa. Di questo io la laudo; ma io non la lodo già che, innanzi che la ne sia voluta ire al letto, ell' abbi fatto tante schifiltà:— Io non voglio! . . . Come farò io? . . . Che mi fate voi fare? . . . Ohimè, mamma mia! . . .—E, se non che la madre le disse el padre del porro, la non entrava in quel letto. Che le venga la contina! Io vorrei ben vedere le donne schizzinose, ma non tanto, ché ci ha tolto la testa, cervel di gatta! Poi, chi dicessi:—Che impiccata sia la più savia donna di Firenze—la direbbe:—Che t'ho io fatto?—Io so che la Pasquina enterrà in Arezzo, ed innanzi che io mi parta da giuoco, io potrò dire, come mona Ghinga:—Di veduta, con queste mani.—Io sto pur bene! Chi mi conoscerebbe? Io paio maggiore, più giovane, più scarzo: e' non sarebbe donna, che mi togliessi danari di letto.—Ma dove troverrò costoro?

LIGURIO: Who could help it? He's wearing a little cloak that doesn't cover his ass. What the hell does he have on his head? He looks like a cross between an owl and a monk, and down below he has a little blade sticking out. Ha! ha! He's muttering something or other. Let's draw aside so we can hear the latest trouble with his wife.

SCENE EIGHT

Messer Nicia in disguise.

NICIA: What a headache that crazy wife of mine has given me. She's sent her maids to her mother's house, and the servant out to the country. I can't blame her for that. But I don't see why she had to put on so many coy airs before she finally got into bed. "I just can't! . . ." "What will I do! . . ." "Oh dear! . . ." "Mamma mia! . . ." If her mother hadn't told her to get her ass moving, she never would have gotten into that damned bed. I hope she gets the pox! I like to see women a bit fussy, but there's a limit! She snapped our heads off, the bird-brained bitch! If anyone shouted: "Hang the most virtuous woman in Florence!" she would answer: "What have I done to you?" But I know that she'll end up by coming around, and before I'm finished with this game, I'll be able to say, like the lady in the story:[30] "I've seen it with my own hands!"— But I'm really looking good! No one would recognize me! I feel taller, younger, slimmer. There isn't a woman in all of Florence who would make me pay to sleep with her. But where can they be?

SCENA NONA

Ligurio, Messer Nicia, Fra' Timoteo, Siro.

LIGURIO: Buona sera, messere.

NICIA: Oh! uh! eh!

LIGURIO: Non abbiate paura, noi siàn noi.

NICIA: Oh! voi sete tutti qui? S' io non vi conoscevo presto, io vi davo con questo stocco, el più diritto che io sapevo! Tu, se' Ligurio? e tu, Siro? e quell'altro? el maestro, eh?

LIGURIO: Messer, sì.

NICIA: Togli! Oh, e' si è contraffatto bene! e' non lo conoscerebbe Va-qua-tu!

LIGURIO: Io gli ho fatto mettere dua noce in bocca, perché non sia conosciuto alla voce.

NICIA: Tu se' ignorante.

LIGURIO: Perché?

NICIA: Che non me 'l dicevi tu prima? Ed are'mene messo anch' io dua: e sai se gli importa non essere conosciuto alla favella!

LIGURIO: Togliete, mettetevi in bocca questo.

NICIA: Che è ella?

LIGURIO: Una palla di cera.

NICIA: Dàlla qua . . . Ca, pu, ca, co, che, cu, cu, spu . . . Che ti venga la seccaggine, pezzo di manigoldo!

LIGURIO: Perdonatemi, ché io ve ne ho data una in scambio, che io non me ne sono avveduto.

NICIA: Ca, ca, pu, pu . . . Di che, che, che, che era?

LIGURIO: D'aloe.

NICIA: Sia, in malora! Spu, pu . . . Maestro, voi non dite nulla?

SCENE NINE

Ligurio, Messer Nicia, Friar in disguise, Siro.

LIGURIO: Good evening, sir!

NICIA: Hey! Who! What!

LIGURIO: Don't be frightened, it's only us.

NICIA: Ah! You're all here! If I hadn't recognized you right away, I would have run you all through and through with my sword! Is that you, Ligurio? And you, Siro? And this other one is the Doctor? Ha!

LIGURIO: Yes, sir.

NICIA: Let me take a look. Oh! He has really disguised himself well. Not even the secret police[31] would recognize him.

LIGURIO: I had him put a couple of nuts in his mouth, so that his voice wouldn't be recognized.

NICIA: That was really stupid of you!

LIGURIO: Why?

NICIA: You should have told me earlier. I would have put a couple of nuts in my mouth, too. You know how important it is not to have our voices recognized!

LIGURIO: Here, take this and stick it in your mouth.

NICIA: What is it?

LIGURIO: A ball of wax.

NICIA: Hand it over. Pfui, kech, yuck, spu! A plague on you, you no good bastard!

LIGURIO: Excuse me, I gave you the wrong one by mistake, without meaning to.

NICIA: Pfui, kech, spu! What . . . what was it made of?

LIGURIO: Camphor.

NICIA: The devil take it! Spu, spu. . . Doctor, you haven't said a word.

FRATE: Ligurio m'ha fatto adirare.

NICIA: Oh! voi contraffate bene la voce.

LIGURIO: Non perdiàn più tempo qui. Io voglio essere el capitano, ed ordinare l'essercito per la giornata. Al destro corno sia preposto Callimaco, al sinistro io, intra le dua corna starà qui el dottore; Siro fia retroguardo, per dar sussidio a quella banda che inclinassi. El nome sia san Cuccù.

NICIA: Chi è san Cuccù?

LIGURIO: È el più onorato santo, che sia in Francia. Andian via, mettiàn l'aguato a questo canto. State a udire: io sento un liuto.

NICIA: Egli è esso. Che vogliàn fare?

LIGURIO: Vuolsi mandare innanzi uno esploratore a scoprire chi egli è, e, secondo ci riferirà, secondo fareno.

NICIA: Chi v'andrà?

LIGURIO: Va' via, Siro. Tu sai quello hai a fare. Considera, essamina, torna presto, referisci.

SIRO: Io vo.

NICIA: Io non vorrei che noi pigliassimo un granchio, che fussi qualche vecchio debole o infermiccio, e che questo giuoco si avessi a rifare domandassera.

LIGURIO: Non dubitate, Siro è valent' uomo. Eccolo, e' torna. Che truovi, Siro?

SIRO: Egli è il più bello garzonaccio, che voi vedessi mai! Non ha venticinque anni, e viensene solo, in pitocchino, sonando el liuto.

NICIA: Egli è il caso, se tu di' el vero. Ma guarda, che questa broda sarebbe tutta gittata addosso a te!

SIRO: Egli è quel ch' io vi ho detto.

TIMOTEO: Ligurio has made me very angry.

NICIA: Hey! You really can disguise your voice.

LIGURIO: Let's not waste any more time here. I'll be the commanding officer, and lead the patrol in tonight's action. I will assign the right column[32] to Callimaco, the left to myself, and Messer Nicia here will stick between the two columns, with Siro bringing up the rear to stiffen up any column if it threatens to go limp. The password will be Saint Cuckoo!

NICIA: Who is Saint Cuckoo?

LIGURIO: The most venerated saint in all of France. Forward, march; let's set up our ambush at this corner. Listen a moment, I hear a guitar.

NICIA: It is! What do we do now?

LIGURIO: We ought to send a scout on ahead to reconnoitre, and we'll make our battle plans according to his report.

NICIA: Who will go?

LIGURIO: Siro, you go on ahead. You know what you have to do. Advance, reconnoitre, rendezvous, and report.

SIRO: Aye aye, sir!

NICIA: I wouldn't like us to catch a crab. We don't want some impotent old geezer, or some cripple, so we'd have to start the game all over again tomorrow night.

LIGURIO: Don't worry, Siro is an able man. Here he is back again. What did you find, Siro?

SIRO: It's the finest young scamp you've ever laid eyes on. He's under twenty-five, and he's walking along all by himself, wearing a short cape, plucking his guitar.

NICIA: He's just what we need, if you're telling the truth. But if you're not, you'll really be in the soup.

SIRO: He's exactly like I've told you.

LIGURIO: Aspettian ch' egli spunti questo canto, e sùbito gli sareno addosso.

NICIA: Tiratevi in qua, maestro: voi mi parete uno uom di legno. Eccolo.

CALLIMACO: "Venir vi possa el diavolo allo letto,
            Dapoi ch' io non vi posso venir io!"

LIGURIO: Sta' forte. Da' qua questo liuto!

CALLIMACO: Ohimè! Che ho io fatto?

NICIA: Tu 'l vedrai! Cuoprigli el capo, imbavaglialo!

LIGURIO: Aggiralo!

NICIA: Dàgli un'altra volta! Dàgliene un'altra! Mettetelo in casa!

FRATE: Messer Nicia, io m'andrò a riposare, ché mi duole la testa, che io muoio. E, se non bisogna, io non tornerò domattina.

NICIA: Sì, maestro, non tornate: noi potren far da noi.

SCENA DECIMA

Fra' Timoteo travestito solo.

FRATE: E' sono intanati in casa, ed io me n'andrò al convento. E voi, spettatori, non ci appuntate, perché in questa notte non ci dormirà persona, sì che gli Atti non sono interrotti dal tempo: io dirò l'uffizio; Ligurio e Siro ceneranno, ché non hanno mangiato oggi; el dottore andrà di camera in sala, perché la cucina vadia netta; Callimaco e madonna Lucrezia non dormiranno, perché io so, se io fussi lui e se voi fussi lei, che noi non dormiremo.

LIGURIO: Let's wait until he has just turned this corner, and then we'll jump on him.

NICIA: Come back over this way, Doctor. What's
wrong? You look as stiff as a board. Here he comes.

CALLIMACO: "I hope you take the devil to your bed,
                 Since I can't make it with you, dear,
                        instead . . ."

LIGURIO: Hold still! Hand over that guitar!

CALLIMACO: Help! What do you want with me?

NICIA: You'll see! Blindfold him, gag his mouth!

LIGURIO: Twirl him around!

NICIA: Give him another turn! One more for good
measure! Now get him into the house!

TIMOTEO: Messer Nicia, I think I'll go take a rest
now, I have a splitting headache. Unless you need me, I
won't be back tomorrow morning, either.

NICIA: All right Doctor, don't come back. We can take
care of the rest ourselves.

SCENE TEN

Friar Timoteo disguised, alone.

TIMOTEO: They have shut themselves up in the house,
and I'll go back home to the monastery. And you, dear
audience, don't say that we are not observing the classical
unities;[33] you had better stick around, because nobody is
going to sleep tonight, so the acts will not be interrupted
by the passage of time. I will go and say Mass. Ligurio and
Siro will have a bite to eat, since they haven't touched a
thing all day. Messer Nicia will go from the bedroom to
the kitchen to see how things are cooking. Callimaco and
Madonna Lucrezia won't sleep, for I know that, if I were
he, and you were she, we wouldn't get any sleep.

CANZONE

Oh dolce notte, oh sante
ore notturne e quete,
ch' i disïosi amanti accompagnate;
in voi s'adunan tante
letizie, onde voi siete
sole cagion di far l'alme beate.
Voi, giusti premii date,
all'amorose schiere,
delle lunghe fatiche;
voi fate, o felici ore,
ogni gelato petto arder d'amore!

SONG

Oh gentle darkness, oh holy
And sweet nocturnal hours
That soothe the burning pain of love's desire,
You bring to lovers solely
Delight, and so your power's
The only draught that quenches passion's fire.
You grant the amorous choir
A well-deserv'd reward for daylight's starkness,
Oh blessed hours of darkness,
Requiting lovers' labors . . .
And hide their ardent kisses from the neighbors.

ATTO QUINTO
SCENA PRIMA

Fra' Timoteo solo.

FRATE: Io non ho potuto questa notte chiudere occhio, tanto è el desiderio, che io ho d'intendere come Callimaco e gli altri l'abbino fatta. Ed ho atteso a consumare el tempo in varie cose: io dissi mattutino, lessi una vita de' Santi Padri, andai in chiesa ed accesi una lampana che era spenta, mutai un velo ad una Nostra Donna, che fa miracoli. Quante volte ho io detto a questi frati che la tenghino pulita! E si maravigliono poi se la divozione manca! Io mi ricordo esservi cinquecento immagine, e non ve ne sono oggi venti: questo nasce da noi, che non le abbiamo saputa mantenere la reputazione. Noi vi solavamo ogni sera doppo la compieta andare a processione, e facevànvi cantare ogni sabato le laude. Botavànci noi sempre quivi, perché vi si vedessi delle immagine fresche; confortavamo nelle confessioni gli uomini e le donne a botarvisi. Ora non si fa nulla di queste cose, e poi ci maravigliamo che le cose vadin fredde! Oh, quanto poco cervello è in questi mia frati! Ma io sento un gran romore da casa messer Nicia. Eccogli, per mia fè! E' cavan fuora el prigione. Io sarò giunto a tempo. Ben si sono indugiati alla sgocciolatura: e' si fa appunto l'alba. Io voglio stare ad udire quel che dicono sanza scoprirmi.

ACT FIVE
SCENE ONE

Friar Timoteo alone.

TIMOTEO: I couldn't close my eyes all night long, I
have been so eager to hear how Callimaco and the others
have made out. I did everything I could to pass the time:
I said my matins, I read a Life of the Holy Fathers, I
went to church and relit a candle that had gone out, and
I changed the veil on a miraculous statue of the Virgin.
How many times have I told those friars to keep her well
cleaned! And then they wonder why attendance is going
down. I remember when there were five hundred holy im-
ages, and nowadays there are barely twenty. It's all our own
fault, because we haven't been smart enough to keep up the
publicity. We always used to hold a procession every evening after vespers, and we would have hymns sung there
every Sabbath. We used to take vows there ourselves, so
that people would see fresh, new plaques all the time, and
we would encourage the men and women to make vows
when they came for confession. Now nobody bothers to
do any of these things, and then we wonder why business
has fallen off! Oh, my fellow friars really don't have any
brains!—But I hear a great racket in Messer Nicia's house.
Here they come, by the blessed Virgin! They are throwing
their prisoner out. I am just in time. They really must
have savored it to the last drop; dawn is already beginning
to break. I am going to stand over there where I can listen
without being seen.

SCENA SECONDA

Messer Nicia, Callimaco, Ligurio, Siro travestiti.

NICIA: Piglialo di costà, ed io di qua, e tu, Siro, lo tieni per il pitocco, di drieto.

CALLIMACO: Non mi fate male!

LIGURIO: Non aver paura, va' pur via.

NICIA: Non andian più là.

LIGURIO: Voi dite bene. Lasciànl'ir qui: diàngli dua volte, che non sappi donde e' si sia venuto. Giralo, Siro!

SIRO: Ecco.

NICIA: Giralo un'altra volta.

SIRO: Ecco fatto.

CALLIMACO: El mio liuto!

LIGURIO: Via, ribaldo, tira via! S' io ti sento favellare, io ti taglierò el collo!

NICIA: E' si è fuggito. Andianci a sbisacciare: e vuolsi che noi usciàn fuori tutti a buona ora, acciò che non si paia che noi abbiam vegghiato questa notte.

LIGURIO: Voi dite el vero.

NICIA: Andate, Ligurio e Siro, a trovar maestro Callimaco, e li dite che la cosa è proceduta bene.

LIGURIO: Che li possiamo noi dire? Noi non sappiamo nulla. Voi sapete che, arrivati in casa, noi ce n'andamo nella volta a bere: voi e la suocera rimanesti alle man' seco, e non vi rivedemo mai se non ora, quando voi ci chiamasti per mandarlo fuora.

NICIA: Voi dite el vero. Oh! io vi ho da dire le belle cose! Mogliama era nel letto al buio. Sostrata m'aspettava al fuoco. Io giunsi su con questo garzonaccio, e, perché e'

SCENE TWO

Messer Nicia, Callimaco disguised, Ligurio, Siro.

NICIA: You grab him on that side, and I'll take this side. Siro, you hold him by the tail of his cape.

CALLIMACO: Don't hurt me!

LIGURIO: Don't worry, just get going, and fast.

NICIA: Let's not go any farther.

LIGURIO: You're right, we'll let him go right here. Let's twirl him around a couple of times, so he won't know where he has come from. Twist him, Siro!

SIRO: There!

NICIA: Once more around, for good measure.

SIRO: There you go!

CALLIMACO: My guitar!

LIGURIO: Scat, you rascal, get going! If I hear one word out of you, I'll slit your gullet.

NICIA: He's run away like a rabbit. Let's go and take off these outfits. We ought to make sure we go out early this morning, so that it doesn't look as if we've been up all night.

LIGURIO: You're right.

NICIA: Ligurio, you and Siro go find Doctor Callimaco, and tell him everything went according to plan.

LIGURIO: What can we tell him? We don't know a thing. As you know, once we were in the house, Siro and I went down to the cellar to open a bottle of wine. You and your mother-in-law stayed around to handle things. We didn't see you again until just now, when you called us to help put him out.

NICIA: That's true. Oh, have I got fine things to tell you! The little woman was in bed, in the dark. Sostrata was waiting for me by the fireplace. I came upstairs with

non andassi nulla in capperuccia, io lo menai in una dispensa, che io ho in sulla sala, dove era un certo lume annacquato, che gittava un poco d'albore, in modo ch' e' non mi poteva vedere in viso.

LIGURIO: Saviamente.

NICIA: Io lo feci spogliare: e' nicchiava; io me li volsi come un cane, di modo che gli parve mille anni di avere fuora e panni, e rimase ignudo. Egli è brutto di viso: egli aveva un nasaccio, una bocca torta . . . Ma tu non vedesti mai le più belle carne: bianco, morbido, pastoso! E dell'altre cose non ne domandare.

LIGURIO: E' non è bene ragionare. Che bisognava vederlo tutto?

NICIA: Tu vuoi el giambo! Poi che io avevo messo mano in pasta, io ne volli toccare el fondo. Poi volli vedere s'egli era sano: s'egli avessi aùto le bolle, dove mi trovavo io? Tu ci metti parole!

LIGURIO: Avevi ragion voi.

NICIA: Come io ebbi veduto che gli era sano, io me lo tirai drieto, ed al buio lo menai in camera, messilo al letto; ed innanzi che mi partissi, volli toccare con mano come la cosa andava, ché io non sono uso ad essermi dato ad intendere lucciole per lanterne.

LIGURIO: Con quanta prudenzia avete voi governata questa cosa!

NICIA: Tocco e sentito che io ebbi ogni cosa, mi uscí di camera, e serrai l'uscio, e me n'andai alla suocera, che era al fuoco, e tutta notte abbiamo attesa a ragionare.

LIGURIO: Che ragionamenti son suti e vostri?

NICIA: Della sciocchezza di Lucrezia, e quanto egli era meglio che, sanza tanti andirivieni, ella avessi ceduto al

that young scamp, and just to be sure we weren't buying a pig in a poke, I took him into a closet next to the bedroom, where there is a very dim light, so he couldn't make out my face.

LIGURIO: Very shrewd.

NICIA: I told him to undress, and when he grumbled, I turned on him like a mad dog. He couldn't rip his clothes off fast enough, until he was stark naked. He had a really ugly face, with an enormous nose and a crooked mouth; but you never saw such a beautiful body, all pink and firm and smooth. As for the other parts, don't ask!

LIGURIO: Let's not talk about it. There was no use poking around.

NICIA: Are you kidding? Since I had gotten my hands into it, I made sure I went right to the bottom of things. I had to make certain that he was healthy: if he had had the pox, where would that have left me? Just tell me that.

LIGURIO: You're absolutely right.

NICIA: When I had made sure he was healthy, I dragged him after me into the bedroom, where it was dark. I put him in bed, and before going back out I made sure I saw with my own hands how things were coming along, because I always like to get the lay of the land for myself.

LIGURIO: I can't get over how cunningly you've handled this whole business.

NICIA: Once I had poked my nose into how things were coming, I left the bedroom, and I locked the door. Then I went to where my mother-in-law was sitting by the fire, and we spent the entire night chatting and waiting.

LIGURIO: Whatever did you talk about all that time?

NICIA: About Lucrezia's silliness, and how much better it would have been for her to give in right away without so

primo. Dipoi ragionamo del bambino, che me lo pare
tuttavia avere in braccio, el naccherino! Tanto che io senti'
sonare le tredici ore; e, dubitando che il dì non sopra-
giugnessi, me n'andai in camera. Che direte voi, che io
non potevo fare levare quel ribaldone?

LIGURIO: Credolo!

NICIA: E' gli era piaciuto l'unto! Pure, e' si levò, io vi
chiamai, e lo abbiamo condutto fuora.

LIGURIO: La cosa è ita bene.

NICIA: Che dirai tu, che me ne incresce?

LIGURIO: Di che?

NICIA: Di quel povero giovane, ch' egli abbia a morire
sì presto, e che questa notte gli abbia a costar sì cara.

LIGURIO: Oh! voi avete e pochi pensieri! Lasciàtene la
cura a lui.

NICIA: Tu di' el vero.—Ma e' mi par ben mille anni di
trovare maestro Callimaco, e rallegrarmi seco.

LIGURIO: E' sarà fra una ora fuora. Ma egli è già chiaro
el giorno: noi ci andreno a spogliare; voi, che farete?

NICIA: Andronne anch' io in casa, a mettermi e panni
buoni. Farò levare e lavare la donna, farolla venire alla
chiesa, ad entrare in santo. Io vorrei che voi e Callimaco
fussi là, e che noi parlassimo al frate, per ringraziarlo e
ristorarlo del bene, che ci ha fatto.

LIGURIO: Voi dite bene: così si farà. A Dio.

much beating around the bush. Then we talked about the baby—ah, I feel as if I were cuddling him in my arms, the little rascal! And so on and so forth, until I heard the bells strike seven, and fearing that day might break any minute, I went up to the bedroom. Would you believe it, I couldn't get that big rogue out of bed?

LIGURIO: I believe it!

NICIA: He really wanted to stew in his own juice! But I got him up at last, called you, and we kicked him out.

LIGURIO: Everything seems to have gone right.

NICIA: Would you believe me, there is something that bothers me?

LIGURIO: What is that?

NICIA: That poor fellow is going to die so soon, and will have to pay such a high price for this one night.

LIGURIO: Oh, that's nothing for you to worry about! Leave that to him.

NICIA: You're right. Well, I just can't wait to see Doctor Callimaco, and congratulate him on our success.

LIGURIO: He'll be out in a little while. But it's getting to be broad daylight. We had better go and change. What are you going to do?

NICIA: I'll go back into the house to put on my Sunday clothes. I'll get the little woman washed and dressed, and have her come to church for the blessing of her womb.[34] I'd like you and Callimaco to be there for that, too, so we can thank the friar for all the good he has done for us, and try to repay him.

LIGURIO: That's a fine idea, we'll do that. So long.

SCENA TERZA

Fra' Timoteo solo.

FRATE: Io ho udito questo ragionamento, e mi è piaciuto tutto, considerando quanta sciocchezza sia in questo
dottore; ma la conclusione ultima mi ha sopra modo dilettato. E poiché debbono venire a trovarmi a casa, io non
voglio stare più qui, ma aspettargli alla chiesa, dove la
mia mercatanzia varrà più.—Ma chi esce di quella casa? E'
mi pare Ligurio, e con lui debb' essere Callimaco. Io non
voglio che mi vegghino, per le ragioni dette: pur, quando
e' non venissino a trovarmi, sempro sarò a tempo ad andare
a trovare loro.

SCENA QUARTA

Callimaco, Ligurio.

CALLIMACO: Come io ti ho detto, Ligurio mio, io
stetti di mala voglia infino alle nove ore; e, benché io avessi
gran piacere, e' non mi parve buono. Ma, poi che io me
le fu' dato a conoscere, e ch' io l'ebbi dato ad intendere
l'amore che io le portavo, e quanto facilmente, per la semplicità del marito, noi potavamo viver felici senza infamia
alcuna, promettendole che, qualunque volta Dio facessi
altro di lui, di prenderla per donna; ed avendo ella, oltre
alle vere ragioni, gustato che differenzia è dalla ghiacitura
mia a quella di Nicia, e da e baci d'uno amante giovane
a quelli d'uno marito vecchio, doppo qualche sospiro,
disse:—Poiché l'astuzia tua, la sciocchezza del mio marito,
la semplicità di mia madre e la tristizia del mio confessoro
mi hanno condutto a fare quello che mai per me medesima

SCENE THREE

Friar Timoteo alone.

TIMOTEO: I heard those remarks and, considering
Messer Nicia's stupidity, I liked them all—especially
those last words he said: they warmed my heart. Since they
are expecting to meet me at home, I had better not stay
here. I'll go and wait for them in church: my goods draw a
better price there, anyway. But who is that coming out of
the house? It looks like Ligurio, and that must be Callimaco with him. I don't want them to see me, for the reasons I have mentioned. And anyway, if they don't come and
get me, I'll always have time to go and get them.

SCENE FOUR

Callimaco, Ligurio.

CALLIMACO: As I was saying, Ligurio my friend, I
felt ill at ease until about three in the morning, and even
though I was having a great deal of pleasure, it didn't seem
right to me. But once I had let her know who I was, and
made her realize the love I felt for her, how easy it would
be for us to live happily ever after, without any scandal,
thanks to her husband's simple-mindedness; and once I
promised I would marry her whenever the good Lord decided to get him out of the way; and aside from all those
valid reasons, once she had had a chance really to appreciate the difference between my technique and Nicia's,
between the kisses of a young lover and those of an old
husband, she sighed a bit and said: "Since your cleverness,
my husband's stupidity, my mother's silliness, and my confessor's guile have led me to do what I would never have

arei fatto, io voglio giudicare che venga da una celeste disposizione, che abbi voluto così, e non sono sufficiente a recusare quello che 'l Cielo vuole che io accetti. Però, io ti prendo per signore, patrone, guida: tu mio padre, tu mio defensore, e tu voglio che sia ogni mio bene; e quel che 'l mio marito ha voluto per una sera, voglio ch' egli abbia sempre. Fara'ti adunque suo compare, e verrai questa mattina a la chiesa, e di quivi ne verrai a desinare con esso noi; e l'andare e lo stare starà a te, e potreno ad ogni ora e sanza sospetto convenire insieme.—Io fui, udendo queste parole, per morirmi per la dolcezza. Non potetti rispondere a la minima parte di quello che io arei desiderato. Tanto che io mi truovo el più felice e contento uomo che fussi mai nel mondo; e, se questa felicità non mi mancassi o per morte o per tempo, io sarei più beato ch' e beati, più santo ch' e santi.

LIGURIO: Io ho gran piacere d'ogni tuo bene, ed ètti intervenuto quello che io ti dissi appunto. Ma che facciàn noi ora?

CALLIMACO: Andian verso la chiesa, perché io le promissi d'essere là, dove la verrà lei, la madre ed il dottore.

LIGURIO: Io sento toccare l'uscio suo: le sono esse, che escono fuora, ed hanno el dottore drieto.

CALLIMACO: Avviànci in chiesa, e là aspetteremole.

SCENA QUINTA

Messer Nicia, Lucrezia, Sostrata.

NICIA: Lucrezia, io credo che sia bene fare le cose con timore di Dio, e non alla pazzeresca.

done by myself, I have to judge that this comes from a
divine providence that willed it so. I am not capable of
refusing what heaven itself wants me to accept. I therefore
take you for my lord, my master and my guide. You shall
act as father and protector to me, and I will be yours completely. What my husband has willed for this one night,
he shall have for good and ever. You must therefore become
his close friend. Come to church with us this morning,
and then return to have lunch at our house. And you will
be able to come and go as you please, and we can meet
at any time, without arousing suspicion." Hearing those
words, I was ready to die for joy. I could not express the
smallest fraction of what I would have liked to reply. And
so I find myself the happiest and most satisfied man who
has ever lived. If this happiness endures, and I stay alive
and well, I will count myself more blessed than all the
saints in Paradise.

LIGURIO: I'm overjoyed at all your good fortune.
Everything has turned out just as I had predicted. Now
what do we do?

CALLIMACO: Let's walk toward the church, because
I promised I would be there when she arrives with her
mother and Messer Nicia.

LIGURIO: I hear their door being unbolted. Here come
the ladies now, with Messer Nicia bringing up the rear.

CALLIMACO: Let's go on to the church and wait for
them there.

SCENE FIVE

Messer Nicia, Lucrezia, Sostrata.

NICIA: Lucrezia, I think it is best to do things like
God-fearing people, and not impulsively.

LUCREZIA: Che s'ha egli a fare, ora?

NICIA: Guarda come la risponde! La pare un gallo!

SOSTRATA: Non ve ne maravigliate: ella è un poco alterata.

LUCREZIA: Che volete voi dire?

NICIA: Dico che gli è bene che io vadia innanzi a parlare al frate, e dirli che ti si facci incontro in sull'uscio della chiesa, per menarti in santo, perché gli è proprio, stamani, come se tu rinascessi.

LUCREZIA: Che non andate?

NICIA: Tu se' stamani molto ardita! Ella pareva iersera mezza morta.

LUCREZIA: Egli è la grazia vostra!

SOSTRATA: Andate a trovare el frate. Ma e' non bisogna, egli è fuora di chiesa.

NICIA: Voi dite el vero.

SCENA SESTA

Fra' Timoteo, Messer Nicia, Lucrezia, Callimaco, Ligurio, Sostrata.

FRATE: Io vengo fuora, perché Callimaco e Ligurio m'hanno detto che el dottore e le donne vengono alla chiesa. Eccole.

NICIA: *Bona dies*, padre!

FRATE: Voi sete le ben venute, e buon pro vi faccia, madonna, che Dio vi dia a fare un bel figliuolo mastio!

LUCREZIA: Dio el voglia!

LUCREZIA: What has to be done now?

NICIA: Listen to how she talks back! She acts like the cock of the walk.

SOSTRATA: Don't be surprised, she has undergone quite a change.

LUCREZIA: What is it you want?

NICIA: I mean it would be better if I went on ahead to speak with the friar. I'll tell him to meet you at the portal of the church, so he can lead you in for the blessing of your womb. It is fitting this morning, since it's as if you have been reborn.

LUCREZIA: Then why don't you go ahead?

NICIA: See how bold you are this morning! Last night she seemed half dead.

LUCREZIA: I have you to thank, haven't I?

SOSTRATA: Go get the friar. Oh, that won't be necessary. There he is outside the church.

NICIA: So he is.

SCENE SIX

Friar Timoteo, Messer Nicia, Lucrezia, Callimaco, Ligurio, Sostrata.

TIMOTEO: (I have come out here because Callimaco and Ligurio told me that Messer Nicia and the ladies were on their way to church. Here they are.)

NICIA: *Bona dies*,[35] padre!

TIMOTEO: Welcome to you all, and my best wishes to you, my lady. May the good Lord grant you a fine baby boy!

LUCREZIA: God willing!

FRATE: E' lo vorrà in ogni modo.

NICIA: Veggh' io in chiesa Ligurio e maestro Callimaco?

FRATE: Messer sì.

NICIA: Accennategli.

FRATE: Venite!

CALLIMACO: Dio vi salvi!

NICIA: Maestro, toccate la mano qui alla donna mia.

CALLIMACO: Volentieri.

NICIA: Lucrezia, costui è quello che sarà cagione che noi aremo uno bastone che sostenga la nostra vecchiezza.

LUCREZIA: Io l'ho molto caro, e vuolsi che sia nostro compare.

NICIA: Or benedetta sia tu! E voglio che lui e Ligurio venghino stamani a desinare con esso noi.

LUCREZIA: In ogni modo.

NICIA: E vo' dare loro la chiave della camera terrena d'in su la loggia, perché possino tornarsi quivi a loro comodità, che non hanno donne in casa, e stanno come bestie.

CALLIMACO: Io l'accetto, per usarla quando mi accaggia.

FRATE: Io ho avere e danari per la limosina.

NICIA: Ben sapete come, domine, oggi vi si manderanno.

LIGURIO: Di Siro non è uomo che si ricordi?

NICIA: Chiegga, ciò che i' ho è suo. Tu, Lucrezia, quanti grossi hai a dare al frate, per entrare in santo?

LUCREZIA: Io non me ne ricordo.

NICIA: Pure, quanti?

LUCREZIA: Dategliene dieci.

TIMOTEO: Where there's a will there's a way.

NICIA: Is that Ligurio and Doctor Callimaco I see in church?

TIMOTEO: Yes, sir.

NICIA: Wave to them to come on over.

TIMOTEO: Come here!

CALLIMACO: God bless you all!

NICIA: Doctor, I want you to shake hands with my wife.

CALLIMACO: The pleasure is all mine.

NICIA: Lucrezia, thanks to this young man, we will have a staff to lean on in our old age.

LUCREZIA: I am more grateful to him than I can say. I am sure that he will be like one of the family.

NICIA: Lord bless you, woman! And I want him and Ligurio to come and have lunch with us this morning.

LUCREZIA: By all means.

NICIA: And I'm going to give them a key to the downstairs guest room off the porch, so they can get back in whenever they feel like it, since they don't have women at home to take care of their needs.

CALLIMACO: I accept, and I will make use of it whenever the occasion arises.

TIMOTEO: Do I receive something, for charity?

NICIA: You know you will, *domine*. It will be sent over to you today.

LIGURIO: Isn't anybody going to remember Siro?

NICIA: Just let him ask me, what I have is his. Lucrezia, how much do you have to give the friar for his blessing?

LUCREZIA: I can't recall.

NICIA: Well, how much?

LUCREZIA: Give him a purse full.

NICIA: Affogaggine!

FRATE: E voi, madonna Sostrata, avete, secondo che mi pare, messo un tallo in sul vecchio.

SOSTRATA: Chi non sarebbe allegra?

FRATE: Andianne tutti in chiesa, e quivi direno l'orazione ordinaria. Dipoi, doppo l'ufizio, ne andrete a desinare a vostra posta.—Voi, aspettatori, non aspettate che noi usciàn più fuora: l'ufizio è lungo, io mi rimarrò in chiesa, e loro, per l'uscio del fianco, se n'andranno a casa. Valete!

NICIA: The devil you say!

TIMOTEO: Madonna Sostrata, it looks to me as if you are sprightly enough to be up to your old tricks!

SOSTRATA: Who wouldn't be tickled?

TIMOTEO: Well, let us all go into the church, and there we will celebrate accordingly. After the service, you can go back home and have a well-earned lunch. As for you, dear audience, don't expect us to come back out again. The service is a long one. Then I'll remain in church, and they'll leave by the side door, and go back home. Farewell!

CLIZIA

CLIZIA

TRANSLATED BY

DAVID SICES

CHARACTERS

PALAMEDE: a young Florentine, friend
of Cleandro

CLEANDRO: son of Nicomaco

EUSTACHIO: Nicomaco's steward

NICOMACO: a wealthy Florentine gentleman

PIRRO: his servant

SOFRONIA: Nicomaco's wife

DAMONE: Nicomaco's neighbor

DORIA: Sofronia's servant

SOSTRATA: Damone's wife

RAMONDO: a wealthy Neapolitan gentleman

CANZONA

Quanto sia lieto el giorno,
che le memorie antiche
fa ch' or per voi sien mostre e celebrate,
si vede, perché intorno
tutte le gente amiche
si sono in questa parte ragunate.
Noi, che la nostra etate
ne' boschi e nelle selve consumiamo,
venuti ancor qui siamo,
io ninfa e noi pastori,
e giàm cantando insieme e nostri amori.

Chiari giorni e quïeti!
Felice e bel paese,
dove del nostro canto el suon s'udia!
Pertanto, allegri e lieti,
a queste vostre imprese
faren col cantar nostro compagnia,
con sì dolce armonia,
qual mai sentita più non fu da voi:
e partirenci poi,
io ninfa e noi pastori,
e tornerenci a' nostri antichi amori.

PROLOGO

Se nel mondo tornassino i medesimi uomini, come tornano i medesimi casi, non passerebbono mai cento anni, che noi non ci trovassimo un'altra volta insieme a fare le medesime cose che ora. Questo si dice, perché già in Atene,

SONG

How blessed is this day
—When happy memory
Of ancient customs may be celebrated—
Shines forth in the array
Of festive pageantry
Our friends from far and wide have here created.
And we who have been fated
To spend our lives in forest and in bosky dell
For you have come to tell,
Like nymphs and swains before us,
The story of our lives in rustic chorus.

Oh! bright and tranquil morns,
Oh! gay and beauteous land
Where once the lilt of our sweet songs resounded!
Just so, our song adorns
With grace and joy your band
Of actors, in this enterprise you've founded,
With harmony sweet-sounded
That ne'er before was heard by mortal ear:
Departing thence from here,
Our nymphs' and shepherds' chorus
Relives the story of those loves before us.

PROLOGUE

If men reappeared in the world in the same way as do
events, not a hundred years would go by before we would
find ourselves together once again, doing the same things
as now.

I say this because in Athens, that noble and most an-

CLIZIA

nobile ed antichissima città in Grecia, fu un gentile uomo,
al quale, non avendo altri figliuoli che uno maschio, capitò
a sorte una picciola fanciulla in casa, la quale da lui infino
alla età di diciassette anni fu onestissimamente allevata.
Occorse dipoi che in uno tratto egli ed il figliuolo se ne
innamororno: nella concorrenzia del quale amore assai casi
e strani accidenti nacquono; i quali trapassati, il figliuolo
la prese per donna, e con quella gran tempo felicissima-
mente visse.

Che direte voi, che questo medesimo caso, pochi anni
sono, seguì ancora in Firenze? E, volendo questo nostro
autore l'uno delli dua rappresentarvi, ha eletto el fiorentino, iudicando che voi siate per prendere maggiore piacere
di questo che di quello: perché Atene è rovinata, le vie, le
piazze, i luoghi non vi si ricognoscono; dipoi, quelli cittadini parlavano in greco, e voi quella lingua non intenderesti. Prendete, pertanto, el caso seguìto in Firenze, e non
aspettate di riconoscere o il casato o gli uomini, perché lo
autore, per fuggire carico, ha convertiti i nomi veri in nomi
fitti. Vuol bene, avanti che la commedia cominci, voi veggiate le persone, acciò che meglio, nel recitarla, le cogno-
sciate.—Uscite qua fuora tutti, che 'l popolo vi vegga.
Eccogli. Vedete come e' ne vengono suavi? Ponetevi costì
in fila, l'uno propinquo all'altro. Voi vedete. Quel primo è
Nicomaco, un vecchio tutto pieno d'amore. Quello che gli è
allato è Cleandro, suo figliuolo e suo rivale. L'altro si chiama
Palamede, amico a Cleandro. Quelli dua che seguono,
l'uno è Pirro servo, l'altro Eustachio fattore, de' quali ciascuno vorrebbe essere marito della dama del suo padrone.
Quella donna, che vien poi, è Sofronia, moglie di Nico-

cient city of Greece, there once was a gentleman, with
no other children save one son, into whose house there
chanced to arrive a young girl, whom he most honorably brought up, until she was seventeen. It then happened that both he and his son fell in love with her at the
same time: and in their amorous rivalry many events and
strange occurences arose, upon whose completion the son
took her to wife, and lived with her most happily for
many a day. [1]

Would you believe that very event occurred not so many
years ago, once again, here in Florence? And since our
author wished to present one of the two of them for you,
he chose the one in Florence, believing you apt to take
greater pleasure in it than the other. For Athens is in ruins:
its streets, its squares, and its buildings can no longer be
recognized. Furthermore, its citizens spoke Greek, and you
would not understand that language. Consider, therefore,
the events which occurred in Florence, but do not expect
to recognize either the household or the people, because,
in order to avoid legal charges, the author has changed the
real names into fictitious ones.

Before the comedy begins, he is eager for you to see
the characters, in order that you may the better recognize
them as it is played. Come on out here, all of you, so the
people can take a look at you. Here they are. You see how
nicely they come forth? Line up over there, one next to the
other. You see: the first one is Nicomaco, an old man all
afire with love. The one beside him is Cleandro, his son
and rival. The next one is called Palamede, Cleandro's
friend. Those two following are, first Pirro the servant,
and next Eustachio the steward: each of them would like
to be the next husband of his master's mistress. The lady
who comes next is Sofronia, wife of Nicomaco. The one

maco. Quella appresso è Doria, sua servente. Di quegli
ultimi duoi che restano, l'uno è Damone, l'altra è Sostrata,
sua donna. Ècci un'altra persona, la quale, per avere a venire ancora da Napoli, non vi si mosterrà. Io credo che
basti, e che voi gli abbiate veduti assai. Il popolo vi li-
cenzia: tornate dentro.

Questa favola si chiama *Clizia*, perché così ha nome
la fanciulla, che si combatte. Non aspettate di vederla,
perché Sofronia, che l'ha allevata, non vuole per onestà che
la venga fuora. Pertanto, se ci fussi alcuno che la vagheg-
giassi, arà pazienza. E' mi resta a dirvi, come lo autore di
questa commedia è uomo molto costumato, e saprebbegli
male, se vi paressi, nel vederla recitare, che ci fussi qualche
disonestà. Egli non crede che la ci sia; pure, quando e'
paressi a voi, si escusa in questo modo. Sono trovate le
commedie, per giovare e per dilettare alli spettatori. Giova
veramente assai a qualunque uomo, e massimamente a' giovanetti, cognoscere la avarizia d'uno vecchio, il furore d'uno
innamorato, l'inganni d'uno servo, la gola d'uno parassito,
la miseria d'uno povero, l'ambizione d'uno ricco, le lusinghe
d'una meretrice, la poca fede di tutti gli uomini. De' quali
essempli le commedie sono piene, e possonsi tutte queste
cose con onestà grandissima rappresentare. Ma, volendo
dilettare, è necessario muovere gli spettatori a riso: il che
non si può fare mantenendo il parlare grave e severo, perché
le parole, che fanno ridere, sono o sciocche, o iniuriose, o
amorose; è necessario, pertanto, rappresentare persone sciocche, malediche, o innamorate: e perciò quelle commedie,
che sono piene di queste tre qualità di parole, sono piene
di risa; quelle che ne mancano, non truovano chi con il
ridere le accompagni.

after her is Doria, her maid. Of the two remaining people, the first is Damone, the other is his wife Sostrata. There is another character who, since he has not yet gotten in from Naples, will not show himself to you.[2] I think that should do; you have seen enough of them now.—The audience gives you leave: go on back inside.—This story is called *Clizia*, because that is the name of the girl who is being fought over. Don't expect to see her, though, for Sofronia, who has brought her up, does not wish her to come out, for modesty's sake. And so, if anyone is sighing for her, he had better resign himself.

It remains for me to inform you that the author of this comedy is a most well-mannered man, and he would be sorely distressed if you were to find, in watching this performance, that it contained any indecency. He does not believe there is any: however, if you should think there were, he begs your pardon in the following manner. Comedies were invented to be of use and of delight to their audiences. It is indeed quite useful for any man, and particularly for young ones, to learn about the avarice of an old man, the frenzy of a lover, the deceit of a servant, the greed of a parasite, the indigence of the poor, the ambition of the rich, the wiles of a whore, and the bad faith of all men. Comedies are filled with such examples, and they all can be represented with the greatest decency. But if the audience is to be delighted, it must be moved to laughter, and that cannot be done while keeping our speeches grave and austere; for speeches which evoke laughter are either foolish, or insulting, or amorous. It is therefore necessary to present characters who are foolish, slanderous, or love-struck. Thus comedies which are full of these three kinds of speech are full of laughter, and those which lack them do not make people laugh along with them.

Volendo, adunque, questo nostro autore dilettare, e fare in qualche parte gli spettatori ridere, non inducendo in questa sua commedia persone sciocche, ed essendosi rimasto di dire male, è stato necessitato ricorrere alle persone innamorate ed alli accidenti, che nello amore nascano. Dove se fia alcuna cosa non onesta, sarà in modo detta che queste donne potranno sanza arrossire ascoltarla. Siate contenti, adunque, prestarci gli orecchi benigni: e, se voi ci satisfarete ascoltando, noi ci sforzeremo, recitando, di satisfare a voi.

And so, since this author of ours wished to delight the audience, and to make it laugh at least in some places; and since he does not introduce foolish characters into this comedy of his, and he refrains from speaking ill, he has had to resort to amorous characters, and to those incidents to which love gives rise. If there should be anything indecent in the play, it will be said in such a way as to let the ladies listen to it without blushing. Be so kind, then, as to lend us your gracious ears; and if you grant us the satisfaction of listening to us, we will make every effort in our performance to give you satisfaction in return.

ATTO PRIMO
SCENA PRIMA

Palamede, Cleandro.

PALAMEDE: Tu esci sì a buon' ora di casa?

CLEANDRO: Tu, donde vieni sì a buon' ora?

PALAMEDE: Da fare una mia faccenda.

CLEANDRO: Ed io vo a farne un'altra, o, a dire meglio, a cercarla di fare, perché, s'io la farò, non ne ho certezza alcuna.

PALAMEDE: È ella cosa che si possa dire?

CLEANDRO: Non so; ma io so bene che la è cosa, che con difficultà si può fare.

PALAMEDE: Orsù, io me ne voglio ire, ché io veggo come lo stare accompagnato t'infastidisce; e per questo io ho sempre fuggito la pratica tua, perché sempre ti ho trovato mal disposto e fantastico.

CLEANDRO: Fantastico no, ma innamorato sì.

PALAMEDE: Togli! Tu mi racconci la cappellina in capo!

CLEANDRO: Palamede mio, tu non sai mezze le messe. Io sono sempre vivuto disperato, ed ora vivo più che mai.

PALAMEDE: Come così?

CLEANDRO: Quello ch' io t'ho celato per lo adrieto, io ti voglio manifestare ora, poiché mi sono redutto al termine che mi bisogna soccorso da ciascuno.

PALAMEDE: Se io stavo mal volentieri teco in prima, io starò peggio ora, perché io ho sempre inteso, che tre sorte di uomini si debbono fuggire: cantori, vecchi ed inna-

ACT ONE
SCENE ONE

Palamede, Cleandro.

PALAMEDE: Why are you leaving your house so early in the morning?

CLEANDRO: Where are you coming from so early in the morning?

PALAMEDE: I have been taking care of some business.

CLEANDRO: And I am on my way to take care of some, or to be more precise, to try to, for I have no assurance whatsoever that I shall be able to do it.

PALAMEDE: Is it something you can talk about?

CLEANDRO: I don't know, but I do know that it is something that will be hard to manage.

PALAMEDE: All right, I had better get going, because I can see you are in no mood for company. That is why I have been avoiding you, since I always find you ill-humored and distracted.

CLEANDRO: I am not distracted, I am in love.

PALAMEDE: You don't say! That is six of one and half a dozen of the other.

CLEANDRO: Palamede, my friend, you don't know the half of it. My life has long been desperate, but now it is worse than ever.

PALAMEDE: What do you mean?

CLEANDRO: Everything that I have kept secret from you till now, I want to reveal to you, since I have been reduced to the point where I can use any help I can get.

PALAMEDE: If I didn't feel like staying around you before, I feel even less like it now. I have always heard that there are three kinds of people you must always avoid:

morati. Perché, se usi con uno cantore e narrigli uno tuo fatto, quando tu credi che t'oda, e' ti spicca uno *ut, re, mi, fa, sol, la*, e gorgogliasi una canzonetta in gola. Se tu sei con uno vecchio, e' ficca el capo in quante chiese e' truova, e va a tutti gli altari a borbottare uno paternostro. Ma di questi duoi lo innamorato è peggio, perché non basta che, se tu gli parli, e' pone una vigna che t'empie gli orecchi di rammarichii e di tanti suoi affanni, che tu sei sforzato a moverti a compassione: perché, s'egli usa con una cantoniera, o ella lo assassina troppo, o ella lo ha cacciato di casa, sempre vi è qualcosa che dire; s'egli ama una donna da bene, mille invidie, mille gelosie, mille dispetti lo perturbano; mai non vi manca cagione di dolersi. Pertanto, Cleandro mio, io userò tanto teco, quanto tu arai bisogno di me, altrimenti io fuggirò questi tuoi dolori.

CLEANDRO: Io ho tenute occulte queste mie passioni infino ad ora per coteste cagioni, per non essere fuggito come fastidioso o uccellato come ridiculo, perché io so che molti, sotto spezie di carità, ti fanno parlare, e poi ti ghignano drieto. Ma, poiché ora la Fortuna m'ha condotto in lato, che mi pare avere pochi rimedii, io te lo voglio conferire, per sfogarmi in parte, e anche perché, se mi bisognassi il tuo aiuto, che tu me lo presti.

PALAMEDE: Io sono parato, poiché tu vuoi, ad ascoltar tutto, e così a non fuggire né disagi né pericoli, per aiutarti.

CLEANDRO: Io lo so. Io credo che tu abbia notizia di quella fanciulla, che noi ci abbiamo allevata.

singers, old men, and lovers. If you hang around a singer, and you talk with him about your affairs, just when you think he is listening to you, he lets loose with a *do*, *re*, *mi*, *fa*, *sol*, *la*, and gurgles a little song in his throat. If you are with an old man, he sticks his head into every church he passes, and he goes and mumbles an "Our Father" at every altar. But a lover is worse than both of them. Not only does he pay no attention whatsoever to what you say, but he chews your ear off with complaints about all of his miseries, so that you can't help feeling pity for him. If he is involved with a whore, either she is driving him crazy or she has driven him out of her house: there is always something to tell you about. If he loves a respectable woman, he is tormented by a thousand envies, a thousand jealousies, a thousand vexations—he never lacks cause for complaint. And so, Cleandro my friend, I will stick around as long as you really need me, but otherwise spare me these troubles of yours.

CLEANDRO: I have kept this passion of mine secret up to now for just that reason. I didn't want to be shunned as a nuisance or mocked as a fool. I know very well that there are a lot of people who let you talk, as if they were sympathetic, and then snicker at you behind your back. But now that Fortune has brought me to a point where I can see almost no possible remedies, I want to let you in on it, partly to get some relief, and also in case I should need your help.

PALAMEDE: If you want, I am ready to listen to the whole story, and to run away from neither discomfort nor danger to help you.

CLEANDRO: I realize that. I think you have heard about that girl we have brought up in our house.

PALAMEDE: Io l'ho veduta. Donde venne?

CLEANDRO: Dirottelo. Quando, dodici anni sono, nel 1494, passò il re Carlo per Firenze, che andava con uno grande essercito alla impresa del Regno, alloggiò in casa nostra uno gentile uomo della compagnia de monsignor di Fois, chiamato Beltramo di Guascogna. Fu costui da mio padre onorato, ed egli, perché uomo da bene era, riguardò ed onorò la casa nostra; e dove molti feciono una inimicizia con quelli Franzesi avevano in casa, mio padre e costui contrassono una amicizia grandissima.

PALAMEDE: Voi avesti una gran ventura più che gli altri, perché quelli che furono messi in casa nostra ci feciono infiniti mali.

CLEANDRO: Credolo; ma a noi non intervenne così. Questo Beltramo ne andò con il suo re a Napoli; e, come tu sai, vinto che Carlo ebbe quel regno, fu constretto a partirsi, perché 'l papa, imperadore, Viniziani e duca di Milano se gli erano conlegati contro. Lasciate, pertanto, parte delle sue gente a Napoli, con il resto se ne venne verso Toscana; e, giunto a Siena, perch' egli intese la Lega avere uno grossissimo essercito sopra il Taro, per combatterlo allo scendere de' monti, gli parve da non perdere tempo in Toscana; e perciò, non per Firenze, ma per la via di Pisa e di Pontremoli, passò in Lombardia. Beltramo, sentito il romore de' nimici, e dubitando, come intervenne, non avere a fare la giornata con quelli, avendo in tra la preda fatta a Napoli questa fanciulla, che allora doveva avere cinque anni, d'una bella aria et tutta gentile,

PALAMEDE: I have seen her. Where did she come from?

CLEANDRO: I will tell you. Twelve years ago, in 1494, when King Charles of France passed through Florence with a great army on the way to his campaign against the Kingdom of Naples,[3] a gentleman accompanying the Count of Foix, by the name of Bertram of Gascony, was billetted in our house. He was treated with honor by my father, and since he was an upstanding man, he respected and honored our household. So whereas many people ended up as enemies of the Frenchmen whom they had in their homes, my father and he became the greatest of friends.

PALAMEDE: You were luckier than the others. The ones who were quartered in our house did us enormous mischief.

CLEANDRO: I believe it! But that didn't happen to us. This Bertram went off with his King to Naples. As you know, once Charles had conquered that kingdom, he was forced to leave, since the Pope, the Emperor, the Venetians, and the Duke of Milan had formed a league against him. Leaving part of his army in Naples, he came back toward Tuscany with the remainder. Arriving in Siena, and learning that the League had a tremendous army along the Taro[4] waiting to attack him as he came down from the mountains, he decided not to waste time in Tuscany. And so he passed into Lombardy, not via Florence, but by way of Pisa and Pontremoli. Bertram, hearing about the enemy, suspected, rightly enough as it turned out, that he would have to do battle with them. Part of the booty he had taken in Naples was this girl, who must have been five years old then, quite pretty and well-bred, and he decided

deliberò di tôrla d'inanzi a' pericoli, e per uno suo servidore la mandò a mio padre, pregandolo che per suo amore dovessi tanto tenerla, che a più commodo tempo mandassi per lei; né mandò a dire se la era nobile o ignobile: solo ci significò che la si chiamava Clizia. Mio padre e mia madre, perché non avevano altri figliuoli che me, sùbito se ne innamororono.

PALAMEDE: Innamorato te ne sarai tu!

CLEANDRO: Lasciami dire! E come loro cara figliuola la trattorono. Io, che allora avevo dieci anni, mi cominciai, come fanno e fanciulli, a trastullare seco, e le posi uno amore estraordinario, il quale sempre con la età crebbe; di modo che, quando ella arrivò alla età di dodici anni, mio padre e mia madre cominciorono ad avermi gli occhi alle mani, in modo che, se io solo gli parlavo, andava sottosopra la casa. Questa strettezza (perché sempre si desidera più ciò che si può avere meno) raddoppiò lo amore, ed hammi fatto e fa tanta guerra, che io vivo con più affanni, che s'io fussi in inferno.

PALAMEDE: Beltramo, mandò mai per lei?

CLEANDRO: Di cotestui non si intese mai nulla: crediamo che morissi nella giornata del Taro.

PALAMEDE: Così dovette essere. Ma dimmi: che vuoi tu fare? A che termine sei? Vuo'la tu tôr per moglie, o vorrestila per amica? Che t'impedisce, avendola in casa? Può essere che tu non ci abbia rimedio?

CLEANDRO: Io t'ho a dire dell'altre cose, che saranno con mia vergogna, perciò ch'io voglio che tu sappi ogni cosa.

PALAMEDE: Di' pure.

to get her out of danger. So he sent her with one of his servants to my father, beseeching him for friendship's sake to keep her until such time as he might conveniently send for her. He didn't say whether she was of humble or noble birth. All he told us was that her name was Clizia. My father and mother, since they had no other children but me, fell in love with her at first sight . . .

PALAMEDE: And I'll wager you did, too!

CLEANDRO: . . . (Let me finish!) and they treated her as their own dear daughter. I was ten years old then. I began by playing with her, as children do, and I conceived an extraordinary love for her, which kept on growing stronger as I grew older. So when she reached the age of twelve, my father and mother began to keep an eye on me, so that if I just talked with her, even, the entire household was turned upside-down. Since people always desire most what they can least have, this restriction redoubled my love, and it has assailed me so, and continues to do so, that I have been suffering greater torment than if I were in Hell.

PALAMEDE: Did Bertram ever send for her?

CLEANDRO: We never heard anything more about him. We believe he died in the battle of the Taro.

PALAMEDE: That must have been the case. But tell me: what do you intend to do? What have you decided? Would you like to marry her, or do you want to have her as a mistress? What is there to stop you, since you have her there in the house? Can it be that you have no remedy for this situation?

CLEANDRO: I have something else to tell you, that I am ashamed to say. But I want you to know everything.

PALAMEDE: Go ahead.

CLEANDRO: E' mi vien voglia—disse colei—di ridere, ed ho male!—Mio padre se n'è innamorato anch' egli.

PALAMEDE: Chi, Nicomaco?!

CLEANDRO: Nicomaco, sì.

PALAMEDE: Puollo fare Iddio?

CLEANDRO: E' lo può fare Iddio e' santi!

PALAMEDE: Oh! questo è il più bel caso, ch' io sentissi mai: e' non se ne guasta se non una casa. Come vivete insieme? che fate? a che pensate? tua madre, sa queste cose?

CLEANDRO: E' lo sa mia madre, le fante, e famigli: egli è una tresca el fatto nostro!

PALAMEDE: Dimmi: infine, dove è ridotta la cosa?

CLEANDRO: Dirottelo. Mio padre, per moglie, quando bene e' non fussi innamorato, non me la concederebbe mai, perché è avaro, ed ella è sanza dota. Dubita anche che la non sia ignobile. Io, per me, la torrei per moglie, per amica, ed in tutti quelli modi ch'io la potessi avere. Ma di questo non accade ragionare ora. Solo ti dirò dove noi ci troviamo.

PALAMEDE: Io l'arò caro.

CLEANDRO: Tosto che mio padre si innamorò di costei, che debbe essere circa uno anno, e desiderando di cavarsi questa voglia, che lo fa proprio spasimare, pensò che non c'era altro rimedio che maritarla ad uno che poi gliene accomunassi, perché tentare d'averla prima che maritata gli debbe parere cosa impia e brutta; e, non sapendo dove si gittare, ha eletto per il più fidato a questa cosa Pirro, nostro servo; e menò tanta segreta questa sua fantasia, che

CLEANDRO: As the lady said, I feel like laughing, but it hurts too much!—My father has fallen in love with her, too.

PALAMEDE: Nicomaco!

CLEANDRO: Yes, Nicomaco.

PALAMEDE: By God, can it be possible!

CLEANDRO: By God and the saints, it is!

PALAMEDE: Oh! That is the most wonderful thing I have ever heard. You have nothing to lose but house and home! How can you go on living together? What are you doing? What are you plans? Does your mother know about all this?

CLEANDRO: My mother knows, and so do the maids and the servants. Our affairs are all in a turmoil.

PALAMEDE: So tell me how things finally stand.

CLEANDRO: I shall tell you. My father, even if he weren't in love with her, would never let me marry her, because he is a miser and she has no dowry. He also is afraid that she is of low birth. As for me, I would take her as a wife, as a mistress, or any way that I could get her. But this is no time for discussion: I will just tell you how matters stand.

PALAMEDE: I would be grateful.

CLEANDRO: As soon as my father fell in love with the girl, which must have been about a year ago, since he was anxious to satisfy his desire—which has him actually panting—he decided that there was no other remedy than to marry her off to someone who would be willing to share her with him afterward; for it must seem an ugly and wicked thing to him to try to have her before she is married. So, not knowing where to turn, he chose our servant Pirro as the person most to be trusted in this business. He followed up this whim of his so secretly that she was

ad uno pelo la fu per condursi, prima che altri se ne accorgessi. Ma Sofronia, mia madre, che prima un pezzo dello innamoramento si era avveduta, scoperse questo agguato, e con ogni industria, mossa da gelosia ed invidia, attende a guastare. Il che non ha potuto far meglio, che mettere in campo uno altro marito, e biasimare quello; e dice volerla dare ad Eustachio, nostro fattore. E benché Nicomaco sia di più autorità, nondimeno l'astuzia di mia madre, gli aiuti di noi altri, che, sanza molto scoprirci, gli facciamo, ha tenuta la cosa in ponte più settimane. Tuttavia Nicomaco ci serra forte, ed ha deliberato, a dispetto di mare e di vento, fare oggi questo parentado, e vuole che la meni questa sera, ed ha tolto a pigione quella casetta, dove abita Damone, vicino a noi; e dice che gliene vuole comperare, fornirla di masserizie, aprirgli una bottega, e farlo ricco.

PALAMEDE: A te che importa che l'abbia più Pirro che Eustachio?

CLEANDRO: Come, che m'importa? Questo Pirro è il maggiore ribaldello che sia in Firenze, perché, oltre ad averla pattuita con mio padre, è uomo che mi ebbe sempre in odio, di modo ch'io vorrei che l'avessi più tosto el diavolo dell'inferno. Io scrissi ieri al fattore, che venissi a Firenze: maravigliomi ch' e' non venne iersera. Io voglio star qui, a vedere s' io lo vedessi comparire. Tu, che farai?

PALAMEDE: Andrò a fare una mia faccenda.

CLEANDRO: Va' in buon' ora.

PALAMEDE: Addio. Temporèggiati il meglio puoi, e, se vuoi cosa alcuna, parla.

within a hair's breadth of being married before anyone ever noticed. But my mother, Sofronia, who had already become aware of his infatuation some time before, discovered the plot. Spurred on by jealousy and spite, she has been using all her wits to try and spoil it. The best she has been able to do is to put another suitor into the running, and to find fault with the first one. She says she wants to give the girl to our steward Eustachio. Nicomaco has greater authority, but my mother's shrewdness, along with the help of the rest of us, has kept the matter in suspense for several weeks. But Nicomaco is pressing us hard. He has made up his mind to have this wedding today, by hook or by crook. He wants the girl to be married this very evening. He has rented the little house where our neighbor Damone lives, and he says he wants to buy it from him, furnish it, open up a shop for him, and make him a rich man.

PALAMEDE: What does it matter to you whether it is Pirro or Eustachio who gets her?

CLEANDRO: What do you mean, what does it matter? That Pirro is the greatest rascal in all Florence. Why, not only has he come to terms with my father, but he has always hated me. So I would sooner the Devil in Hell had her. Yesterday I wrote to our steward and asked him to come to Florence. I am surprised he didn't get here last night. I am going to stay here until I see him arrive. What are you going to do?

PALAMEDE: I have some business to take care of.

CLEANDRO: Go, and godspeed.

PALAMEDE: Farewell: try to hold out as long as you can, and if you need anything at all, let me know.

SCENA SECONDA

Cleandro solo.

CLEANDRO: Veramente chi ha detto che lo innamorato
ed il soldato si somigliono ha detto il vero. El capitano
vuole che i suoi soldati sien giovani, le donne vogliono che
i loro amanti non sieno vecchi. Brutta cosa vedere un vecchio soldato, bruttissima è vederlo innamorato. I soldati
temono lo sdegno del capitano, gli amanti non meno quello
delle loro donne. I soldati dormono in terra allo scoperto,
gli amanti su per muricciuoli. I soldati perseguono infino
a morte i loro nimici, gli amanti i loro rivali. I soldati, per
la oscura notte, nel più gelato verno, vanno per il fango,
esposti alle acque ed a' venti, per vincere una impresa, che
faccia loro acquistare la vittoria; gli amanti, per simil' vie
e con simili e maggior' disagi, di acquistare la loro amata
cercano. Ugualmente, nella milizia e nello amore è necessario il secreto, la fede e l'animo; sono e pericoli uguali,
ed il fine il più delle volte è simile: il soldato more in una
fossa, lo amante more disperato. Così dubito io che non
intervenga a me. Ed ho la dama in casa, veggola quanto io
voglio, mangio sempre seco! Il che credo che mi sia maggior dolore: perché, quanto è più propinquo l'uomo ad uno
suo desiderio, più lo desidera, e, non lo avendo, maggior
dolore sente. A me bisogna pensare per ora di sturbare
queste nozze; dipoi, nuovi accidenti mi arrecheranno nuovi
consigli e nuova fortuna.—È egli possibile che Eustachio
non venga di villa? E scrissigli che ci fussi infino iersera!
Ma io lo veggo spuntare là, da quel canto. Eustachio! o
Eustachio!

SCENE TWO

Cleandro alone.

CLEANDRO: The man who said that lovers are like soldiers certainly was speaking the truth. The captain wants his soldiers to be young, women want their lovers not to be old. It is an ugly thing to see an old man a soldier; it is uglier still to see him in love. Soldiers fear the captain's scorn, no less do lovers their mistresses'. Soldiers sleep outdoors on the ground, lovers on the garden wall. Soldiers pursue their enemies to the death, and lovers their rivals. Soldiers go in the dark of night through the mud of iciest winter, exposed to rain and wind, in order to carry out an exploit which will lead them to victory; lovers, by similar paths, and with similar and even greater discomforts, seek to conquer their beloved lady. Courage, faith, and secrecy are equally necessary in the military and in love: the perils are equal, and the end is most often the same. The soldier dies in a ditch, the lover dies in despair. I am afraid that is what will happen to me. And yet I have the lady in my house, I see her all I like, I eat with her every day. I believe that is an even greater torment: for the closer a man is to his desire, the more he desires it; and since he cannot have it, he feels greater torment. Now I have to find a way to prevent this marriage. Afterward, new circumstances may bring me new ideas and new opportunities. How can it be that Eustachio has not yet come from the country? I wrote him to be here by last night! But I see him coming around the corner. Eustachio! Oh, Eustachio!

SCENA TERZA

Eustachio, Cleandro.

EUSTACHIO: Chi mi chiama? O Cleandro!

CLEANDRO: Tu hai penato tanto a comparire!

EUSTACHIO: Io venni infino iersera, ma io non mi
sono appalesato, perché, poco innanzi che io avessi la tua
lettera, ne avevo avuta una da Nicomaco, che mi imponeva
uno monte di faccende; e perciò io non volevo capitargli
innanzi, se prima io non ti vedevo.

CLEANDRO: Hai ben fatto. Io ho mandato per te,
perché Nicomaco sollecita queste nozze di Pirro; le quale
tu sai non piacciono a mia madre, perché, poiché di questa
fanciulla si ha a fare bene ad uno uomo nostro, vorrebbe
che la si dessi a chi la merita più. Ed invero le tue con-
dizioni sono altrimenti fatte che quelle di Pirro; ché, a
dirlo qui fra noi, egli è uno sciagurato.

EUSTACHIO: Io ti ringrazio; e veramente io non avevo
il capo a tôr donna, ma, poiché tu e madonna volete, io
voglio ancora io. Vero è ch' io non vorrei anche arrecarmi
nimico Nicomaco, perché poi, alla fine, el padrone è egli.

CLEANDRO: Non dubitare, perché mia madre ed io
non siamo per mancarti, e ti trarremo d'ogni pericolo. Io
vorrei bene che tu ti rassettassi uno poco. Tu hai cotesto
gabbano, che ti cade di dosso, hai el tocco polveroso, una
barbaccia . . . Va' al barbieri, làvati el viso, sètolati cotesti
panni, acciò che Clizia non ti abbia a rifiutare per porco.

EUSTACHIO: Io non sono atto a rimbiondirmi.

CLEANDRO: Va', fa' quel ch' io ti dico, e poi te ne vai
in quella chiesa vicina, e quivi mi aspetta. Io me ne andrò
in casa, per vedere a quel che pensa el vecchio.

SCENE THREE

Eustachio, Cleandro.

EUSTACHIO: Who is calling me? Oh, Cleandro!

CLEANDRO: What took you so long getting here?

EUSTACHIO: I got here last night, but I didn't show my face; because shortly before I got your letter, I had gotten one from Nicomaco charging me with a bunch of errands to do. So I didn't want to run into him, until I had seen you first.

CLEANDRO: You did the right thing. I sent for you because Nicomaco is pushing this marriage with Pirro, which, as you know, my mother doesn't favor. Since this girl is to be granted to one of our men, she would like her to be given to the one who most deserves her; and in truth your situation is quite a different matter from Pirro's. Between you and me, he is a scoundrel.

EUSTACHIO: Thank you. To tell the truth, I had no intention of marrying, but since you and my lady want it, so do I. On the other hand, I would not like to make an enemy of Nicomaco, though, because he is the master after all.

CLEANDRO: Don't worry, my mother and I aren't going to let you down; we will take care of any trouble you get into. I would like you to tidy up, though. You have this old cloak that is falling off your back, your cap is all dusty, and you need a shave. Go to the barber's, wash your face, and brush these clothes off, so that Clizia won't turn you down for being a pig.

EUSTACHIO: I am not likely to get any handsomer.

CLEANDRO: Go on, do as I tell you, and then go off into that church nearby and wait for me there. I will go into the house and see what the old man is up to.

CANZONA

Chi non fa prova, Amore,
della tua gran possanza, indarno spera
di far mai fede vera
qual sia del Cielo il più alto valore;
né sa come si vive insieme e more,
come si segue el danno, il ben si fugge,
come s'ama se stesso
men d'altrui, come spesso
paura e speme i cori adiaccia e strugge:
né sa come ugualmente uomini e dèi
paventan l'arme di che armato sei.

SONG[5]

No man can, without trying
The sweetness of thy power, Love, imagine
In any rightful fashion
High heaven's greatest virtue, love undying;
Nor can he know mix'd death and life, while
    sighing,
Or how we flee our welfare as from error,
And think more of our lover
Than self; over and over
Our hearts are racked with hope and then with
    terror;
For thou strik'st fear into the very marrow
Of gods and mortals with thy bow and arrow.

ATTO SECONDO
SCENA PRIMA

Nicomaco solo.

NICOMACO: Che domine ho io stamani intorno agli
occhi? E' mi pare avere e bagliori, che non mi lasciono
vedere lume, e iersera io arei veduto el pelo nell'uovo. Are'
io beuto troppo? Forse che sì. O Dio, questa vecchiaia ne
viene con ogni mal mendo! Ma io non sono ancora sì vecchio, ch' io no rompessi una lancia con Clizia. È egli però
possibile che io mi sia innamorato a questo modo? E, quello
che è peggio, mogliama se ne è accorta, ed indovinasi perch'
io voglia dare questa fanciulla a Pirro. Infine, e' non mi va
solco diritto. Pure, io ho a cercare di vincere la mia.—
Pirro! o Pirro! vien' giù, esci fuora!

SCENA SECONDA

Pirro, Nicomaco.

PIRRO: Eccomi!

NICOMACO: Pirro, io voglio che tu meni questa sera
moglie in ogni modo.

PIRRO: Io la merrò ora.

NICOMACO: Adagio un poco!—A cosa, a cosa,—disse
'l Mirra. E' bisogna anche fare le cose in modo che la casa
non vadia sottosopra. Tu vedi: mogliama non se ne contenta, Eustachio la vuole anch' egli, parmi che Cleandro lo
favorisca, e' ci si è volto contro Iddio e 'l diavolo. Ma sta'
tu pur forte nella fede di volerla; non dubitare, ch' io varrò

ACT TWO

SCENE ONE

Nicomaco alone.

NICOMACO: What the devil is wrong with my eyes this morning? I seem to have flashes that don't let me see the light, and yet last night I could see well enough to split hairs. Could I have had too much to drink? Maybe so. Oh Lord, old age is creeping up on me, with all its complaints! But I am not too old yet to break a lance with Clizia. How is it possible for me to have fallen in love this way? And what is worse, the wife has noticed it, and she has figured out why I want to give that girl to Pirro. All in all, I have a tough row to hoe ahead of me. But I have to try and get what I want. Pirro! Oh, Pirro! Come down here, come on out!

SCENE TWO

Pirro, Nicomaco.

PIRRO: Here I am!

NICOMACO: Pirro, I want you to take a bride this evening, come what may.

PIRRO: I'll take her right now.

NICOMACO: Hold on a minute! "One thing at a time," as the lady said.[6] Everything has to be done in such a way that the whole house isn't turned upside-down, too. You see, the wife isn't too keen on it; Eustachio wants the girl, too. It seems to me that Cleandro is in his favor, God and the Devil have lined up against us. But you just stand firm and have faith that you will get her; don't worry, I can take

per tutti loro, perché, al peggio fare, io te la darò a loro dispetto, e chi vuole ingrognare, ingrogni!

PIRRO: Al nome di Dio, ditemi quel che voi volete che io facci.

NICOMACO: Che tu non ti parta di quinci oltre, acciò che, s' io ti voglio, che tu sia presto.

PIRRO: Così farò; ma mi era scordato dirvi una cosa.

NICOMACO: Quale?

PIRRO: Eustachio è in Firenze.

NICOMACO: Come, in Firenze? Chi te l'ha detto?

PIRRO: Ser Ambruogio, nostro vicino in villa, e mi dice che entrò dentro alla porta iersera con lui.

NICOMACO: Come, iersera? Dove è egli stato stanotte?

PIRRO: Chi lo sa?

NICOMACO: Sia, in buon' ora. Va' via, fa' quello ch' io t'ho detto. Sofronia arà mandato per Eustachio, e questo ribaldo ha stimato più le lettere sue che le mie, che gli scrissi che facessi mille cose, che mi rovinano, se le non si fanno. Al nome di Dio, io ne lo pagherò! Almeno sapessi io dove egli è, e quel che fa! Ma ecco Sofronia, che esce di casa.

SCENA TERZA

Sofronia, Nicomaco.

SOFRONIA: Io ho rinchiusa Clizia e Doria in camera. E' mi bisogna guardare questa povera fanciulla dal figliuolo, dal marito, da' famigli: ognuno l'ha posto il campo intorno.

care of all of them. Because, if worse comes to worst, I will give her to you in spite of them, and if anyone wants to grumble, let him grumble!

PIRRO: So be it, just tell me what you want me to do.

NICOMACO: I want you not to budge from here, so that you can be ready if I need you.

PIRRO: I will do that. Oh, I forgot to tell you one thing.

NICOMACO: What?

PIRRO: Eustachio is here in Florence.

NICOMACO: What! In Florence? Who told you?

PIRRO: Master Ambrogio, our neighbor out in the country. He tells me he came in through the city gates with him yesterday evening.

NICOMACO: What! Yesterday evening? Where did he spend the night?

PIRRO: How should I know?

NICOMACO: All right, then. Go on and do what I told you. Sofronia must have sent for Eustachio, and that rascal has paid more heed to her letter than to mine, where I told him to do a bunch of things that would ruin me if they weren't done. By God, I will pay him for this! If only I knew where he is and what he is doing. But here comes Sofronia out of the house.

SCENE THREE

Sofronia, Nicomaco.

SOFRONIA: (I have shut Clizia and Doria up in their room. I have to keep that girl away from my son, my husband, and the servants: everyone wants to get his hands on her.)

NICOMACO: Ove si va?

SOFRONIA: Alla messa.

NICOMACO: Ed è per carnesciale: pensa quel che tu farai di quaresima!

SOFRONIA: Io credo che s'abbia a fare bene d'ogni tempo, e tanto è più accetto farlo in quelli tempi che gli altri fanno male. Ma e' mi pare che, a fare bene, noi ci facciamo da cattivo lato!

NICOMACO: Come? Che vorresti tu che si facessi?

SOFRONIA: Che non si pensassi a chiacchiere; e, poiché noi abbiamo in casa una fanciulla buona, d'assai, e bella, abbiamo durato fatica ad allevarla, che si pensi di nolla gittare or via; e, dove prima ogni uomo ci lodava, ogni uomo ora ci biasimerà, veggendo che noi la diàno ad uno ghiotto, sanza cervello, e non sa fare altro che un poco radere, che è un'arte che non ne viverebbe una mosca!

NICOMACO: Sofronia mia, tu erri. Costui è giovane, di buono aspetto (e, se non sa, è atto a imparare), vuol bene a costei: che son tre gran parte in uno marito, gioventù, bellezza ed amore. A me non pare che si possa ire più là, né che di questi partiti se ne truovi ad ogni uscio. Se non ha roba, tu sai che la roba viene e va; e costui è uno di quegli, che è atto a farne venire; ed io non lo abbandonerò, perch' io fo pensiero, a dirti il vero, di comperarli quella casa, che per ora ho tolta a pigione da Damone, nostro vicino, ed empierolla di masserizie; e di più, quando mi costassi quattrocento fiorini, per metterliene . . .

SOFRONIA: Ah, ah, ah!

NICOMACO: Tu ridi?

NICOMACO: Where are you off to?

SOFRONIA: To mass.

NICOMACO: And yet it is only Carnival; imagine what you will do during Lent!

SOFRONIA: I believe people should do the right thing at all times, and it is all the more important in times like these, when others are doing wrong. But it seems to me that if we really want to do right, we are going about it the wrong way!

NICOMACO: What? What would you like us to do?

SOFRONIA: We ought to think less about wasting our breath. Since we have such a good and beautiful young girl in the house, whom we have taken the trouble of bringing up, we should think about not throwing her away now. Everyone used to praise us, but now everyone will blame us for giving her away to a witless good-for-nothing, who doesn't know much more than how to give a shave, and who couldn't provide for a fly!

NICOMACO: Sofronia my dear, you are so wrong. He is young, and quite presentable. He may not know much, but he is ready to learn; and he loves her. Those are three excellent qualities in a husband: youth, beauty, and love. It doesn't seem to me that we can do better, and matches like this don't grow on trees. He may not have any property, but you know that property comes and goes; and he is one of those people to whom it is likely to come. I am not going to abandon him, either. To tell the truth, I have been thinking of buying him that house which I rented from our neighbor Damone, and furnishing it. And moreover, if it costs me four hundred florins to set him up . . .

SOFRONIA: Ha, ha, ha!

NICOMACO: You are laughing?

SOFRONIA: Chi non riderebbe? Dove liene vuoi tu mettere?

NICOMACO: Sì, che vuoi tu dire? . . . per metterliene in su 'n una bottega, non sono per guardarvi.

SOFRONIA: È egli possibile però che tu voglia con questo partito strano tôrre al tuo figliuolo più che non si conviene, e dare a costui più che non si merita? Io non so che mi dire: io dubito che non ci sia altro, sotto.

NICOMACO: Che vuoi tu che ci sia?

SOFRONIA: Se ci fussi chi non lo sapessi, io glielo direi; ma, perché tu lo sai, io non te lo dirò.

NICOMACO: Che so io?

SOFRONIA: Lasciamo ire! Che ti muove a darla a costui? Non si potrebbe con questa dote o con minore maritarla meglio?

NICOMACO: Sì, credo. Nondimeno, e' mi muove l'amore, ch' io porto all'una ed all'altro, che avendoceli allevati tutti a dua, mi pare da beneficarli tutti a dua.

SOFRONIA: Se cotesto ti muove, non ti hai tu ancora allevato Eustachio, tuo fattore?

NICOMACO: Sì, ho; ma che vuoi tu che la faccia di cotestui, che non ha gentilezza veruna ed è uso a stare in villa fra' buoi e tra le pecore? Oh! se noi gliene dessimo, la si morrebbe di dolore.

SOFRONIA: E con Pirro si morrà di fame. Io ti ricordo che le gentilezze delli uomini consistono in avere qualche virtù, sapere fare qualche cosa, come sa Eustachio, che è uso alle faccende in su' mercati, a fare masserizia, ad avere cura delle cose d'altri e delle sua, ed è uno uomo, che viverebbe in su l'acqua: tanto che tu sai che gli ha un

SOFRONIA: Who wouldn't? Just how are you planning to "set him up"?

NICOMACO: Why, what do you mean? . . . To set him up in business, I am not going to let that stop me.

SOFRONIA: Is it really possible that you want to take more from your son than is proper, with this crazy match, and to give that fellow more than he deserves? I don't know what to think: I suspect there is something else beneath it all.

NICOMACO: What do you suppose there could be?

SOFRONIA: If there were someone here who didn't know, I would tell him. But since you know, I won't bother.

NICOMACO: What do I know?

SOFRONIA: Never mind! Whatever prompts you to give her to this man? With a dowry like that, or even less, couldn't you find her a better husband?

NICOMACO: Yes, I suppose I could. But I am prompted by the love I have for both of them. Since I have brought them both up, I think I should do well by both of them.

SOFRONIA: If that is what prompts you, haven't you brought up your steward Eustachio, too?

NICOMACO: Yes, I have. But what do you want her to do with a man like that, who has no manners and is used to staying out in the country with the cows and the sheep? Why, if we gave her to him, she would die of grief.

SOFRONIA: And with Pirro she will die of starvation. Let me remind you that men's manners consist in having some ability, and knowing how to do something, like Eustachio, who is used to doing business in the markets, running the farm, taking care of other people's affairs and his own, and is a man who can keep his head above water.

buono capitale. Pirro, dall'altra parte, non è mai se non in sulle taverne, su pe' giuochi, un cacapensieri, che morrebbe di fame nello Altopascio!

NICOMACO: Non ti ho io detto quello che io li voglio dare?

SOFRONIA: Non ti ho io risposto che tu lo getti via? Io ti concludo questo, Nicomaco, che tu hai speso in nutrir costei, ed io ho durato fatica in allevarla; e per questo, avendoci io parte, io voglio ancora io intendere come queste cose hanno ad andare: o io dirò tanto male e commetterò tanti scandoli, che ti parrà essere in mal termine, che non so come tu ti alzi el viso. Va', ragiona di queste cose con la maschera!

NICOMACO: Che mi di' tu? Se' tu impazata? Or mi fa' tu venir voglia di dargliene in ogni modo; e, per cotesto amore, voglio io che la meni stasera, e merralla, se ti schizzassino gli occhi!

SOFRONIA: O la merrà, o e' non la merrà.

NICOMACO: Tu mi minacci di chiacchiere; fa' ch' io non dica. Tu credi forse che io sia cieco, e che io non conosca e giuochi di queste tua bagatelle? Io sapevo bene che le madre volevano bene a' figliuoli, ma non credevo che le volessino tenere le mani alle loro disonestà?

SOFRONIA: Che di' tu? Che cosa è disonesta?

NICOMACO: Deh! non mi fare dire. Tu m'intendi ed io t'intendo. Ognuno di noi sa a quanti dì è san Biagio. Fac-

Indeed, you know that he has a good bit of capital. Pirro, on the other hand, never goes anywhere but to taverns or gambling dens. He is a dilly-dallier who would die of starvation in the Promised Land.[7]

NICOMACO: Didn't I tell you what I am going to give him?

SOFRONIA: Didn't I answer you that you are throwing it away? Let me tell you this in conclusion, Nicomaco: you may have spent money feeding that girl, but I put a lot of effort into bringing her up! And so, since I had my part in it, I also want to have a say in how things are going to go. Or else I will speak so much ill and spread so much scandal that you will think you have gotten into real trouble, and I don't know how you will be able to hold your head up. Go and discuss that with that clown of yours!

NICOMACO: What are you saying to me? Have you lost your head? Now you really make me feel like giving her to him one way or another. I love them so much that I want to marry them off this evening, and married they will be, even if your eyes pop out of your head!

SOFRONIA: Maybe he will marry her, and maybe he won't.

NICOMACO: You are threatening me with scandal. Watch out that I don't talk too. Maybe you think I am blind, and that I don't know what has been going on, with your fooling around. I had always heard about mothers being fond of their sons, but I didn't think they went so far as to lend a hand to their dirty business.

SOFRONIA: What is that you say? What dirty business?

NICOMACO: Please don't make me say it! You understand and I understand. Neither of us was born yesterday.[8]

ciamo, per tua fè, le cose d'accordo, ché, se noi entriamo
in cetere, noi sareno la favola del popolo.

SOFRONIA: Entra in che cetere tu vuoi. Questa fanciulla non s' ha a gittar via, o io manderò sottosopra, non
che la casa, Firenze.

NICOMACO: Sofronia, Sofronia, chi ti pose questo
nome non sognava! Tu se' una soffiona, e se' piena di
vento!

SOFRONIA: Al nome d'Iddio, io voglio ire alla messa!
Noi ci rivedreno.

NICOMACO: Odi un poco: sarebbeci modo a
raccapezzare questa cosa, e che noi non ci facessimo tenere
pazzi?

SOFRONIA: Pazzi no, ma tristi sì.

NICOMACO: Ei ci sono in questa terra tanti uomini
dabbene, noi abbiamo tanti parenti, e' ci sono tanti buoni
religiosi! Di quello che noi non siamo d'accordo noi, do-
mandianne loro, e per questa via o tu o io ci sgarereno.

SOFRONIA: Che? vogliamo noi cominciare a bandire
queste nostre pazzie?

NICOMACO: Se noi non vogliam tôrre amici o parenti,
togliamo uno religioso, e non si bandiranno; e rimettiamo
in lui questa cosa in confessione.

SOFRONIA: A chi andremo?

NICOMACO: E' non si può andare ad altri che a fra'
Timoteo, che è nostro confessoro di casa, ed è uno san-
terello, ed ha fatto già qualche miracolo.

SOFRONIA: Quale?

NICOMACO: Come, quale? Non sai tu che, per le sue
orazioni, mona Lucrezia di messer Nicia Calfucci, che era
sterile, ingravidò?

For your sake let us get together in this matter, because if we get carried away we will be the talk of the whole town.

SOFRONIA: You can get carried away all you want. That girl is not to be thrown away, or I will turn, not only the house, but all of Florence upside-down.

NICOMACO: Sofronia, Sofronia, whoever gave you that name had the right idea![9] You certainly make *me* suffer with that big mouth of yours, you windbag.

SOFRONIA: All right, then, I am going to mass! You will see me again later on.

NICOMACO: Listen a minute. Isn't there some way to patch this matter up, and not make people think we are crazy?

SOFRONIA: Not crazy, but certainly nasty.

NICOMACO: There are so many upright people in this city, we have so many relations, there are so many good men of the cloth! Let us ask them about our disagreement, and that way one or the other of us will see the light.

SOFRONIA: Why should we want to start advertising this foolishness of ours?

NICOMACO: If we don't want to choose friends or relatives, let's get a priest, and then it won't be advertised. Let's put this business to him in confession.

SOFRONIA: Who can we go to?

NICOMACO: There is no one else we can go to but Friar Timoteo, who is our family confessor.[10] He is a little saint, and has already worked a few miracles.

SOFRONIA: What miracles?

NICOMACO: What do you mean, what miracles? Don't you know that through his prayers the wife of Messer Nicia, Madonna Lucrezia, who was sterile, became pregnant?

SOFRONIA: Gran miracolo, un frate fare ingravidare una donna! Miracolo sarebbe, se una monaca la facessi ingravidare ella!

NICOMACO: È egli possibile che tu non mi attraversi sempre la via con queste novelle?

SOFRONIA: Io voglio ire alla messa, e non voglio rimettere le cose mia in persona.

NICOMACO: Orsù, va' e torna: io ti aspetterò in casa. Io credo che sia bene non si discostare molto, perché non trafugassino Clizia in qualche lato.

SCENA QUARTA

Sofronia sola.

SOFRONIA: Chi conobbe Nicomaco uno anno fa, e lo pratica ora, ne debbe restare maravigliato, considerando la gran mutazione, che gli ha fatta, perché soleva essere uno uomo grave, resoluto, respettivo. Dispensava il tempo suo onorevolmente, e si levava la mattina di buon' ora, udiva la sua messa, provedeva al vitto del giorno; dipoi, s' egli aveva faccenda in piazza, in mercato, o a' magistrati, e' le faceva; quanto che no, o e' si riduceva con qualche cittadino tra ragionamenti onorevoli, o e' si ritirava in casa nello scrittoio, dove raguagliava sue scritture, riordinava suoi conti; dipoi, piacevolmente con la sua brigata desinava; e, desinato, ragionava con il figliuolo, ammunivalo, davagli a conoscere gli uomini, e con qualche essemplo antico e moderno gl'insegnava vivere; andava dipoi fuora, consumava tutto il giorno o in faccende o in diporti gravi ed onesti; venuta la sera, sempre l'Avemaria lo trovava in casa: stavasi un poco con esso noi al fuoco, se gli era di verno; dipoi, se n'entrava nello scrittoio, a rivedere le faccende sue; alle tre

SOFRONIA: Some miracle, for a friar to get a woman pregnant! It would be a miracle if it were a nun that got her pregnant!

NICOMACO: Isn't there some way to keep you from always throwing these stories in my face?

SOFRONIA: I am going to go to mass, and I don't want to put my business in anyone's hands.

NICOMACO: Go ahead, I will wait for you at home. (I think I had better not go too far away, so that they don't carry Clizia off somewhere.)

SCENE FOUR

Sofronia alone.

SOFRONIA: If anyone who knew Nicomaco a year ago were to meet him now, he would certainly be amazed at the great change that has come over him. He used to be a serious, resolute, considerate man. He spent his time honorably. He would get up early in the morning, go to hear mass, see to the provisions for the day. Then, if he had business in town, in the market, or at city hall, he would do it; and if he didn't, he would either walk about talking in a dignified way with some townsman or other, or he would come back home to his study, where he would tally his accounts and balance his books. Then he would have lunch with his friends, and after lunch he would converse with his son, he would give him lessons and instruct him all about men; using ancient and modern examples, he would teach him how to behave. Then he would go out and spend the rest of the day either in business or in serious, worthwhile activities; when evening came, he would always be home for the rosary, he would remain with us by the hearth if it were winter, then he would go off into his

ore si cenava allegramente. Questo ordine della sua vita era
uno essemplo a tutti gli altri di casa, e ciascuno si vergo-
gnava non lo imitare. E così andavano le cose ordinate e
liete. Ma, dipoi che gli entrò questa fantasia di costei, le
faccende sue si straccurano, e poderi si guastono, e trafichi
rovinano; grida sempre, e non sa di che; entra ed esce di
casa ogni dì mille volte, sanza sapere quello che si vada
faccendo; non torna mai ad ora, che si possa cenare o desinare a tempo; se tu gli parli, o e' non ti risponde, o e' ti
risponde non a proposito. I servi, vedendo questo, si fanno
beffe di lui, il figliuolo ha posto giù la reverenzia, ognuno
fa a suo modo, ed infine niuno dubita di fare quello che
vede fare a lui: in modo che io dubito, se Iddio non ci
remedia, che questa povera casa non rovini. Io voglio pure
andare alla messa, e raccomandarmi a Dio quanto io posso.
—Io veggo Eustachio e Pirro, che si bisticciano: be' mariti
che si apparecchiano a Clizia!

SCENA QUINTA

Pirro, Eustachio.

PIRRO: Che fa' tu in Firenze, trista cosa?

EUSTACHIO: Io non l'ho a dire a te.

PIRRO: Tu se' così razzimato! Tu mi pari un cesso
ripulito!

EUSTACHIO: Tu hai sì poco cervello, che io mi maraviglio ch' e fanciulli non ti gettino drieto e sassi.

study to look over his business again; at nine o'clock we would have a hearty supper. The orderliness of his life was an example to everyone else in the house, and anyone who didn't imitate him felt ashamed. And so, things went along in an orderly and happy fashion. But ever since this fancy for that girl has gotten into him, his affairs have gone to the dogs, his farms have gone to seed, and his business has gone to ruin. He is always shouting, and he doesn't know what about. He is in and out of the house a thousand times a day without knowing what he is doing, he never comes home at an hour when we can have dinner or supper on time, if you talk to him he doesn't answer you or he answers you without rhyme or reason. Seeing all this, the servants make fun of him, and his son has lost all respect for him. Everyone does as he pleases, and all in all no one hesitates to do what Nicomaco can be seen doing. It has gotten so that I am afraid, if the good Lord doesn't do something about it, that this poor house is going to go to rack and ruin. Well, I am going to go to mass and commend myself to God as best I can. I see Eustachio and Pirro there, having a quarrel: fine husbands to be offering to Clizia!

SCENE FIVE

Pirro, Eustachio.

PIRRO: What are you doing in Florence, you miserable wretch?

EUSTACHIO: I don't have to tell you.

PIRRO: You are dressed up so fancy, you look like a newly-polished latrine.

EUSTACHIO: You have so few brains, I am amazed that little boys don't run after you throwing stones!

PIRRO: Presto ci avvedremo chi arà più cervello, o tu o io.

EUSTACHIO: Prega Iddio che 'l padrone non muoia, ché tu andrai un dì accattando!

PIRRO: Hai tu veduto Nicomaco?

EUSTACHIO: Che ne vuoi tu sapere, se io l'ho veduto o no?

PIRRO: E' ti toccherà bene a te a saperlo, che se e' non si rimuta, se tu non torni in villa da te, e' vi ti farà portare a' birri.

EUSTACHIO: E' ti dà una gran briga questo mio essere in Firenze!

PIRRO: E' dà più briga ad altri che a me.

EUSTACHIO: E però ne lascia el pensiero ad altri.

PIRRO: Pure le carne tirano.

EUSTACHIO: Tu guardi, e ghigni.

PIRRO: Guardo che tu saresti el bel marito.

EUSTACHIO: Orbè, sai quello ch' io ti voglio dire? "Ed anche il duca murava!" Ma, s' ella prende te, la sarà salita in su' muricciuoli. Quanto sarebbe meglio che Nicomaco la affogassi in quel suo pozzo! Almeno la poverina morrebbe ad uno tratto.

PIRRO: Doh! villan poltrone, profumato nel litame! Part' egli avere carni, da dormire allato a sì dilicata figlia?

EUSTACHIO: Ell' arà bene carni teco! che, se la sua trista sorte te la dà, o ella in uno anno diventerà puttana, o ella si morrà di dolore: ma del primo ne sarai tu d'accordo seco, ché, per uno becco pappataci, tu sarai desso!

PIRRO: We will soon see who has more brains, you
or me.

EUSTACHIO: Just pray to God for the master to live a
long life, or else you will have to go begging some day!

PIRRO: Have you seen Nicomaco?

EUSTACHIO: What does it matter to you whether I
have seen him or not?

PIRRO: You had better find out soon, because, unless
he changes his mind, if you don't get yourself back to the
country, he will have the law take you there.

EUSTACHIO: My being in Florence like this really
seems to bother you!

PIRRO: It will bother someone else more than me.

EUSTACHIO: Then let someone else worry about it.

PIRRO: Still, I can't help feeling sorry for you.

EUSTACHIO: That is why you stand there snickering
at me.

PIRRO: I am snickering at what a fine husband you
would be.

EUSTACHIO: Well, then, do you know what I will say
to you?—There is no shame in getting your hands dirty.[11]—
But if she takes you, she will really be in the gutter. It
would be a lot better for her if Nicomaco drowned her in
his well! At least the poor girl would die a quick death.

PIRRO: Pooh, you lazy hick, you smell of manure! Do
you think your body is fit to sleep next to such a dainty
girl?

EUSTACHIO: She will get a fine body with you! If her
bad luck puts her in your hands, either she will become a
whore within a year, or she will die of grief. But you will
certainly go along with her in the first case, for if ever
there was a contented cuckold, it is you!

PIRRO: Lasciamo andare! Ognuno aguzzi e sua ferruzzi: vedreno a chi e' dirà meglio. Io me ne voglio ire in casa, ch' io t'arei a rompere la testa.

EUSTACHIO: Ed io mi tornerò in chiesa.

PIRRO: Tu fai bene a non uscire di franchigia!

CANZONA

Quanto in cor giovinile è bello amore,
tanto si disconviene
in chi degli anni suoi passato ha il fiore.
Amore ha sua virtute agli anni uguale,
e nelle fresche etati assai s'onora,
e nelle antiche poco o nulla vale:
sì che, o vecchi amorosi, el meglio fora
lasciar la impresa a' giovinetti ardenti,
ch' a più fort' opra intenti,
far ponno al suo signor più largo onore.

PIRRO: Enough said, let each one sharpen his tools, and we shall see who has the last laugh. I am going to go back into the house, so I don't have to break your neck.

EUSTACHIO: And I'm going to go back into church.

PIRRO: That's it, you don't want to lose the right of asylum!

SONG

How beautiful is love in youthful heart!
And how incongruous
In one who's long since passed life's flowering part.
    Love's power parallels declining years,
And in our time of bloom evokes esteem,
But with old age its honor disappears.
And so, ye amorous old men, 'twould seem
The better part of valor to leave wooing
To ardent youths' pursuing,
For they're a fitter butt for Cupid's dart.

ATTO TERZO
SCENA PRIMA

Nicomaco, Cleandro.

NICOMACO: Cleandro! o Cleandro!

CLEANDRO: Messere!

NICOMACO: Esci giù, esci giù, dico io! Che fai tu, tanto el dì, in casa? Non te ne vergogni tu, che dài carico a cotesta fanciulla? Sogliono a simili dì di carnasciale e giovani tuoi pari andarsi a spasso veggendo le maschere, o ire a fare al calcio. Tu se' uno di quelli uomini, che non sai far nulla, e non mi pari né morto né vivo.

CLEANDRO: Io non mi diletto di coteste cose, e non me ne dilettai mai, e piacemi più lo stare solo, che con coteste compagnie; e tanto più stavo ora volentieri in casa, veggendovi stare voi, per potere, se voi volevi cosa alcuna, farla.

NICOMACO: Deh! guarda dove l'aveva! Tu se' el buon figliuolo! Io non ho bisogno di averti tuttodì drieto! Io tengo dua famigli ed uno fattore, per non avere a comandare a te.

CLEANDRO: Al nome d'Iddio! e' non è però che quello ch' io fo no 'l faccia per bene.

NICOMACO: Io non so per quel che tu te 'l fai, ma io so bene che tua madre è una pazza, e rovinerà questa casa. Tu faresti el meglio a ripararci.

CLEANDRO: O lei, o altri.

NICOMACO: Chi altri?

CLEANDRO: Io non so.

ACT THREE
SCENE ONE

Nicomaco, Cleandro.

NICOMACO: Cleandro, hey, Cleandro!

CLEANDRO: Sir!

NICOMACO: Come on down, come on down, I tell you. What are you doing in the house all this time? Aren't you ashamed of yourself, being such a burden on that poor girl? On Carnival days like this, a young man such as you ought to be roaming about looking at the maskers, or kicking the ball around with the others.[12] You are one of those men who can't find anything to do. I can't tell whether you are dead or alive.

CLEANDRO: I am not interested in such things, and I never have been. I would rather stay by myself than in company like that. I was all the happier to stay at home, since you were there, so that I could do whatever you might happen to want me to do.

NICOMACO: Please, don't do me any favors! Such a good son! I don't need to have you trailing around after me all day long! I keep two servants and a steward just so I won't have to give you orders.

CLEANDRO: So be it! But it isn't as if I weren't doing what I am doing for good reason.

NICOMACO: I don't know what reason you are doing it for. But I do know that your mother is a madwoman, and will bring this house to ruin. You would do best to prevent it.

CLEANDRO: Either she, or someone else.

NICOMACO: Who else?

CLEANDRO: I don't know.

NICOMACO: E' mi pare bene che tu no 'l sappi. Ma che di' tu di questi casi di Clizia?

CLEANDRO: Vedi che vi capitamo!

NICOMACO: Che di' tu? Di' forte, ch' io t'intenda.

CLEANDRO: Dico ch' io non so che me ne dire.

NICOMACO: Non ti par egli che questa tua madre pigli un granchio, a non volere che Clizia sia moglie di Pirro?

CLEANDRO: Io non me ne intendo.

NICOMACO: Io son chiaro! tu hai preso la parte sua! E' ci cova sotto altro che favole! Parrebbet' egli però che la stessi bene con Eustachio?

CLEANDRO: Io non lo so, e non me ne intendo.

NICOMACO: Di che diavolo t'intendi tu?

CLEANDRO: Non di cotesto.

NICOMACO: Tu ti sei pur inteso di far venire in Firenze Eustachio, e trafugarlo, perché io non lo vegga, e tendermi lacciuoli, per guastare queste nozze. Ma te e lui caccerò io nelle Stinche; a Sofronia renderò io la sua dota, e manderolla via, perché io voglio essere io signore di casa mia, e ognuno se ne sturi gli orecchi! E voglio che questa sera queste nozze si faccino, o io, quando non arò altro rimedio, caccerò fuoco in questa casa. Io aspetterò qui tua madre, per vedere s' io posso essere d'accordo con lei; ma, quando io non possa, ad ogni modo ci voglio l'onor mio, ché io non intendo ch' e paperi menino a bere l'oche. Va', pertanto, se tu desideri el bene tuo e la pace di casa, a pregarla che facci a mio modo. Tu la troverrai in chiesa, ed io aspetterò

NICOMACO: I am sure you don't know. But what do you say about this business with Clizia?

CLEANDRO: (Now we are getting there!)

NICOMACO: What is that you say? Speak louder so I can hear you.

CLEANDRO: I said I don't know what to say about it.

NICOMACO: Don't you think that mother of yours is making a blunder by not wanting Clizia to marry Pirro?

CLEANDRO: I don't know anything about it.

NICOMACO: It's pretty clear to me that you have taken her side. There must be some other story underneath all this! You don't really believe that she would be better off with Eustachio?

CLEANDRO: I can't say, and I don't know anything about any of this.

NICOMACO: What the devil do you know about?

CLEANDRO: Not about this.

NICOMACO: But you know enough to have Eustachio come to Florence, and to hide him so I wouldn't see him, and to set a trap for me to spoil this marriage. But I will have the two of you thrown in jail; I will give Sofronia her dowry back and send her packing; I intend to be the master in my own house; and let everyone unplug his ears, because I want the marriage to take place this evening; or else, if I have no other remedy, I will set fire to this house! I am going to wait here for your mother, and see if I can come to some agreement with her; but if I can't, one way or another I will see to it that I get some respect, because it is a sad house where the hen crows louder than the cock. So if you know what is good for you, and you want peace in this house, you had better go and ask her to do as I say. You will find her in church, and I shall wait for you and

te e lei qui in casa. E, se tu vedi quel ribaldo di Eustachio,
digli che venghi a me, altrimenti non farà bene e casi suoi.

CLEANDRO: Io vo.

SCENA SECONDA

Cleandro solo.

CLEANDRO: O miseria di chi ama! Con quanti affanni
passo io il mio tempo! Io so bene che qualunque ama una
cosa bella, come è Clizia, ha di molti rivali, che gli dànno
infiniti dolori; ma io non intesi mai che ad alcuno avvenissi
di avere per rivale il padre; e, dove molti giovani hanno
trovato appresso al padre qualche rimedio, io vi truovo el
fondamento e la cagione del male mio; e, se mia madre mi
favorisce, la non fa per favorire me, ma per disfavorire la
impresa del marito. E perciò io non posso scoprirmi in
questa cosa gagliardamente, perché sùbito la crederrebbe
che io avessi fatti quelli patti con Eustachio, che mio padre
ha fatti con Pirro; e, come la credesse questo, mossa dalla
coscienza, lascerebbe ire l'acqua alla china, e non se ne
travaglierebbe più, e io al tutto sarei spacciato, e ne pi-
glierei tanto dispiacere, ch' io non crederrei più vivere. Io
veggio mia madre, che esce di chiesa: io voglio parlare
seco, ed intendere la fantasia sua, e vedere quali rimedii
ella apparecchi contro a' disegni del vecchio.

her here in the house. And if you see that rascal Eustachio, tell him to come and see me; otherwise he will never hear the end of it!

CLEANDRO: I am going.

SCENE TWO

Cleandro alone.

CLEANDRO: Oh, what misery lovers have! I spend my time going through so many torments! I know that anyone who loves a creature as fair as Clizia has many rivals to cause him endless sorrow; but I never yet have heard of anyone with the ill fortune to have his own father as a rival. Many young men have found some help from their fathers, whereas I find in mine the very basis and cause of my troubles; and even though my mother serves my interests, she is not doing it as a service to me, but as a disservice to her husband's interests. And so I cannot reveal myself boldly in this matter, for she would immediately guess that I had made the same agreement with Eustachio as my father has with Pirro. And if she thought that, her conscience would make her let things slide, and she wouldn't trouble herself any more. Then I would be completely done for, and I would be so disheartened that I don't think I could go on living. There is my mother coming out of church. I am going to talk to her, and find out what she has thought up, and see what remedies she is preparing against the old man's plans.

SCENA TERZA

Cleandro, Sofronia.

CLEANDRO: Dio vi salvi, madre mia!

SOFRONIA: O Cleandro! Vieni tu di casa?

CLEANDRO: Madonna sì.

SOFRONIA: Sèvvi tu stato tuttavia, poi ch' io vi ti lasciai?

CLEANDRO: Sono.

SOFRONIA: Nicomaco, dove è?

CLEANDRO: È in casa, e per cosa che sia accaduta non è uscito.

SOFRONIA: Lascialo fare, al nome d'Iddio! Una ne pensa el ghiotto, e l'altra el tavernaio. Hatt' egli detto cosa alcuna?

CLEANDRO: Un monte di villanie; e parmi che gli sia entrato el diavolo addosso. E' vuole mettere nelle Stinche Eustachio e me, a voi vuole rendere la dota, e cacciarvi via, e minaccia, nonché altro, di cacciare fuoco in casa, e mi ha imposto ch' io vi truovi e vi persuada a consentire a queste nozze, altrimenti non si farà per voi.

SOFRONIA: Tu, che ne di'?

CLEANDRO: Dicone quello che voi, perché io amo Clizia come sorella, e dorrebbemi infino all'anima, che la capitassi in mano di Pirro.

SOFRONIA: Io non so come tu te la ami; ma io ti dico bene questo, che s' io credessi trarla delle mani di Nicomaco, e metterla nelle tua, che io non me ne impaccerei. Ma io penso che Eustachio la vorrebbe per sè, e che il tuo amore, per la sposa tua (che siamo per dartela presto), si potessi cancellare.

SCENE THREE

Cleandro, Sofronia.

CLEANDRO: God save you, mother!

SOFRONIA: Oh, Cleandro, have you just left the house?

CLEANDRO: Yes, Madam.

SOFRONIA: Have you been there all the time since I left you?

CLEANDRO: I have.

SOFRONIA: Where is Nicomaco?

CLEANDRO: He is in the house, and he has not left it for any reason whatsoever.

SOFRONIA: Let him be, as the good Lord wills! Every man to his own tastes. Has he said anything at all to you?

CLEANDRO: A bunch of nasty things. I think the devil has gotten into him. He wants to put Eustachio and me in jail; as for you, he is going to give you back your dowry and throw you out, and he threatens, if need be, to set fire to the house. He has ordered me to find you and convince you to consent to this marriage. Otherwise you had better watch out.

SOFRONIA: What do you have to say about that?

CLEANDRO: The same as you, because I love Clizia like a sister, and I would be deeply grieved if she fell into Pirro's hands.

SOFRONIA: I am not sure how you love her, but let me tell you this: if I thought I was pulling her out of Nicomaco's hands just to put her in yours, I would not get involved. But I think that Eustachio would like her for himself, and that your love for the wife that we are soon going to give you will cancel out this one.

CLEANDRO: Voi pensate bene; e però io vi prego, che voi facciate ogni cosa, perché queste nozze non si faccino; e, quando non si possa fare altrimenti che darla ad Eustachio, dìesili; ma, quando si possa, sarebbe meglio, secondo me, lasciarla stare così, perché l'è ancora giovinetta, e non le fugge il tempo: potrebbono e Cieli farle trovare e sua parenti, e, quando e' fussino nobili, arebbono un poco obligo con voi, trovando che voi l'avessi maritata o ad uno famiglio, o ad uno contadino!

SOFRONIA: Tu di' bene: io ancora ci avevo pensato, ma la rabbia di questo vecchio mi sbigottisce. Nondimeno, e' mi si aggirano tante cose per il capo, che io credo che qualcuna gli guasterà ogni suo disegno. Io me ne voglio ire in casa, perché io veggo Nicomaco aliare intorno all'uscio. Tu, va' in chiesa, e di' ad Eustachio che venga a casa, e non abbia paura di cosa alcuna.

CLEANDRO: Così farò.

SCENA QUARTA

Nicomaco, Sofronia.

NICOMACO: Io veggo mogliama, che torna: io la voglio un poco berteggiare, per vedere, se le buone parole mi giovano. O fanciulla mia, ha' tu però a stare sì malinconosa, quando tu vedi la tua speranza? Sta' un poco meco!

SOFRONIA: Lasciami ire!

NICOMACO: Fèrmati, dico!

SOFRONIA: Io non voglio: tu mi par' cotto!

NICOMACO: Io ti verrò drieto.

SOFRONIA: Se' tu impazzato?

NICOMACO: Pazzo, perch' io ti voglio troppo bene?

CLEANDRO: I am sure that you are right, and so I beg
you to do everything possible to keep this wedding from
taking place. If there is no other way out than to give
her to Eustachio, give her to him. But if it is possible, it
would be better (in my opinion) to let her be, because she
is still young and there is plenty of time left. With God's
help, she may find her family, and if they should be noble,
they would not be too grateful to you for marrying her off
to a servant or a peasant!

SOFRONIA: You are right. I had thought of that, too,
but that old man's madness is just too much for me! Nevertheless, I have so many things turning about in my mind,
I think any one of them could spoil his plans. I am going
to go into the house, because I see Nicomaco snooping
around the front door. You go to church and tell Eustachio
to come to the house; he has nothing to fear from anyone.

CLEANDRO: I shall do that.

SCENE FOUR

Nicomaco, Sofronia.

NICOMACO: (I see the wife is back. I think I shall fool
around with her a bit, to see if sweet talk does any good.)
Oh, little girl of mine, how can you look so melancholy
when you see your sweetheart standing before you? Stay
here a moment with me.

SOFRONIA: Let me go.

NICOMACO: Stand still, I tell you!

SOFRONIA: I don't want to. You look drunk to me.

NICOMACO: I am going to come after you.

SOFRONIA: Have you gone crazy?

NICOMACO: Crazy, because I want you so much?

SOFRONIA: Io non voglio che tu me ne voglia.

NICOMACO: Questo non può essere!

SOFRONIA: Tu m'uccidi! Uh, fastidioso!

NICOMACO: Io vorrei che tu dicessi il vero.

SOFRONIA: Credotelo.

NICOMACO: Eh! guatami un poco, amor mio.

SOFRONIA: Io ti guato, ed odoroti anche: tu sai di buono! Bembè, tu mi riesci!

NICOMACO: Ohimè, ché la se ne è avveduta! Che maladetto sia quel poltrone, che me l'arrecò dinanzi!

SOFRONIA: Onde son venuti questi odori, di che sai tu, vecchio impazzato?

NICOMACO: E' passò dianzi uno di qui, che ne vendeva: io gli trassinai, e mi rimase di quello odore addosso.

SOFRONIA: Egli ha già trovato la bugia! Non ti vergogni tu di quello che tu fai da uno anno in qua? Usi sempre con sei giovanetti, vai alla taverna, ripariti in casa femmine, e dove si giuoca, spendi sanza modo. Begli essempli, che tu dài al tuo figliuolo! Date moglie a questi valenti uomini!

NICOMACO: Ah! moglie mia, non mi dir tanti mali ad un tratto! Serba qualche cosa a domani! Ma non è egli ragionevole che tu faccia più tosto a mio modo, che io a tuo?

SOFRONIA: Sì, delle cose oneste.

NICOMACO: Non è egli onesto maritare una fanciulla?

SOFRONIA: Sì, quando ella si marita bene.

NICOMACO: Non starà ella bene con Pirro?

SOFRONIA: No.

NICOMACO: Perché?

SOFRONIA: I don't want you to want me.

NICOMACO: I can't help it!

SOFRONIA: You are killing me! Ugh, you are disgusting!

NICOMACO: I would like you to tell the truth.

SOFRONIA: I can imagine.

NICOMACO: Ah! Look at me a moment, my love!

SOFRONIA: I am looking at you, and I can smell you, too. What an aroma! You certainly are making an impression on me!

NICOMACO: (Damn! She has noticed! The devil take that good-for-nothing who brought it to me!)

SOFRONIA: Where did you get that stench you smell of, you crazy old fool?

NICOMACO: A man who was selling the stuff passed by here; I was dealing with him, and some of the smell rubbed off on me.

SOFRONIA: (He has already made up a lie.)—Aren't you ashamed of what you have been doing this past year? You always hang around those young men, you go to the tavern, you frequent whorehouses and gambling dens, and you spend money without any regard. A fine example to set for your son! Give a wife to worthy men like these!

NICOMACO: Oh, my darling wife, don't accuse me of everything all at once! Keep something in reserve for tomorrow! But isn't it more sensible for you to do things my way than for me to do them your way?

SOFRONIA: Yes, decent things.

NICOMACO: Isn't it decent to marry a girl off?

SOFRONIA: Yes, when she is married off well.

NICOMACO: Won't she be well off with Pirro?

SOFRONIA: No.

NICOMACO: Why not?

SOFRONIA: Per quelle cagioni, ch' io t'ho dette altre volte.

NICOMACO: Io m'intendo di queste cose più di te. Ma, se io facessi tanto con Eustachio, ch' e' non la volessi?

SOFRONIA: E se io facessi con Pirro tanto, che non la volessi anch' egli?

NICOMACO: Da ora innanzi, ciascuno di noi si pruovi, e chi di noi dispone el suo, abbi vinto.

SOFRONIA: Io son contenta. Io vo in casa a parlare a Pirro, e tu parlerai con Eustachio, che io lo veggo uscir di chiesa.

NICOMACO: Sia fatto.

SCENA QUINTA

Eustachio, Nicomaco.

EUSTACHIO: Poiché Cleandro mi ha detto che io vadia a casa e non dubiti, io voglio fare buono core, ed andarvi.

NICOMACO: Io volevo dire a questo ribaldo una carta di villanie, e non potrò, poiché io l'ho a pregare. Eustachio!

EUSTACHIO: O padrone!

NICOMACO: Quando fusti tu in Firenze?

EUSTACHIO: Iersera.

NICOMACO: Tu hai penato tanto a lasciarti rivedere! Dove se' tu stato tanto?

EUSTACHIO: Io vi dirò. Io mi cominciai iermattina a sentir male: e' mi doleva el capo, avevo una anguinaia, e parevami avere la febre; ed essendo questi tempi sospetti di peste, io ne dubitai forte; e iersera venni a Firenze, e mi

SOFRONIA: For the reasons I have already given you.

NICOMACO: I know more about these things than you do. But what if I made it so that Eustachio didn't want her any more?

SOFRONIA: And what if I made it so that Pirro didn't, either?

NICOMACO: From now on, let each of us try to do that: and the one who convinces his man will be the winner.

SOFRONIA: That is fine with me. I am going into the house to talk to Pirro, and you talk to Eustachio. I see him coming out of church.

NICOMACO: Let's do that.

SCENE FIVE

Eustachio, Nicomaco.

EUSTACHIO: (Since Cleandro has told me to go into the house and not to worry, I am going to screw up my courage and go in.)

NICOMACO: (I wanted to say a bunch of nasty things to that rascal, but I can't now, because I have to plead with him.) Eustachio!

EUSTACHIO: Oh, master!

NICOMACO: When did you get to Florence?

EUSTACHIO: Last night.

NICOMACO: You took so long to let us see you again: where have you been all this time?

EUSTACHIO: I will tell you. Yesterday morning, I began to feel ill: I had a headache, I had a pain in my groin, and I felt as if I had a fever. So since there is a suspicion of plague right now, I was really worried. Last night I came to Florence, and I stayed at the inn. I didn't want to show

stetti all'osteria, né mi volli rappresentare, per non fare
male a voi o a la famiglia vostra, se pure e' fussi stato
desso. Ma, grazia di Dio, ogni cosa è passata via, e sen-
tomi bene.

NICOMACO: E' mi bisogna fare vista di crederlo. Ben
facesti tu! Se' or bene guarito?

EUSTACHIO: Messer sì.

NICOMACO: Non del tristo. Io ho caro che tu ci sia.
Tu sai la contenzione, che è tra me e mogliama circa al dar
marito a Clizia: ella la vuole dare a te, ed io la vorrei dare
a Pirro.

EUSTACHIO: E dunque, volete meglio a Pirro che
a me?

NICOMACO: Anzi, voglio meglio a te che a lui. Ascolta
un poco. Che vuoi tu fare di moglie? Tu hai oggimai tren-
totto anni, ed una fanciulla non ti sta bene; ed è ragionevole
che, come la fussi stata teco qualche mese, che la cercassi un
più giovane di te, e viveresti disperato. Dipoi, io non mi
potrei più fidare di te, perderesti lo aviamento, diventeresti
povero, ed andresti, tu ed ella, accattando.

EUSTACHIO: In questa terra, chi ha bella moglie non
può essere povero: e del fuoco e della moglie si può essere
liberale con ognuno, perché quanto più ne dài, più te ne
rimane.

NICOMACO: Dunque, vuoi tu fare questo parentado,
per farmi dispiacere?

EUSTACHIO: Anzi, lo vo' fare, per fare piacere a me!

NICOMACO: Or tira, vanne in casa. Io ero pazzo, s' io
credevo avere da questo villano una risposta piacevole. Io
muterò teco verso. Ordina di rimettermi e conti, e di
andarti con Dio; e fa' stima d'essere il maggior nimico,
ch'io abbia, e ch' io ti abbia a fare il peggio, che io posso.

myself for fear of harming you or your family, in case if turned out to to be the plague. But thank God, it all went away and I feel fine.

NICOMACO: (I have to act as if I believe him.) You did the right thing! Are you really completely cured now?

EUSTACHIO: Yes, sir.

NICOMACO: (Not of lying.) I am so glad you are here. You know about the argument between me and the wife about giving Clizia a husband. She wants to give her to you, and I would like to give her to Pirro.

EUSTACHIO: So you like Pirro better than me?

NICOMACO: Not at all, I like you better than him. Listen. What do you want with a wife? You are already thirty-eight, and a young girl is no good for you. It stands to reason that, after she was with you for a few months, she would look for a man younger than you, and you would become despondent. And then I couldn't have confidence in you any more. You would lose your standing, you would become a pauper, and the two of you would go begging.

EUSTACHIO: In this town, a man who has a beautiful wife can never be a pauper. With your hearthfire and your wife, you can be generous with everyone, because the more you give, the more you have.

NICOMACO: So you want to go ahead with this marriage, and displease me?

EUSTACHIO: Not at all. I want to do it to please me!

NICOMACO: Get away now, go on into the house. (I was crazy to think I would have a satisfactory answer from this peasant.) I am going to change my way of dealing with you. Get ready to turn in your accounts to me and to get going. From now on you can consider yourself among my worst enemies, and I will make life as miserable as I can for you.

EUSTACHIO: A me non dà briga nulla, purch' io abbia Clizia.

NICOMACO: Tu arai le forche!

SCENA SESTA

Pirro, Nicomaco.

PIRRO: Prima ch' io facessi ciò che voi volete, io mi lascerei scorticare!

NICOMACO: La cosa va bene. Pirro sta nella fede. Che hai tu? Con chi combatti tu, Pirro?

PIRRO: Combatto ora con chi voi combattete sempre.

NICOMACO: Che dic' ella? Che vuol ella?

PIRRO: Pregami che io non tolga Clizia per donna.

NICOMACO: Che l'hai tu detto?

PIRRO: Che io mi lascerei prima ammazzare, che io la rifiutassi.

NICOMACO: Ben dicesti.

PIRRO: Se io ho ben detto, io dubito non avere mal fatto, perché io mi sono fatto nimico la vostra donna, ed il vostro figliuolo, e tutti gli altri di casa.

NICOMACO: Che importa a te? Sta' bene con Cristo, e fatti beffe de' santi!

PIRRO: Sì, ma se voi morissi, i santi mi tratterebbono assai male.

NICOMACO: Non dubitare, io ti farò tal parte, ch' e santi ti potranno dare poca briga; e, se pur e' volessino, e magistrati e le leggi ti difenderanno, purch' io abbia facultà, per tuo mezzo, di dormire con Clizia.

EUSTACHIO: That doesn't bother me at all, as long as I can get Clizia.

NICOMACO: You will get the gallows!

SCENE SIX

Pirro, Nicomaco.

PIRRO: I would sooner let myself be flayed alive than do what you want.

NICOMACO: (Things are going well! Pirro is keeping his word.) What is the matter? Who are you quarreling with, Pirro?

PIRRO: I am quarreling now with the one you are always quarreling with.

NICOMACO: What did she say? What does she want?

PIRRO: She was asking me not to marry Clizia.

NICOMACO: How did you answer her?

PIRRO: That I would sooner let myself be slaughtered than turn her down.

NICOMACO: That was the right thing to tell her.

PIRRO: Maybe it was the right thing to tell her, but I am afraid it was the wrong thing to do, because I have made an enemy of your wife, your son, and everyone else in the house.

NICOMACO: What does that matter to you? You can't please everyone in the world.

PIRRO: No, but if you were to die, everyone else in the world would make life pretty hard for me.

NICOMACO: Don't worry, I will leave you enough so that the others can't cause you much trouble. And even if they tried, the courts and the law will protect you—just as long as you make it possible for me to sleep with Clizia.

PIRRO: Io dubito che voi non possiate, tanta infiammata vi veggio contro la donna.

NICOMACO: Io ho pensato che sarà bene, per uscire una volta di questo farnetico, che si getti per sorte di chi sia Clizia: da che la donna non si potrà discostare.

PIRRO: Se la sorte vi venissi contro?

NICOMACO: Io ho speranza in Dio, che la non verrà.

PIRRO: O vecchio impazzato! vuol che Dio tenga le mani a queste sua disonestà! Io credo, che se Dio s'impaccia di simil' cose, che Sofronia ancora speri in Dio.

NICOMACO: Ella si speri! E, se pur la sorte mi venissi contro, io ho pensato al rimedio. Va', chiamala, e dilli che venga fuora con Eustachio.

PIRRO: O Sofronia! Venite, voi ed Eustachio, al padrone.

SCENA SETTIMA

Sofronia, Nicomaco, Eustachio, Pirro.

SOFRONIA: Eccomi: che sarà di nuovo?

NICOMACO: E' bisogna pur pigliare verso a questa cosa. Tu vedi, poiché costoro non si accordano, e' conviene che noi ci accordiano.

SOFRONIA: Questa tua furia è estraordinaria. Quel che non si farà oggi, si farà domani.

NICOMACO: Io voglio farla oggi.

SOFRONIA: Faccisi, in buon' ora. Ecco qui tutti a duoi e competitori. Ma come vuoi tu fare?

NICOMACO: Io ho pensato, poiché noi non consentiàno l'uno all'altro, che la si rimetta nella Fortuna.

PIRRO: I am afraid you won't be able to, the way your wife seems to be furious with you.

NICOMACO: I have decided, in order to clear up this nonsense once and for all, that it would be a good idea to choose whom Clizia will belong to by lots. Then my wife will have to go along with it.

PIRRO: But what if luck goes against you?

NICOMACO: I am hoping that the good Lord won't let that happen.

PIRRO: (Oh, what a crazy old man! He wants God to take a hand in his dirty business!) I think that if the Lord gets involved in such matters, Sofronia has as much hope as you do.

NICOMACO: Let her hope! Even if luck should go against me, I have thought of a remedy. Go and call her, tell her to come on out with Eustachio.

PIRRO: Sofronia, you and Eustachio come see the master.

SCENE SEVEN

Sofronia, Eustachio, Nicomaco, Pirro.

SOFRONIA: Here I am. What now?

NICOMACO: We have to find a way to deal with this matter. You can see that, if these two can't agree, we will have to reach some agreement ourselves.

SOFRONIA: This haste of yours is extraordinary. What can't be done today can be done tomorrow.

NICOMACO: I want to do it today.

SOFRONIA: Then let it be done right away. Here are both of the suitors. So what do you intend to do?

NICOMACO: I have decided that, since we cannot agree on one or the other, we should leave it up to Fortune.

SOFRONIA: Come, nella Fortuna?

NICOMACO: Che si ponga in una borsa e nomi loro, ed in un'altra el nome di Clizia ed una polizza bianca; e che si tragga prima el nome d'uno di loro, e che, a chi tocca Clizia, se l'abbia, e l'altro abbi pazienza. Che pensi tu? Non rispondi?

SOFRONIA: Orsù, io son contenta.

EUSTACHIO: Guardate quel che voi fate.

SOFRONIA: Io guardo, e so quel ch' io fo. Va' 'n casa, scrivi le polizze, e reca dua borse, ch' io voglio uscire di questo travaglio, o io enterrò in uno maggiore.

EUSTACHIO: Io vo.

NICOMACO: A questo modo ci accordereno noi. Prega Dio, Pirro, per te.

PIRRO: Per voi!

NICOMACO: Tu di' bene, a dire per me: io arò una gran consolazione che tu l'abbia.

EUSTACHIO: Ecco le borse e le sorte.

NICOMACO: Da' qua. Questa, che dice? Clizia. E quest' altra? È bianca. Sta bene. Mettile in questa borsa di qua. Questa, che dice? Eustachio. E quest' altra? Pirro. Ripiegale, e mettile in quest' altra. Serrale, tienvi sù gli occhi, Pirro, che non ci andassi nulla in capperuccia; e' ci è chi sa giucare di macatelle!

SOFRONIA: Gli uomini sfiducciati non son buoni.

NICOMACO: Son parole, coteste! Tu sai che non è ingannato, se non chi si fida. Chi vogliàn noi che tragga?

SOFRONIA: Tragga chi ti pare.

SOFRONIA: What do you mean, to Fortune?

NICOMACO: Let us put their names in one pouch, and in another the name of Clizia and a blank slip. Then first we will draw the name of one of them, and whoever gets Clizia can have her, and the other one will give up. What do you think? Won't you answer?

SOFRONIA: All right, I accept.

EUSTACHIO: Watch what you are doing.

SOFRONIA: I am watching, and I know what I am doing. Go into the house, write out the slips, and bring back two pouches, because I want to put an end to this dispute, or I will start a bigger one.

EUSTACHIO: I am going.

NICOMACO: This way we will come to an agreement. Pray God to help you, Pirro.

PIRRO: To help you!

NICOMACO: You are right, to help me. It will be a great comfort for me for you to have her.

EUSTACHIO: Here are the pouches and the slips.

NICOMACO: Hand them over. What does this one say? "Clizia." And this one? It is blank. Fine. Put them in this pouch here. What does this say? "Eustachio." And this one? "Pirro." Fold them up and put them in this other one. Close them up tight, keep your eye on them, Pirro, so they don't get lost in the shuffle. There are some tricky players around here.

SOFRONIA: A man who has no confidence is a wicked man.

NICOMACO: That is a lot of empty words: you know that a man who has confidence is the one who gets tricked. Who should we let draw the lots?

SOFRONIA: Anyone you want.

NICOMACO: Vien' qua, fanciullo.

SOFRONIA: E' bisognerebbe che fussi vergine.

NICOMACO: O vergine o no, io non v'ho tenute le mani. Tra' di questa borsa una polizza, detto che io ho certe orazioni: —O santa Apollonia, io prego te e tutti e santi e le sante avvocate de' matrimonii, che concediate a Clizia tanta grazia, che di questa borsa esca la polizza di colui, che sia per essere più a piacere nostro. —Trài, col nome di Dio! Dàlla qua. Ohimè, io son morto! Eustachio.

SOFRONIA: Che avesti? O Dio! fa' questo miracolo, acciò che costui si disperi.

NICOMACO: Tra' di quell' altra. Dàlla qua. Bianca. Oh, io sono resucitato! Noi abbiam vinto, Pirro! Buon pro ti faccia! Eustachio è caduto morto. Sofronia, poiché Dio ha voluto che Clizia sia di Pirro, vogli anche tu.

SOFRONIA: Io voglio.

NICOMACO: Ordina le nozze.

SOFRONIA: Tu hai sì gran fretta: non si potrebb' egli indugiare a domani?

NICOMACO: No, no, no! Non odi tu che no? Che? vuoi tu pensare a qualche trappola?

SOFRONIA: Vogliàn noi fare le cose da bestie? Non ha ella a udir la messa del congiunto?

NICOMACO: La messa della fava! La la può udire un altro dì! Non sai tu che si dà le perdonanze a chi si confessa poi, come a chi s' è confessato prima?

SOFRONIA: Io dubito che la non abbia l'ordinario delle donne.

NICOMACO: Come here, boy.

SOFRONIA: It ought to be a virgin.

NICOMACO: Virgin or not, I have never laid a hand on him. Draw a lot from this pouch, as soon as I have said a few prayers:—Oh, Saint Apollonia, I pray to you and all the patron saints of marriage that you grant such grace to Clizia that the lot which is drawn from this pouch bears the name of the one who will give us the most pleasure.—Draw the lot, in God's name. Give it to me. Ayay! I am a dead man! Eustachio!

SOFRONIA: What is the matter with you? (Oh, Lord, send a miracle, and let him give up all hope.)

NICOMACO: Draw a lot from the other one. Give it to me. Blank. Oh! I have been restored to life, we have won! Pirro, more power to you; Eustachio is a dead duck. Sofronia, since God has willed that Clizia belongs to Pirro, you should, too.

SOFRONIA: I do.

NICOMACO: Arrange the wedding.

SOFRONIA: You are in such a hurry; couldn't it wait until tomorrow?

NICOMACO: No, no, no! Don't you hear me: no! Why? Do you want to think up some trick?

SOFRONIA: We don't want to do things foolishly, do we? Doesn't she have to hear the nuptial mass?

NICOMACO: Nuptial mass, my ass! She can hear it some other day! Don't you know that forgiveness is granted to those who confess afterward, just as it is to those who confess before?

SOFRONIA: I am afraid she may have her female monthlies.

NICOMACO: Adoperi lo straordinario delli uomini! Io voglio che la meni stasera. E' par che tu non mi intenda.

SOFRONIA: Menila, in mal' ora! Andianne in casa, e fa' questa imbasciata tu a questa povera fanciulla, che non fia da calze!

NICOMACO: La fia da calzoni! Andiano dentro.

SOFRONIA: Io non voglio già venire, perché io vo' trovar Cleandro, perché e' pensi, se a questo male è rimedio alcuno.

CANZONA

Chi già mai donna offende,
a torto o a ragion, folle è se crede
trovar per prieghi o pianti in lei merzede.
   Come la scende in questa mortal vita,
con l'alma insieme porta
Superbia, Ingegno e di perdono Oblio;
Inganno e Crudeltà le sono scorta,
e tal le dànno aita,
che d'ogni impresa appaga el suo desio;
e, se sdegno aspro e rio
la muove, o gelosia, addopra e vede,
e la sua forza mortal forza eccede.

NICOMACO: That is nothing some male nightlies won't cure! I want her to be married this evening. You don't seem to have understood me.

SOFRONIA: Let her be married and be damned. Let us go into the house, and you can give the news to that poor girl. But don't expect a tip for it!

NICOMACO: She is the one who will get the tip. Let us go in.

SOFRONIA: (I am not going to go along yet, because I want to find Cleandro and see if he can find any cure for this ill.)

SONG

Whoe'er offends a lady
For right or wrong's a fool to seek compassion,
Or think by prayers or tears to stem her passion.
When woman comes down to this mortal sphere,
Her soul bears in its essence
Disdain and haughtiness, rejecting pardon:
Deceit and cruelty bide in her presence
To lend such aid and cheer
As quench desires and defenses harden.
And if disdain, the warden
So harsh of virtue, or if jealousy should stir her,
She mounts her guard, and dreadful powers spur her.

ATTO QUARTO
SCENA PRIMA

Cleandro, Eustachio.

CLEANDRO: Come è egli possibile che mia madre sia stata sì poco avveduta, che la si sia rimessa a questo modo alla sorta d'una cosa, che ne vadi in tutto l'onore di casa nostra?

EUSTACHIO: Egli è comé io t'ho detto.

CLEANDRO: Ben sono sventurato! Ben sono infelice! Vedi s' i' trovai appunto uno, che mi tenne tanto a bada, che si è, sanza mia saputa, concluso el parentado, e delibererate le nozze ed ogni cosa! E seguirà secondo el desiderio del vecchio! O Fortuna, tu suòi pure, sendo donna, essere amica de' giovani: a questa volta tu se' stata amica de' vecchi! Come non ti vergogni tu, ad avere ordinato che sì dilicato viso sia da sì fetida bocca scombavato, sì dilicate carne da sì tremanti mani, da sì grinze e puzzolente membra tocche? Perché, non Pirro, ma Nicomaco, come io mi stimo, la possederà. Tu non mi possevi fare la maggior ingiuria, avendomi con questo colpo tolto ad un tratto l'amata e la roba, perché Nicomaco, se questo amore dura, è per lasciare delle sue sustanze più a Pirro che a me. E' mi par mille anni di vedere mia madre, per dolermi e sfogarmi con lei di questo partito.

EUSTACHIO: Confòrtati, Cleandro, ché mi parve che la ne andassi in casa ghignando, in modo che mi pare essere certo che 'l vecchio non abbia ad avere questa pera monda, come e' crede. Ma ecco che viene fuora, egli e Pirro, e son tutti allegri.

ACT FOUR
SCENE ONE

Cleandro, Eustachio.

CLEANDRO: How can my mother have been so foolish as to leave a matter like this up to chance, when the entire honor of our house is at stake?

EUSTACHIO: It is just as I have told you.

CLEANDRO: How unfortunate, how miserable I am! You see, I happened to run into someone who held me up just long enough for the marriage to be arranged and the wedding to be planned without my knowledge, and everything has gone exactly the way the old man wanted! Oh Fortune, since you are a woman, you really ought to be the mistress of young men: but this time you were the old man's mistress! Aren't you ashamed of arranging for such a delicate face to be drooled over by such a foul-smelling mouth, for such a delicate body to be fondled by such quivering hands, by such wrinkled and stinking limbs? Because it won't be Pirro who possesses her, but Nicomaco, unless I miss my guess. You couldn't do me a greater injury, since by one blow you take from me both my beloved and my inheritance. For if this love lasts, Nicomaco is bound to leave more of his fortune to Pirro than to me. I can hardly wait to see my mother, and get some relief by complaining about this match.

EUSTACHIO: If it is any consolation Cleandro, it seems to me that she was snickering as she went into the house. So I don't think the old man is so certain to pluck this fruit, as ripe as he may think it is. But here he comes with Pirro, and they are as happy as can be.

CLEANDRO: Vanne, Eustachio, in casa: io voglio stare da parte, per intendere qualche loro consiglio, che facessi per me.

EUSTACHIO: Io vo.

SCENA SECONDA

Nicomaco, Cleandro, Pirro.

NICOMACO: Oh, come è ella ita bene! Hai tu veduto come la brigata sta malinconosa, come mogliama sta disperata? Tutte queste cose accrescono la mia allegrezza; ma molto più sarò allegro, quando io terrò in braccio Clizia, quando io la toccherò, bacerò, strignerò. O dolce notte! giugnerovv' io mai? E questo obligo, che io ho teco, io sono per pagarlo a doppio!

CLEANDRO: O vecchio impazzato!

PIRRO: Io lo credo; ma io non credo già che voi possiate fare cosa nessuna questa sera, né ci veggo commodità alcuna.

NICOMACO: Come?! Io ti vo' dire come io ho pensato di governare la cosa.

PIRRO: Io l'arò caro.

CLEANDRO: Ed io molto più, ché potrei udir cosa, che guasterebbe e fatti d'altri, e racconcerebbe e mia.

NICOMACO: Tu cognosci Damone, nostro vicino, da chi io ho tolto la casa a pigione per tuo conto?

PIRRO: Sì, cognosco.

NICOMACO: Io fo pensiero che tu la meni stasera in quella casa, ancora ch' egli vi abiti e che non l'abbia sgombera, perch' io dirò ch' io voglio che tu la meni in casa, dove l'ha a stare.

PIRRO: Che sarà poi?

CLEANDRO: Rizza gli orecchi, Cleandro!

CLEANDRO: You go into the house, Eustachio. I want
to stand aside to hear whatever plans they are hatching
that might be of use to me.

EUSTACHIO: All right.

SCENE TWO

Nicomaco, Pirro, Cleandro.

NICOMACO: Oh, everything has gone so well! Did you
see how melancholy the bunch of them are, how desperate
the wife is? All these things increase my happiness; but I
will be much happier still when I hold Clizia in my arms,
when I can fondle her, kiss her, embrace her. Oh, sweet
night, will I ever get there? As for that debt I have to you,
I am ready to pay it double!

CLEANDRO: (Oh, the old fool!)

PIRRO: I believe you, but I don't think you can do anything tonight, or at least I don't see any way to manage it.

NICOMACO: Why not? I will tell you how I have decided to arrange things.

PIRRO: I would be grateful.

CLEANDRO: (So would I, even more, so I can find out
how to spoil your plans and get my own back in order.)

NICOMACO: You know our neighbor, Damone, whose
house I have rented on your account?

PIRRO: Yes, I do.

NICOMACO: I have been thinking that you should take
her to that house tonight, even though he is still living
there and hasn't moved out. I will say that I want you to
take her to the house where she is supposed to live.

PIRRO: What then?

CLEANDRO: (Prick up your ears, Cleandro!)

NICOMACO: Io ho imposto a mogliama che chiami Sostrata, moglie di Damone perché gli aiuti ad ordinare queste nozze ed acconciare la nuova sposa; ed a Damone dirò che solleciti che la donna vi vadia. Fatto questo, e cenato che si sarà, la sposa da queste donne sarà menata in casa di Damone, e messa teco in camera e nel letto; ed io dirò di volere restare con Damone ad albergo, e Sostrata ne verrà con Sofronia qui in casa. Tu, rimaso solo in camera, spegnerai il lume, e ti baloccherai per camera, faccendo vista di spogliarti; intanto io, pian piano, me ne verrò in camera, e mi spoglierò, ed enterrò allato a Clizia. Tu ti potrai stare pianamente in sul lettuccio. La mattina, avanti giorno, io mi uscirò del letto, mostrando di volere ire ad orinare, rivestirommi, e tu enterrai nel letto.

CLEANDRO: O vecchio poltrone! Quanta è stata la mia felicità intendere questo tuo disegno! Quanta la tua disgrazia ch' io l'intenda.

PIRRO: E' mi pare che voi abbiate divisata bene questa faccenda. Ma e' conviene che voi vi armiate in modo, che voi paiate giovane, perché io dubito che la vecchiaia non si riconosca, al buio.

CLEANDRO: E' mi basta quel che io ho inteso: io voglio ire a raguagliare mia madre.

NICOMACO: Io ho pensato a tutto, e fo conto, a dirti il vero, di cenare con Damone, ed ho ordinato una cena a mio modo. Io piglierò prima una presa d'uno lattovaro, che si chiama satirionne.

PIRRO: Che nome bizzarro è cotesto?

NICOMACO: Gli ha più bizzarri e fatti, perché gli è un lattovaro, che farebbe, quanto a quella faccenda, ringiovanire uno uomo di novanta anni, nonché di settanta,

NICOMACO: I have told the wife to ask Damone's wife Sostrata to help her arrange this wedding and prepare the bride; and I will tell Damone to urge his wife to do it. When that is done, and we have had supper, Sostrata will take the bride to Damone's house, and bring her into the bedroom and put her in bed with you. I will say that I am going to stay at the inn with Damone, and Sostrata will come back home with Sofronia. Once you are alone in the bedroom, put out the light and dawdle around the room, acting as if you are getting undressed. Meanwhile, I will sneak into the room, get undressed, and hop into bed with Clizia. You can stay quietly on the little cot. In the morning, before dawn comes, I will get out of bed, as if I want to go pee, I will get dressed again, and you will get into the bed.

CLEANDRO: (Oh, you old scoundrel! What good luck for me to have heard this plan of yours! What bad luck for you that I did!)

PIRRO: It seems to me you have really devised a fine plan. But you had better get your weapon cocked so that you seem like a young man; because I am afraid your old age will be evident even in the dark.

CLEANDRO: (What I have heard is enough. I am going to inform my mother.)

NICOMACO: I have thought of everything. As a matter of fact, I am planning on having supper with Damone, and I have ordered a meal of my own concoction. First I will take a dose of a potion called satyrion.

PIRRO: What strange kind of name is that?

NICOMACO: The stuff is even stranger than its name! It is a potion that, as far as this business is concerned, would rejuvenate a man of ninety, let alone a man of sev-

come ho io. Preso questo lattovaro, io cenerò poche cose,
ma tutte sustanzevole: in prima, una insalata di cipolle
cotte; dipoi, una mistura di fave e spezierie . . .

PIRRO: Che fa cotesto?

NICOMACO: Che fa? Queste cipolle, fave e spezierie,
perché sono cose calde e ventose, farebbono far vela ad una
caracca genovese. Sopra queste cose si vuole uno pippione
grosso arrosto, così verdemezzo, che sanguini un poco.

PIRRO: Guardate che non vi guasti lo stomaco, perché
bisognerà, o che vi sia masticato, o che voi lo 'ngoiate
intero: non vi vegg' io tanti o sì gagliardi denti in bocca!

NICOMACO: Io non dubito di cotesto, ché, bench'
io non abbia molti denti, io ho le mascella che paiono
d'acciaio.

PIRRO: Io penso che, poi che voi ne sarete ito, ed io
entrato nel letto, che io potrò fare sanza toccarla, perché io
ho viso di trovare quella povera fanciulla fracassata.

NICOMACO: Bàstiti, ch' io arò fatto l'ufficio tuo e quel
d'un compagno.

PIRRO: Io ringrazio Dio, poiché mi ha dato una moglie
in modo fatta, ch' io non arò a durare fatica né a 'mpre-
gnarla, né a darli le spese.

NICOMACO: Vanne in casa, sollecita le nozze, ed io par-
lerò un poco con Damone, ch' io lo veggo uscir di casa sua.

PIRRO: Così farò.

SCENA TERZA

Nicomaco, Damone.

NICOMACO: Egli è venuto quello tempo, o Damone,
che mi hai a mostrare, se tu mi ami. E' bisogna che tu

enty like me. After I take the potion, I will eat a few—
but very substantial—things. First a salad of cooked
onions, then a mixture of beans and spices.

PIRRO: What does that do?

NICOMACO: What does it do? Onions, beans, and
spices, since they are hot and windy things, would get the
sails up on a Genoan frigate. On top of that, I need a fat
roasted pigeon, half-cooked, still a little bit bloody.

PIRRO: Watch out you don't spoil your stomach, because either it will have to be chewed for you, or you will
have to swallow it whole. I don't see all that many good
teeth in your mouth!

NICOMACO: I am not worried about that. Even if I
don't have many teeth, I have jaws like steel.

PIRRO: It looks to me as if, once you have left and I
have gotten into bed, I won't need to lay a hand on her,
because I am sure I will find the poor girl in tatters.

NICOMACO: Let us just say that I will have done your
work for you, and your best friend's as well.

PIRRO: I thank God for giving me a wife for whom I
won't have to strain myself either providing for her or getting her pregnant.

NICOMACO: You go into the house and hurry the wedding preparations, and I will talk with Damone for a moment. I see him coming out of his house.

PIRRO: I shall do that.

SCENE THREE

Nicomaco, Damone.

NICOMACO: The time has come, Damone, for you
to show me whether you are my friend. You will have to

sgomberi la casa, e non vi rimanga né la tua donna, né altra persona, perché io vo' governare questa cosa, come io t'ho già detto.

DAMONE: Io son parato a fare ogni cosa, purché io ti contenti.

NICOMACO: Io ho detto a mogliama che chiami Sostrata tua, che vadia ad aiutarla ordinare le nozze. Fa' che la vadia sùbito, come la chiama, e che vadia con lei la serva, sopratutto.

DAMONE: Ogni cosa è ordinato: chiamala a tua posta.

NICOMACO: Io voglio ire infino allo speziale a fare una faccenda, e tornerò ora: tu aspetti qui, che mogliama eschi fuora, e chiami la tua. Ecco che la viene: sta' parato. Addio.

SCENA QUARTA

Sofronia, Damone.

SOFRONIA: Non maraviglia che 'l mio marito mi sollecitava ch' io chiamassi Sostrata di Damone! E' voleva la casa libera, per potere giostrare a suo modo. Ecco Damone di qua. O specchio di questa città, e colonna del suo quartieri, che accomoda la casa sua a sì disonesta e vituperosa impresa! Ma io gli tratterò in modo, che si vergogneranno sempre di loro medesimi. E voglio or cominciare ad uccellare costui.

DAMONE: Io mi maraviglio che Sofronia si sia ferma, e non venga avanti a chiamare la mia donna . . . Ma ecco che la viene. Dio ti salvi, Sofronia!

SOFRONIA: E te, Damone! Ove è la tua donna?

move out of your house; neither you, your wife, nor anyone else can stay there, because I want to set things up in the way I have already told you about.

DAMONE: I am ready to do everything exactly as you wish.

NICOMACO: I have told the wife to call your Sostrata to come over and help her arrange the wedding. Make sure she goes right away when she is called, and especially that the maid goes along with her.

DAMONE: Everything is taken care of; call her when you want.

NICOMACO: I am going to go and get something at the druggist's; I will be right back. You wait here for my wife to come out and call yours. Here she comes; be prepared. Goodbye.

SCENE FOUR

Sofronia, Damone.

SOFRONIA: (No wonder my husband was urging me to call Damone's wife, Sostrata! He wanted the house free so that he could fool around at his leisure. And here is Damone, the paragon of this city and the pillar of the community, who lends his house out to such indecent and shameless goings-on! But I will fix them so that they will be ashamed of themselves forever. I am going to start by having some fun with this fellow.)

DAMONE: (I am surprised that Sofronia is just standing there, and hasn't come over to call my wife. Ah, here she comes.) God be with you, Sofronia!

SOFRONIA: And with you, too, Damone! Where is your wife?

DAMONE: La è in casa, ed è parata a venire, se tu la chiami, perché el tuo marito me ne ha pregato. Vo io a chiamarla?

SOFRONIA: No, no! la debbe avere faccenda.

DAMONE: Non ha faccenda alcuna.

SOFRONIA: Lasciala stare, io non le voglio dare briga: io la chiamerò, quando fia tempo.

DAMONE: Non ordinate voi le nozze?

SOFRONIA: Sì, ordiniamo.

DAMONE: Non hai tu necessità di chi ti aiuti?

SOFRONIA: E' vi è brigata un mondo, per ora.

DAMONE: Che farò ora io? Ho fatto uno errore grandissimo a cagione di questo vecchio impazzato, bavoso, cisposo, e sanza denti. E' mi ha fatto offerire la donna per aiuto a costei, che non la vuole, in modo che la crederrà ch'io vadi mendicando un pasto, e terrammi uno sciagurato.

SOFRONIA: Io ne rimando costui tutto inviluppato. Guarda come ne va ristretto nel mantello! E' mi resta ora ad uccellare un poco el mio vecchio. Eccolo che viene dal mercato. Io voglio morire, se non ha comperato qualche cosa, per parere gagliardo o odorifero!

SCENA QUINTA

Nicomaco, Sofronia.

NICOMACO: Io ho comperato el lattovaro e certa unzione appropriata a fare risentire le brigate. Quando si va armato alla guerra, si va con più animo la metà. —Io ho veduta la donna: ohimè, che la m'arà sentito!

DAMONE: She is in the house. She is all ready to come out if you call her, because your husband asked me about it. Should I go and call her?

SOFRONIA: No, no! She must have things to do.

DAMONE: She has nothing at all to do.

SOFRONIA: Leave her alone, I don't want to give her any trouble. I will call her when it is time.

DAMONE: Aren't you arranging the wedding?

SOFRONIA: Yes, we are.

DAMONE: Don't you need someone to help you?

SOFRONIA: There are all too many people there right now.

DAMONE: (What should I do now? I have made a big mistake, thanks to that crazy, drooling, bleary-eyed, tooth-less old man. He has made me offer my wife to help this woman, who doesn't want her, and so she will believe that I am just begging for a meal, and think I am a good-for-nothing.)

SOFRONIA: (Now I have sent this fellow away all mixed up. Look how he is skulking off with his cloak pulled about him! Now I still have to have a bit of fun with my old man. Here he comes back from the market. I would stake my life that he has bought something to get his pecker up, the stinker!)

SCENE FIVE

Nicomaco, Sofronia.

NICOMACO: I have bought the potion, and a certain unguent that would wake up a regiment. If you go to war with the right weapons, you go with twice the courage.— There is my wife: oh, oh, I hope she didn't hear me!)

SOFRONIA: Sì, ch' io t'ho sentito, e con tuo danno e vergogna, s' io vivo insino a domattina!

NICOMACO: Sono ad ordine le cose? Hai tu chiamata questa tua vicina, che ti aiuti?

SOFRONIA: Io la chiamai, come tu mi dicesti; ma questo tuo caro amico le favellò non so che nell'orecchio, in modo che la mi rispose che non poteva venire.

NICOMACO: Io non me ne maraviglio, perché tu se' un poco rozza, e non sai accomodarti con le persone, quando tu vuoi alcuna cosa da loro.

SOFRONIA: Che volevi tu, ch' io lo toccassi sotto 'l mento? Io non son usa a fare carezze a' mariti d'altri. Va', chiamala tu, poiché ti giova andare drieto alle moglie d'altri, ed io andrò in casa ad ordinare il resto.

SCENA SESTA

Damone, Nicomaco.

DAMONE: Io vengo a vedere, se questo amante è tornato dal mercato. Ma eccolo davanti all'uscio. Io venivo appunto a te.

NICOMACO: Ed io a te, uomo da farne poco conto! Di che t'ho io pregato? Di che t'ho io richiesto? Tu m'hai servito così bene!

DAMONE: Che cose è?

NICOMACO: Tu mandasti mogliata! Tu hai vòta la casa di brigata, che fu un solazzo! In modo che, alle tua cagione, io son morto e disfatto!

DAMONE: Va', t'impicca! Non mi dices' tu, che mogliata chiamerebbe la mia?

NICOMACO: La l'ha chiamata, e non è voluta venire.

SOFRONIA: (Yes, I heard you, and you will be sorry and ashamed, if I live until tomorrow morning!)

NICOMACO: Is everything in order? Have you called your neighbor to help you?

SOFRONIA: I called her, as you told me, but that dear friend of yours whispered something or other in her ear, so she answered me that she couldn't come.

NICOMACO: I am not surprised, because you are a bit clumsy and don't know how to get along with people when you want something from them.

SOFRONIA: What did you want me to do, chuck him under the chin? I'm not in the habit of pawing other people's husbands. Go and call her yourself, since you are good at tailing after other people's wives. I will go into the house to arrange the rest.

SCENE SIX

Damone, Nicomaco.

DAMONE: (I have come to see whether our lover is back from the market. Ah, there he is in front of his door.) I was just coming for you!

NICOMACO: And so was I, you good-for-nothing! What did I ask you for? What did I tell you to do? You really have done a fine job for me!

DAMONE: What is the matter?

NICOMACO: So that is how you send your wife! So you got everybody out of the house! What a relief! The result is that, thanks to you, I am a dead duck.

DAMONE: Go and be hanged! Didn't you tell me your wife would call mine?

NICOMACO: She did call her, and she wouldn't come.

DAMONE: Anzi, che gliene offersi! Ella, non volle che la venissi; e così mi fai uccellare, e poi ti duoli di me. Che 'l diavolo ne 'l porti, te e le nozze ed ognuno!

NICOMACO: Infine, vuoi tu che la venga?

DAMONE: Sì, voglio, in mal' ora! ed ella, e la fante, e la gatta, e chiunque vi è! Va', se tu hai a fare altro: io andrò in casa, e, per l'orto, la farò venire or ora.

NICOMACO: Ora, m'è costui amico! Ora, andranno le cose bene! —Ohimè! ohimè! che romore è quel che è in casa?

SCENA SETTIMA

Doria, Nicomaco.

DORIA: Io son morta! Io son morta! Fuggite, fuggite! Toglietele quel coltello di mano! Fuggitevi, Sofronia!

NICOMACO: Che hai tu, Doria? Che ci è?

DORIA: Io son morta!

NICOMACO: Perché se' tu morta?

DORIA: Io son morta, e voi spacciato!

NICOMACO: Dimmi quel che tu hai!

DORIA: Io non posso per lo affanno! Io sudo! Fatemi un poco di vento col mantello!

NICOMACO: Deh! dimmi quel che tu hai, ch' io ti romperò la testa!

DORIA: Ah! padron mio, voi siate troppo crudele!

NICOMACO: Dimmi quel che tu hai, e qual romore è in casa!

DAMONE: Not at all! She offered to, but she didn't want her to come. So you get me to make a fool of myself, and then you complain. The devil take you, your wedding, and the whole business!

NICOMACO: Well, once and for all, do you want her to come?

DAMONE: Yes, I do; and she and the maid and the cat and all the rest of them be damned! Go on, if you have something else to do: I will go home and have her come over right away through the garden.

NICOMACO: Now that he is friendly again, everything will be fine. Oh, oh! What is that noise I hear in the house?

SCENE SEVEN

Doria, Nicomaco.

DORIA: I am dying, I am dying! Run for your life! Take that knife out of her hand! Run away, Sofronia!

NICOMACO: What is the matter with you, Doria? What is it?

DORIA: I am dying!

NICOMACO: Why are you dying?

DORIA: I am dying, and you are done for!

NICOMACO: Tell me what is wrong.

DORIA: I can't, I am too frightened! I am all in a sweat! Fan me a little with your cloak!

NICOMACO: Please, tell me what is wrong, or I will break your neck!

DORIA: Oh, master, you are too cruel!

NICOMACO: Tell me what is wrong, and what all that noise is in the house.

DORIA: Pirro aveva dato l'anello a Clizia, ed era ito ad accompagnare el notaio infino all'uscio di drieto. Ben sai che Clizia, non so da che furore mossa, prese uno pugnale, e, tutta scapigliata, tutta furiosa, grida: —Ove è Nicomaco? Ove è Pirro? Io gli voglio ammazzare! —Cleandro, Sofronia, tutte noi la volavamo pigliare, e non potemo. La si è arrecata in uno canto di camera, e grida che vi vuole ammazzare in ogni modo, e per paura chi fugge di qua e chi di là. Pirro si è fuggito in cucina, e si è nascosto drieto alla cesta de' capponi. Io son mandata qui, per avvertirvi, che voi non entriate in casa.

NICOMACO: Io son il più misero di tutti gli uomini! Non si può egli trarle di mano il pugnale?

DORIA: Non, per ancora.

NICOMACO: Chi minacc' ella?

DORIA: Voi e Pirro.

NICOMACO: Oh! che disgrazia è questa! Deh! figliuola mia, io ti prego che tu torni in casa, e con buone parole vegga, che se le cavi questa pazzia del capo, e che la ponga giù il pugnale; ed io ti prometto ch' io ti comperrò un paio di pianelle ed uno fazzoletto. Deh! va', amor mio!

DORIA: Io vo: ma non venite in casa, se io non vi chiamo.

NICOMACO: O miseria! O infelicità mia! Quante cose mi si intraversano, per fare infelice questa notte, ch' io aspettavo felicissima! Ha ella posto giù il coltello? Vengo io?

DORIA: Non, ancora! non venite!

NICOMACO: O Iddio! che sarà poi? Poss' io venire?

DORIA: Pirro had given the ring to Clizia, and had gone to accompany the notary to the back door. Well, don't you know that Clizia got into some sort of a frenzy, and grabbed a knife, and started shouting, all wild and disheveled:—Where is Nicomaco? Where is Pirro? I am going to murder them!—Cleandro, Sofronia, and all of us tried to grab her, but we couldn't. She has backed herself into a corner of the room, and she keeps shouting that she wants to murder you come what may, and everyone is running around frightened out of his wits. Pirro escaped into the kitchen and is hiding behind the chicken crates. They sent me out here to warn you not to go into the house.

NICOMACO: I am the most miserable man in the world! Can't you get the knife out of her hand?

DORIA: Not so far.

NICOMACO: Who is she threatening?

DORIA: You and Pirro.

NICOMACO: Oh, what a catastrophe this is! Please, my dear girl, I beg you, go back into the house and see if you can get this crazy idea out of her head with a few kind words, and get her to put down the knife. I promise I will buy you a pair of slippers and a kerchief. Please, go, my love!

DORIA: I am going; but don't come into the house unless I call you.

NICOMACO: (Oh misery, oh woe is me! So many things are getting in my way, to turn what I thought would be my lucky night into an unlucky one!) Has she put down the knife? May I come in?

DORIA: Not yet, don't come in!

NICOMACO: (Oh Lord, what can it be?) May I come in now?

DORIA: Venite, ma non entrate in camera, dove ella è.
Fate che la non vi vegga. Andate in cucina, da Pirro.

NICOMACO: Io vo.

SCENA OTTAVA

Doria sola.

DORIA: In quanti modi uccelliamo noi questo vecchio!
Che festa è egli vedere e travagli di questa casa! Il vecchio
e Pirro sono paurosi in cucina; in sala son quelli, che apparecchiano la cena; ed in camera sono le donne, Cleandro,
ed il resto della famiglia; ed hanno spogliato Siro, nostro
servo, e de' sua panni vestita Clizia, e de' panni di Clizia
vestito Siro, e vogliono che Siro ne vadia a marito in scambio di Clizia; e perché il vecchio e Pirro non scuoprino
questa fraude, gli hanno, sotto ombra che Clizia sia cru-
ciata, confinati in cucina. Che belle risa! Che bello inganno!—Ma ecco fuora Nicomaco e Pirro.

SCENA NONA

Nicomaco, Doria, Pirro.

NICOMACO: Che fai tu costì, Doria? Clizia è quietata?

DORIA: Messer sì, ed ha promesso a Sofronia di volere
fare ciò che voi volete. Egli è ben vero che Sofronia giudica
che sia bene che voi e Pirro non li capitiate innanzi, acciò
che non se li riaccendessi la collera; poi, messa che la fia al
letto, se Pirro non la saprà dimesticare, suo danno!

NICOMACO: Sofronia ci consiglia bene, e così faremo.
Ora, vattene in casa; e, perché gli è cotto ogni cosa, sol-

DORIA: Come in, but don't go into the room where she is. Don't let her see you. Go into the kitchen with Pirro.

NICOMACO: I shall.

SCENE EIGHT

Doria alone.

DORIA: We certainly are making a fool of this old man in every possible way! What a treat it is to see the turmoil in this house! The old man and Pirro are skulking in the kitchen, in the hall they are preparing the dinner, and in the bedroom are the women, Cleandro, and the rest of the household. They took Siro our servant's clothes off him, dressed Clizia in them, and put Siro in Clizia's; and they are going to have Siro take Clizia's place as the bride. In order for the old man and Pirro not to discover this hoax, they have confined them in the kitchen, under the pretense that Clizia is in a rage. What a fine joke! What a beautiful trick! But here come Nicomaco and Pirro.

SCENE NINE

Nicomaco, Doria, Pirro.

NICOMACO: What are you doing out here, Doria? Has Clizia quieted down?

DORIA: Yes, sir, and she has promised Sofronia to do whatever you want. To tell you the truth, Sofronia thinks it is better for you and Pirro not to get too close to her, so that her anger won't be rekindled. Then, once she has been put to bed, if Pirro can't tame her, too bad for him!

NICOMACO: Sofronia is giving us good advice, we will do that. Now you go on into the house. Since the meal is

lecita che si ceni; Pirro ed io ceneremo a casa Damone;
e, come gli hanno cenato, fa' che la menino fuora. Sollecita, Doria, per l'amore d'Iddio, ché sono già sonate le
tre ore, e non è bene stare tutta notte in queste pratiche.

DORIA: Voi dite el vero. Io vo.

NICOMACO: Tu, Pirro, riman' qui: io andrò a bere un
tratto con Damone. Non andare in casa, acciò che Clizia
non si infuriassi di nuovo; e, se cosa alcuna accade, corri a
dirmelo.

PIRRO: Andate, io farò quanto mi imponete. Poiché
questo mio padrone vuole ch' io stia sanza moglie e sanza
cena, io son contento. Né credo che in uno anno intervenghino tante cose, quante sono intervenute oggi; e dubito
non ne intervenghino dell'altre, perché io ho sentito per
casa certi sghignazzamenti, che non mi piacciano. —Ma
ecco ch' io veggo apparire un torchio: e debbe uscir fuora
la pompa, la sposa ne debbe venire. Io voglio correre per
il vecchio. O Nicomaco! O Damone! Venite da basso! La
sposa ne viene.

SCENA DECIMA

Nicomaco, Sofronia, Sostrata, Damone.

NICOMACO: Eccoci. Vanne, Pirro, in casa, perché
io credo che sia bene cha la non ti vegga. Tu, Damone,
pàramiti innanzi, e parla tu con queste donne. Eccoli tutti
fuora.

SOFRONIA: O povera fanciulla! la ne va piangendo.
Vedi che la non si lieva el fazzoletto dagli occhi.

cooked already, get them all to have dinner right away. Pirro and I will eat at Damone's house. When they have finished eating, have them take her outside. Get it done quickly, Doria, for the love of God; it is already nine o'clock,[13] and it is not a good idea to make these things drag out all night.

DORIA: You are right. I am going.

NICOMACO: Pirro, you stay here. I am going to have a little drink with Damone. Don't go into the house, so that Clizia won't fly into a rage again. If anything at all should happen, run and let me know.

PIRRO: Go ahead, I will do as you have asked me. (Since this master of mine wants me to go without a wife and without dinner, I am satisfied. I didn't believe as many things could happen in a year as have happened today. But I am afraid that even more is going to happen to me, because I heard some snickering in the house which I didn't like. But I see a torch appearing there; the procession must be coming out. The bride ought to be on her way. I will go run and get the old man.) Nicomaco, oh Damone, come on, come down! The bride is arriving.

SCENE TEN

Nicomaco, Damone, Sofronia, Sostrata.

NICOMACO: Here we are. Pirro, you go on into the house, because I think it is better for you not to be seen. Damone, you get in front of me, and talk with these women. Here they all are outside.

SOFRONIA: Oh, the poor girl, she is walking along crying! See, she can't take her handkerchief away from her eyes.

SOSTRATA: Ella riderà domattina! Così usano di fare le fanciulle. Dio vi dia la buona sera, Nicomaco e Damone!

DAMONE: Voi siate le ben venute. Andatevene sù, voi donne, mettete al letto la fanciulla, e tornate giù. Intanto, Pirro sarà ad ordine anche egli.

SOSTRATA: Andiamo, col nome d'Iddio.

SCENA UNDECIMA

Nicomaco, Damone.

NICOMACO: Ella ne va molto malinconosa. Ma hai tu veduto come l'è grande? La si debbe essere aiutata con le pianelle.

DAMONE: La pare anche a me maggiore, che la non suole. O Nicomaco, tu se' pur felice! La cosa è condotta dove tu vuoi. Pòrtati bene, altrimenti tu non vi potrai tornare più.

NICOMACO: Non dubitare! Io sono per fare el debito, ché, poi ch' io presi il cibo, io mi sento gagliardo come una spada.—Ma ecco le donne, che tornano.

SCENA DUODECIMA

Nicomaco, Sostrata, Damone, Sofronia.

NICOMACO: Avetela voi messa al letto?

SOSTRATA: Sì, abbiamo.

DAMONE: Bene sta; noi fareno questo resto. Tu, Sostrata, vanne con Sofronia a dormire, e Nicomaco rimarrà qui meco.

SOFRONIA: Andianne, ché par lor mille anni di avercisi levate dinanzi.

SOSTRATA: She will be laughing tomorrow! That is the way girls always act. God give you a good evening, Nicomaco and Damone!

DAMONE: Welcome to you all. Go on upstairs, ladies, put the girl to bed, and then come on back down. Meanwhile Pirro will get ready, too.

SOSTRATA: Let us go, for the Lord's sake.

SCENE ELEVEN

Nicomaco, Damone.

NICOMACO: She is walking off so sadly. But did you see how tall she is? She must be wearing high slippers.

DAMONE: She seemed taller than usual to me, too. Oh, Nicomaco, what a lucky man you are! Things have turned out just as you wanted. Do a good job; otherwise you won't be able to go back there any more.

NICOMACO: Don't you worry! I am ready to do all that is required! Why, ever since I had that meal, I have been feeling as lusty as a lance. But here come the ladies back again.

SCENE TWELVE

Nicomaco, Sostrata, Sofronia, Damone.

NICOMACO: Did you put her in bed?

SOSTRATA: Yes, we did.

DAMONE: Fine. We will take care of the rest. Sostrata, you go over and sleep with Sofronia, and Nicomaco will stay here with me.

SOFRONIA: Let's go, they just can't wait to get rid of us.

DAMONE: Ed a voi il simile. Guardate a non vi far male.

SOSTRATA: Guardatevi pur voi, che avete l'arme: noi siamo disarmate.

DAMONE: Andiamone in casa.

SOFRONIA: E noi ancora. Va' pur là, Nicomaco, tu troverrai riscontro, perché questa tua dama sarà come le mezzine da Santa Maria Impruneta.

CANZONA

Sì suave è lo inganno,
al fin condotto immaginato e caro,
ch' altri spoglia d'affanno,
e dolce face ogni gustato amaro!
O remedio alto e raro,
tu monstri el dritto calle all'alme erranti;
tu, col tuo gran valore,
nel far beato altrui, fai ricco Amore;
tu vinci, sol con tua consigli santi,
pietre, veneni, e incanti.

DAMONE: The same to you. Watch out that you don't do each other any harm.

SOSTRATA: You watch out, yourselves. You have the weapons, and we don't.

DAMONE: Let's go on into the house.

SOFRONIA: And we will, too. Go on ahead, Nico-maco, you will find your match, because that lady of yours will be like the pitchers of Santa Maria in Pruneta, with a long spout on the bottom.[14]

SONG [15]

How gentle is deception
When carried to fruition as intended,
For it defies perception
And soothes the blissful dupes we have befriended.
Oh draught by heaven blended,
You show the quickest way to true contentment,
And with your magic power
You comfort those whose wealth we would devour:
And vanquish, by your devious presentment,
Stone walls, and arm'd resentment.

ATTO QUINTO
SCENA PRIMA

Doria sola.

DORIA: Io non risi mai più tanto, né credo mai più ridere tanto; né, in casa nostra, questa notte si è fatto altro che ridere. Sofronia, Sostrata, Cleandro, Eustachio, ognuno ride. E si è consumata la notte in misurare el tempo, e dicevàno:—Ora entra in camera Nicomaco, or si spoglia, or si corica allato alla sposa, or le dà battaglia, ora è combattuto gagliardamente.—E, mentre noi stavamo in su questi pensieri, giunsono in casa Siro e Pirro, e ci raddoppiorno le risa; e, quel che era più bel vedere, era Pirro, che rideva più di Siro: tanto che io non credo che ad alcuno sia tocco, questo anno, ad avere il più bello, né il maggiore piacere. Quelle donne mi hanno mandata fuora, sendo già giorno, per vedere quel che fa il vecchio, e come egli comporta questa sciagura.—Ma ecco fuora egli e Damone. Io mi voglio tirare da parte, per vedergli, ed avere materia di ridere di nuovo.

SCENA SECONDA

Damone, Nicomaco, Doria.

DAMONE: Che cosa è stata questa, tutta notte? Come è ella ita? Tu stai cheto. Che rovigliamenti di vestirsi, di aprire uscia, di scender e salire in sul letto sono stati questi, che mai vi siate fermi? Ed io, che nella camera terrena vi dormivo sotto, non ho mai potuto dormire; tanto che

ACT FIVE
SCENE ONE

Doria alone.

DORIA: I have never laughed so hard in my life, and I don't believe I ever shall again. In fact, nobody did anything else but laugh in our house all last night. Sofronia, Sostrata, Cleandro, Eustachio—everyone has been laughing. We spent the night counting the minutes as they went by, and we would say:—Now Nicomaco is going into the bedroom, now he is getting undressed, now he is lying down next to his bride, now he is mounting his attack, now they are wrestling together lustily.—And while we were absorbed in those thoughts, Siro and Pirro arrived at the house, and they started us laughing twice as hard. What was best of all was to see Pirro laughing at Siro; I really don't think anyone has been given a greater or finer pleasure this year. The ladies have sent me out, now that it is daylight, to see what the old man is up to, and how he is bearing up under this misfortune. But here he comes, with Damone. I am going to withdraw to one side, to see them and have something new to laugh at.

SCENE TWO

Damone, Nicomaco, Doria.

DAMONE: What has been happening all night? How did it go? You are silent. What was all that commotion of dressing, opening doors, getting in and out of bed—there was never a moment's peace. I was sleeping in the downstairs bedroom just below, and I couldn't get a wink of

per dispetto mi levai, e truovoti, che tu esci fuori tutto
turbato. Tu non parli? Tu mi par' morto. Che diavolo
hai tu?

NICOMACO: Fratel mio, io non so dove io mi fugga,
dove io mi nasconda, o dove io occulti la gran vergogna,
nella quale io sono incorso. Io sono vituperato in eterno,
non ho più rimedio, né potrò mai più innanzi a mogliama,
a' figliuoli, a' parenti, a' servi capitare. Io ho cerco il vituperio mio, e la mia donna me lo ha aiutato a trovare:
tanto che io sono spacciato; e tanto più mi duole, quanto
di questo carico tu anche ne participi, perché ciascuno
saprà che tu ci tenevi le mani.

DAMONE: Che cosa è stata? Hai tu rotto nulla?

NICOMACO: Che vuoi tu ch' io abbia rotto? che rotto
avess' io el collo!

DAMONE: Che è stato, adunque? Perché non me lo di'?

NICOMACO: Uh! uh! uh! Io ho tanto dolore ch' io non
credo poterlo dire.

DAMONE: Deh! tu mi pari un bambino! Che domine
può egli essere?

NICOMACO: Tu sai l'ordine dato, ed io, secondo
quell'ordine, entrai in camera, e chetamente mi spogliai;
ed in cambio di Pirro, che sopra el lettuccio s'era posto a
dormire, non vi essendo lume, allato alla sposa mi coricai.

DAMONE: Orbè, che fu poi?

NICOMACO: Uh! uh! uh! Accosta'migli. Secondo
l'usanza de' nuovi mariti, vollile porre le mani sopra il
petto, ed ella, con la sua, me le prese, e non mi lasciò.
Vollila baciare, ed ella con l'altra mano mi spinse el viso

sleep; so finally, out of desperation, I got up, and here I find you outside, all in a state. You don't speak, you look like a dead man: what the devil is wrong?

NICOMACO: Brother, I don't know where to run, and where to hide myself or the awful shame I have gotten myself into. I am disgraced for all eternity, there is no remedy left for me, and I will never be able to show my face again to the wife, the children, the relatives, or the servants. I went looking for my own disgrace, and my wife helped me to find it. So now I really may as well give up. It hurts me all the more, that you have a share in my guilt, too, because everyone will know that you took a hand in all of this.

DAMONE: What happened? Did you break something?

NICOMACO: What did you expect me to break? I wish I had broken my neck!

DAMONE: What in the world happened? Why don't you tell me?

NICOMACO: Boo, hoo, hoo! I have so much grief that I don't think I can tell you.

DAMONE: Please, you are acting like a child! What the devil can it be?

NICOMACO: You know the plans we made. Following them out, I went into the bedroom, and quietly I got undressed. In place of Pirro, who had lain down to sleep on the little cot, in the dark, I got into bed next to the bride.

DAMONE: Well, so, what then?

NICOMACO: Boo, hoo, hoo! I drew closer to her; as bridegrooms generally do, I tried to put my hands on her breasts, and she grabbed hold of both my hands with one of hers, and wouldn't let go. I tried to kiss her, and she pushed my face back with her other hand. I tried to jump

indrieto. Io me li volli gittare tutto addosso: ella mi porse un ginocchio, di qualità che la m'ha infranto una costola. Quando io viddi che la forza non bastava, io mi volsi a' prieghi, e con dolce parole ed amorevole, pur sottovoce, che la non mi cognoscessi, la pregavo fussi contenta fare e piacer' miei, dicendoli:—Deh! anima mia dolce, perché mi strazii tu? Deh! ben mio, perché non mi concedi tu volentieri quello, che l'altre donne a' loro mariti volentieri concedano?—Uh! uh! uh!

DAMONE: Rasciùgati un poco gli occhi.

NICOMACO: Io ho tanto dolore, ch' io non truovo luogo, né posso tenere le lacrime. Io potetti cicalare: mai fece segno di volerme, nonché altro, parlare. Ora, veduto questo, io mi volsi alle minacce, e cominciai a dirli villania, e che le farei, e che le direi. Ben sai che, ad un tratto, ella raccolse le gambe, e tirommi una coppia di calci, che, se la coperta del letto non mi teneva, io sbalzavo nel mezzo dello spazzo.

DAMONE: Può egli essere?

NICOMACO: E ben che può essere! Fatto questo, ella si volse bocconi, e stiacciossi col petto in su la coltrice, che tutte le manovelle dell'Opera non l'arebbono rivolta. Io, veduto che forza, preghi e minacci non mi valevano, per disperato le volsi le stiene, e deliberai di lasciarla stare, pensando che verso el dì la fussi per mutare proposito.

DAMONE: Oh, come facesti bene! Tu dovevi, el primo tratto, pigliar cotesto partito, e, chi non voleva te, non voler lui!

NICOMACO: Sta' saldo, la non è finita qui: or ne viene el bello. Stando così tutto smarrito, cominciai, fra per il dolore e per lo affanno avuto, un poco a sonniferare. Ben

right on top of her: she hit me with her knee hard enough to break one of my ribs. When I saw that force wouldn't do the trick, I turned to prayer, and with sweet, loving words (whispering, though, so that she wouldn't recognize me) I begged her to let me have my way with her, saying:— Please, my sweet love, why are you tormenting me this way? Please, my treasure, why don't you give me willingly what other women willingly give their husbands?—Boo, hoo, hoo!

DAMONE: Dry your eyes a little!

NICOMACO: I hurt so much that there is no way I can stop crying. No matter how I sweet-talked her, she never gave any sign of wanting even to answer me. So, seeing that, I turned to threats and started to say nasty things about what I would say and do to her. Would you believe that all of a sudden she pulled back her legs, and gave me a couple of kicks, so that if the bed cover hadn't held me in, I would have landed right in the middle of the floor!

DAMONE: Can it be possible?

NICOMACO: It most certainly can! After that, she turned over on her belly, and hung on so tightly to the mattress that all the winches working on the Cathedral couldn't have turned her over. Seeing that neither force, prayers, nor threats did any good, in desperation I turned my back on her; and decided to let her be, thinking that toward morning she might change her mind.

DAMONE: Oh, you did the right thing! That is what you ought to have done from the start. If she didn't want you, you shouldn't have wanted her!

NICOMACO: Hold on, that isn't the end of it! Now comes the best part. Feeling so bewildered that way, what with all the pain and the distress, I started to fall asleep.

sai che, ad un tratto, io mi sento stoccheggiare un fianco,
e darmi qua, sotto el codrione, cinque o sei colpi de' mala-
detti. Io, così fra il sonno, vi corsi sùbito con la mano, e
trovai una cosa soda ed acuta, di modo che, tutto spaven-
tato, mi gittai fuora del letto, ricordandomi di quello
pugnale, che Clizia aveva il dì preso, per darmi con esso.
A questo romore, Pirro, che dormiva, si risentì; al quale
io dissi, cacciato più dalla paura che dalla ragione, che cor-
ressi per uno lume, ché costei era armata, per ammazzarci
tutti a dua. Pirro corse, e, tornato con il lume, in scambio
di Clizia vedemo Siro, mio famiglio, ritto sopra il letto,
tutto ignudo, che per dispregio (uh! uh! uh!) e' mi faceva
bocchi (uh! uh! uh!) e manichetto dietro.

DAMONE: Ah! ah! ah!

NICOMACO: Ah! Damone, tu te ne ridi?

DAMONE: E' m'incresce assai di questo caso; nondimeno egli è impossibile non ridere.

DORIA: Io voglio andare a raguagliare di quello, che io
ho udito, la padrona, acciò che se le raddoppino le risa.

NICOMACO: Questo è il mal mio, che toccherà a rider-
sene a ciascuno, ed a me a piagnerne! E Pirro e Siro, alla
mia presenzia, or si dicevano villania, or ridevano; dipoi,
così vestiti a bardosso, se n'andorno, e credo che sieno iti a
trovare le donne, e tutti debbono ridere. E così ognuno
rida, e Nicomaco pianga!

DAMONE: Io credo che tu creda che m'incresca di te e
di me, che sono, per tuo amore, entrato in questo lecceto.

NICOMACO: Che mi consigli ch' io faccia? Non mi
abbandonare, per lo amor d'Iddio!

But just then, all of a sudden, I felt myself being jabbed
in the rump, and I got five or six of the damnedest pokes
right here under the tailbone! Half-asleep like that, I quickly
reached my hand down there, and I discovered a hard,
pointed object. I was so frightened that I jumped out of
bed, remembering the knife that Clizia had grabbed to
stab me with. What with all the noise, Pirro woke up,
and I told him, more out of fear than for any good reason,
to run and get a lamp, since she was armed and ready to
murder us both. Pirro ran off, and when he got back with
the lamp, instead of Clizia who do I see but Siro, my
servant, standing erect all naked on the bed, and out of
spite (boo, hoo, hoo!) he was making faces (boo, hoo,
hoo!) and giving me the finger.[16]

NICOMACO: Ha, ha, ha!

NICOMACO: Ah, Damone, you are laughing?

DAMONE: I am awfully sorry about what happened,
but it is impossible not to laugh.

DORIA: (I am going to tell the mistress about what I
have heard, so that she can have an even bigger laugh than
before.)

NICOMACO: That is the worst of it all: everyone else
is going to laugh at it, and I am going to cry. And then,
right in front of me, Pirro and Siro started to insult each
other, and then they would start to laugh. Afterward, they
threw some clothes on, and they ran off. I think they went
to find the ladies, and they all must be laughing. So let
everyone laugh, and Nicomaco cry!

DAMONE: I am sure you know how sorry I am for you,
and for me, too, since I got into this mess as a favor to
you.

NICOMACO: What do you advise me to do? Don't
abandon me, for the love of God!

DAMONE: A me pare, che se altro di meglio non nasce, che tu ti rimetta tutto nelle mani di Sofronia tua, e dicale che, da ora innanzi, e di Clizia e di te faccia ciò che la vuole. La doverrebbe anch' ella pensare all'onore tuo, perché, sendo suo marito, tu non puoi avere vergogna, che quella non ne participi.—Ecco che la vien fuora. Va', parlale, ed io n'andrò intanto in piazza ed in mercato, ad ascoltare s'io sento cosa alcuna di questo caso, e ti verrò ricoprendo el più ch' io potrò.

NICOMACO: Io te ne priego.

SCENA TERZA

Sofronia, Nicomaco.

SOFRONIA: Doria, mia serva, mi ha detto che Nicomaco è fuora, e che egli è una compassione a vederlo. Io vorrei parlargli, per vedere quel ch' e' dice a me di questo nuovo caso.—Eccolo di qua. O Nicomaco!

NICOMACO: Che vuoi?

SOFRONIA: Dove va' tu sì a buon' ora? Esci tu di casa senza fare motto alla sposa? Hai tu saputo, come lo abbia fatto questa notte con Pirro?

NICOMACO: Non so.

SOFRONIA: Chi lo sa, se tu non lo sai, che hai messo sottosopra Firenze, per fare questo parentado? Ora che gli è fatto, tu te ne mostri nuovo e malcontento!

NICOMACO: Deh, lasciami stare! Non mi straziare!

SOFRONIA: Tu, se' quello che mi strazii, che, dove tu dovresti racconsolarmi, io ho da racconsolare te; e, quando

DAMONE: My advice would be, if nothing better comes along, for you to place yourself completely in Sofronia's hands, and tell her that from now on you will do whatever she says about both Clizia and yourself. She ought to be concerned about your reputation, too, because, since you are her husband, you cannot incur any shame without her being party to it. Here she comes now. Go and talk to her; meanwhile, I will go to the marketplace and into town to see if I hear anything about this story. I will try and cover it up as much as I can.

NICOMACO: Please do.

SCENE THREE

Sofronia, Nicomaco.

SOFRONIA: (Doria, my maid, told me that Nicomaco is out here and that he is a pity to behold. I would like to talk to him to see what he has to say to me about these new events. There he is.) Oh, Nicomaco!

NICOMACO: What do you want?

SOFRONIA: Where are you going so early in the morning? Are you leaving the house without saying a word to the bride? Did you find out how things went last night for Pirro?

NICOMACO: I don't know.

SOFRONIA: If you don't know, who does? You turned Florence upside-down to arrange this marriage. Now that it is done, you look queer and unhappy about it!

NICOMACO: Please! Leave me alone; don't torment me!

SOFRONIA: You are the one who is tormenting me because, instead of consoling me, as you should be doing,

tu gli aresti a provedere, e' tocca a me, che vedi ch' io
porto loro queste uova.

NICOMACO: Io crederrei che fussi bene che tu non
volessi il giuoco di me affatto. Bastiti averlo avuto tutto
questo anno, e ieri e stanotte più che mai.

SOFRONIA: Io non lo volli mai, el giuoco di te; ma tu,
sei quello che lo hai voluto di tutti noi altri, ed alla fine
di te medesimo! Come non ti vergognavi tu, ad avere allevata in casa tua una fanciulla con tanta onestade, ed in
quel modo che si allevano le fanciulle da bene, di volerla
maritare poi ad uno famiglio cattivo e disutile, perché fussi
contento che tu ti giacessi con lei? Credevi tu però a fare
con ciechi o con gente, che non sapessi interrompere le
disonestà di questi tuoi disegni? Io confesso avere condotti
tutti quelli inganni, che ti sono stati fatti, perché, a volerti
fare ravvedere, non ci era altro modo, se non giugnerti in
sul furto, con tanti testimonii, che tu te ne vergognassi, e
dipoi la vergogna ti facessi fare quello, che non ti arebbe
potuto fare fare niuna altra cosa. Ora, la cosa è qui: se tu
vorrai ritornare al segno, ed essere quel Nicomaco, che tu
eri da uno anno indrieto, tutti noi vi torneremo, e la cosa
non si risaprà; e, quando la si risapessi, egli è usanza errare
ed emendarsi.

NICOMACO: Sofronia mia, fa' ciò che tu vuoi: io sono
parato a non uscire fuora de' tua ordini, pure che la cosa
non si risappia.

SOFRONIA: Se tu vuoi fare cotesto, ogni cosa è
acconcio.

NICOMACO: Clizia, dove è?

SOFRONIA: Manda'la, sùbito che si fu cenato iersera,
vestita con panni di Siro, in uno monistero.

it is I who must console you, and when you ought to be providing for them, it is up to me: as you can see, I am bringing them these eggs.

NICOMACO: I should think it might be better for you not to make a complete fool of me. Isn't it enough for you to have done it all this past year, and yesterday, and last night more than ever?

SOFRONIA: I never wanted to make a fool of you. You were the one who tried to do it to every one of us, and you ended up doing to yourself! Aren't you ashamed of having brought up a girl in your house with such decency, as proper girls are brought up, and then trying to marry her off to a nasty and useless servant, just so he would let you sleep with her? Did you think you were dealing with blind men, or with people who wouldn't be able to stop those dirty plans of yours? I confess that I staged all those tricks that were played on you, because there was no other way to make you see the light except to catch you in the act with so many witnesses that you would be ashamed, and shame would make you do what nothing else would. Now this is how things are. If you make a clean start, and go back to being the Nicomaco you once were a year ago, we shall all go back, too, and nobody will know a thing. And even if it were to be known, it is normal to err and make amends.

NICOMACO: Sofronia, my darling, do whatever you want. I am ready to do anything you say, as long as nobody knows about this business.

SOFRONIA: If you will do that, everything will be all right.

NICOMACO: Where is Clizia?

SOFRONIA: I sent her down to a convent right after dinner last night, dressed in Siro's clothes.

NICOMACO: Cleandro, che dice?

SOFRONIA: È allegro che queste nozze sien guaste, ma egli è ben doloroso, che non vede come e' si possa avere Clizia.

NICOMACO: Io lascio avere ora a te il pensiero delle cose di Cleandro; nondimeno, se non si sa chi costei è, non mi parebbe da dargliene.

SOFRONIA: E' non pare anche a me; ma conviene differire il maritarla, tanto che si sappia di costei qualcosa, o che gli sia uscita questa fantasia; ed intanto si farà annullare il parentado di Pirro.

NICOMACO: Governala come tu vuoi. Io voglio andare in casa a riposarmi, che per la mala notte, ch' io ho avuta, io non mi reggo ritto, ed anche perché io veggo Cleandro ed Eustachio uscir fuora, con i quali io non mi voglio abboccare. Parla con loro tu, di' la conclusione fatta da noi, e che basti loro avere vinto, e di questo caso più non me ne ragionino.

SCENA QUARTA

Cleandro, Sofronia, Eustachio.

CLEANDRO: Tu hai udito come el vecchio n'è ito chiuso in casa; e debbe averne tocco una rimesta da Sofronia. E' par tutto umile! Accostianci a lei, per intendere la cosa. Dio vi salvi, mia madre! Che dice Nicomaco?

SOFRONIA: È tutto scorbacchiato, il povero uomo! Pargli essere vituperato; hammi dato il foglio bianco, e vuole ch' io governi per lo avvenire a mio senno ogni cosa.

NICOMACO: What does Cleandro have to say?

SOFRONIA: He is happy this wedding is spoiled, but he is really sorry that he can't see how to get Clizia for himself.

NICOMACO: I will leave what to do with Cleandro's affairs up to you now. Nevertheless, as long as we don't know who that girl is, I don't see how we can give her to him.

SOFRONIA: I don't either. But we will have to put off marrying her until we learn something about her, or until he has gotten over this fancy. Meanwhile, we will have Pirro's marriage annulled.

NICOMACO: Do what you want with her. I am going to go into the house and rest, because after the bad night I have spent I can't stand up straight. Besides, I see Cleandro and Eustachio coming out, and I don't feel like getting into a discussion with them. You speak to them. Tell them the conclusion we have reached. Let them be satisfied with having won, and tell them not to talk to me about this business any more.

SCENE FOUR

Cleandro, Sofronia, Eustachio.

CLEANDRO: Did you hear how the old man went and shut himself in the house? He must have gotten an earful from Sofronia! He really looked sheepish! Let's go and ask her about it. God save you mother! What does Nicomaco have to say?

SOFRONIA: The poor man is in an awful state; he feels as if he has been disgraced. He has given me carte blanche; and he wants me to manage everything my way from now on.

EUSTACHIO: E' l'andrà bene! Io doverrò avere Clizia!

CLEANDRO: Adagio un poco! E' non è boccone da te.

EUSTACHIO: Oh, questa è bella! Ora, che io credetti avere vinto, ed io arò perduto, come Pirro?

SOFRONIA: Né tu, né Pirro l'avete avere; né tu, Cleandro, perché io voglio che la stia così.

CLEANDRO: Fate almeno che la torni a casa, acciò ch'io non sia privo di vederla.

SOFRONIA: La vi tornerà, e non vi tornerà, come mi parrà. Andianne noi a rassettare la casa; e tu, Cleandro, guarda, se tu vedi Damone, perché gli è bene parlargli, per rimanere, come s'abbia a ricoprire il caso seguìto.

CLEANDRO: Io sono mal contento.

SOFRONIA: Tu ti contenterai un'altra volta.

SCENA QUINTA

Cleandro, Damone.

CLEANDRO: Quando io credo essere navigato, e la Fortuna mi ripigne nel mezzo al mare e tra più turbide e tempestose onde! Io combattevo prima con lo amore di mio padre; ora combatto con la ambizione di mia madre. A quello io ebbi per aiuto lei, a questo sono solo: tanto che io veggo meno lume in questo, che io non vedevo in quello. Duolmi della mia mala sorte, poiché io nacqui, per non avere mai bene; e posso dire, da che questa fanciulla ci venne in casa, non avere cognosciuti altri diletti, che di

EUSTACHIO: That will be fine! I will get to have Clizia!

CLEANDRO: Just a minute now! She is not a morsel for you!

EUSTACHIO: Oh, what a fine thing! Just when I thought I had won, am I going to lose like Pirro?

SOFRONIA: Neither you nor Pirro is going to have her. Nor you, either, Cleandro, because I want her to stay as she is.

CLEANDRO: At least let her come back home, so that I won't be deprived of the sight of her.

SOFRONIA: Maybe she will come home, and maybe she won't, as I see fit. Let us go straighten up the house. Cleandro, you see if you can find Damone, because it is a good idea to talk to him and see how we can keep this story covered up.

CLEANDRO: I am so unhappy.

SOFRONIA: You can be happy some other time!

SCENE FIVE

Cleandro, Damone.

CLEANDRO: Just when I thought my ship had come in, fortune blows me back out onto the high seas, in the midst of darker and stormier waves! First I had to contend with my father's passion, now I have to contend with my mother's ambition. I had her to help me against him, but now I stand alone. And so I see less reason to hope in this instance than in the other one. How my evil fortune grieves me; I seem born never to get what I want. I can truly say that ever since that girl set foot in our house, I have known no delight other than thinking of her, and

pensare a lei; dove sono sì radi stati e piaceri, che i giorni di quegli si annoverrebbono facilmente.—Ma chi veggo io venire verso me? È egli Damone? Egli è esso, ed è tutto allegro. Che ci è, Damone, che novelle portate? Donde viene tanta allegrezza?

DAMONE: Né migliori novelle, né più felice, né che io portassi più volentieri potevo sentire!

CLEANDRO: Che cosa é?

DAMONE: Il padre di Clizia vostra è venuto in questa terra, e chiamasi Ramondo, ed è gentiluomo napolitano, ed è ricchissimo, ed è solamente venuto, per ritrovare questa sua figliuola.

CLEANDRO: Che ne sai tu?

DAMONE: Sòllo, ch' io gli ho parlato, ed ho inteso il tutto, e non c'è dubbio alcuno.

CLEANDRO: Come sta la cosa? Io impazzo per la allegrezza.

DAMONE: Io voglio che voi la intendiate da lui. Chiama fuora Nicomaco e Sofronia, tua madre.

CLEANDRO: Sofronia! o Nicomaco! Venite da basso a Damone.

SCENA SESTA

Nicomaco, Damone, Ramondo, Sofronia.

NICOMACO: Eccoci! Che buone novelle?

DAMONE: Dico che 'l padre di Clizia, chiamato Ramondo, gentiluomo napolitano, è in Firenze, per ritrovare quella; ed hogli parlato, e già l'ho disposto di darla per moglie a Cleandro, quando tu voglia.

NICOMACO: Quando e' fia cotesto, io sono contentissimo. Ma dove è egli?

my pleasures have been so rare that I can easily count their days. But who is that I see coming toward me? Is it Damone? It is, and he is all smiles. What is it, Damone? What news do you bring? What is the cause of all this joy?

DAMONE: I could never have heard better or happier news, or news that I might more willingly bring!

CLEANDRO: What is it?

DAMONE: The father of your Clizia has arrived in this city. His name is Ramondo. He is a Neapolitan gentleman, very rich, and he has come here just to find his daughter again.

CLEANDRO: How do you know that?

DAMONE: I know it because I talked with him and heard it all myself. There is not the slightest doubt about it.

CLEANDRO: How can it be? I am beside myself with joy!

DAMONE: I want you to hear it from him yourself. Call Nicomaco and your mother Sofronia outside.

CLEANDRO: Sofronia, oh Nicomaco! Come downstairs, it is Damone.

SCENE SIX

Nicomaco, Damone, Sofronia, Ramondo.

NICOMACO: Here we are! What is the good news?

DAMONE: I was saying that Clizia's father, named Ramondo, a Neapolitan gentleman, is in Florence to find her. I have spoken to him, and I have already convinced him to give her as a wife to Cleandro, if you are willing.

NICOMACO: If that is what it is, I am delighted. But where is he?

DAMONE: Alla "Corona"; e gli ho detto ch' e' venga in qua. Eccolo che viene. Egli è quello che ha dirieto quelli servidori. Facciànceli incontro.

NICOMACO: Eccoci. Dio vi salvi, uomo da bene!

DAMONE: Ramondo, questo è Nicomaco, e questa è la sua donna, ed hanno con tanto onore allevato la figliuola tua; e questo è il loro figliuolo, e sarà tuo genero, quando ti piaccia.

RAMONDO: Voi siate tutti e ben trovati! E ringrazio Iddio, che mi ha fatto tanta grazia, che, avanti ch' io muoia, rivegga la figliuola mia, e possa ristorare questi gentiluomini, che l'hanno onorata. Quanto al parentado, a me non può essere più grato, acciò che questa amicizia, fra noi per i meriti vostri cominiciata, per il parentado si mantenga.

DAMONE: Andiamo dentro, dove da Ramondo tutto il caso intenderete appunto, e queste felice nozze ordinerete.

SOFRONIA: Andiamo. E voi, spettatori, ve ne potrete andare a casa, perché, sanza uscir più fuora, si ordineranno le nuove nozze, le quali fieno femmine, e non maschie, come quelle di Nicomaco.

CANZONA

Voi, che sì intente e quete,
anime belle, essemplo onesto umile,
mastro saggio e gentile
di nostra umana vita udito avete;
e per lui conoscete
qual cosa schifar dèsi, e qual seguire,

DAMONE: At the Crown. I told him to come here. Here he is now. He is the one who has all those servants following him! Let us go and greet them.

NICOMACO: Here we are. God bless you, my worthy man!

DAMONE: Ramondo, this is Nicomaco, and this is his lady. It is they who have brought up your daughter with such honor. And this is their son, who will be your son-in-law, if it pleases you.

RAMONDO: How glad I am to have found you all! I thank God that He has given me such grace as to see my daughter once again, before I die, and to let me reward these gentle people who have so honored her. As for the marriage, I couldn't be more pleased, for thus our friendship, initiated between us through your great merit, shall be strengthened by the bonds of matrimony.

DAMONE: Let us go inside, so you can hear the entire story in all its details from Ramondo, and you can plan this joyous wedding.

SOFRONIA: Let us go! And you, dear audience, can go on back home, because we shall not leave the house again until we have arranged this new wedding. And this time it will be man and wife, not man and man, like Nicomaco's!

SONG

Oh you, whose lofty souls
Have harkened to our true though humble story,
Its message monitory
Recorded henceforth in your memory's rolls,
You now may know which goals
May rightly be pursued, and which to flee,

per salir dritti al cielo,
e sotto rado velo
più altre assai, ch' or fora lungo a dire:
di cui preghian tal frutto appo voi sia,
qual merta tanta vostra cortesia.

That we may go to heaven;
And 'neath the comic leaven
Were other truths too numerous for me
To tell now; so, kind audience, we pray
You reap the fruit you merit from our play.

THE MANDRAKE

APPENDIX I

PROLOGUE (adapted for performance) [1]

God make you merry, audience:
I ask it, since tonight's success
In staging these divertissements
Depends upon your happiness.
You see, our tone is Machiavellian
Right from the Prologue's opening lines!
That wicked, calculating hellion
Twists actors to his base designs.
Tonight you're going to see some action
(I choose that latter term with care)
That proves the irresistible attraction
To wayward youth, of ladies fair.
Our scene is in Renascence Florence,
The House of Medici's one-time fief:
Our set designer's talent warrants
Suspension of your disbelief.
This stately house upon my right
Belongs to a rather witless lawyer
Whose charming wife will spend the night
With a learned young man, who to enjoy her . . .
But I'm starting to anticipate!
There are some other shady people
Who are also scheduled to participate:
A venal friar haunts that steeple;
A most ingenious parasite

Devises one scheme after another;
But even he would fail outright,
Without the lady's bawdy mother!
Our hero, fresh from school in Paris,
Lives at this other, left-hand door.
His boundless ardor may embarrass,
But as the French say: "Vive l'amour!"
He doesn't stop at anything
To get the girl he's yearning for;
He'll even stoop to kidnapping
To reach the . . . end he's burning for.
The name of our unscrupulous lover's
Messer Callimaco Guadagni.
You'll find the names of all the others
On the second page of your programmē.
Our author called his play *Mandragola*;
The plot, you'll find, is not complex:
A Machiavellian comic sagola
Of passion, guile, deceit and sex.
The man, of course, was known far more
For his wicked *Prince*, and for his *Histories*,
As well as for an *Art of War*;
But he also mastered theater's mysteries.
He set the pace for lusty drama
When the modern comic style was . . . laid.
He paints a vivid panorama
Four hundred fifty years can't fade.
Both he and our benign producer
Will stake their annual salary
That you will laugh at our seducer
And the others in our rogues' gallery.
The play, alas! was once much criticized

For lack of all morality,
Since Machiavelli boldly witticized
Adultery and carnality.
We'll leave it to the idealists
To cover up sin and moral scar:
Our author is among the realists
Who show us humans as they are.
Let's get on now with our comedy,
I'm almost running out of rhyme;
(If you can find a rhyme for comedy
Then you're a better poet than I'm!).

APPENDIX II

ALTERNATIVE ENDING (for performance) [2]

TIMOTEO: Well, let us all go into church, and there
we will celebrate accordingly. After the service, you can go
back home and have a well-earned lunch.

And as for you, my dearest friends,
No need for you to tarry here:
You've been the ideal audience,
Your laughter made that perfectly clear.
We won't come out here any more:
My service lasts at least an hour,
Then they will leave by another door,
The lovers to their illicit bower.
So now we bid you fond farewell,
And hope, despite our drama's flaws,
You've liked the tale we had to tell:
Just signify by your applause.

NOTES

NOTES TO *THE WOMAN FROM ANDROS*

1. Sosia echoes Solon's famous saying; see Diogenes Laertius, *Lives*.

2. Translates one of Terence's famous maxims, *veritas odium parit* (v.68); cf. p. 404 below.

3. Translates a frequently quoted phrase that has become proverbial in Latin, *hinc illae lacrumae* (v. 126).

4. Terence arranges the last sentence of Simo's speech so that it reads as his own comment, not, as Machiavelli has it, as part of Panfilo's reported speech.

5. Translates as idiom *si forza con le mani e co' piè* taken directly from a phrase common in Terence, his *manibus pedibusque obnixe* (v.161); it occurs again in Act Four, Scene One—see p. 404 below. Evidently Machiavelli likes the mental picture the phrase conjures up because he uses it again in *Mandragola* I, 1 where it is translated "in any way he could."

6. Manuscripts of Terence's plays, and most Renaissance editions of plays, do not indicate stage directions. Modern editors sometimes add them at points where the author signals the entrance on stage of a new actor. Thus, many scenes end with a reference to "inside" indicating that one actor is about to enter his "house," that is, exit. Sometimes scenes end with an announcement, "here comes so-and-so," to let us know of the arrival of a new actor. Similarly, some scenes begin with the actor announcing "I'm coming back . . . " usually in order to find something out.

7. An example of Machiavelli enlivening Terence. He does so in the first version by *cazzo* "cock" and here by *zugo* for *quid hic volt* (v. 184); cf. p. 405 below.

8. See Introduction, p. 9.

9. Machiavelli's *a lettere di speziali* elaborates Terence's *aperte* (v. 195), "plainly," and enhances the idiomatic flavor of his translation.

10. Terence may have had Andromache's plea to Hector in mind; *Iliad* VI. 429. Cf. Callimaco's recounting to Ligurio of the words Lucrezia uses to accept him as her lover in *La Mandragola* V, 4, pp. 267–69.

11. Translates *nam pollicitus sum suscepturum* (v. 401), meaning "for I've promised to acknowledge the child"; on this point, see the Introduction, p. 10.

12. Machiavelli's rendering of a rich pun in the Latin *ut pro hoc malo mihi det malum* (v. 431), "so as to get myself in bad for my bad news"; *malum* also refers to the corporal punishment meted out to slaves.

13. The translation of Machiavelli's *discepolo* for Terence's *discipuli* (v. 487) by "crew" is an attempt to suggest the theatrical metaphor of picking up on cues that is more apparent in the Latin than the Italian.

14. Machiavelli follows the textual tradition that assigns this speech to Simo; it is generally held to be a continuation of Davus' speech.

15. A typically Terentian sentiment; cf. p. 403 above.

16. Machiavelli's various translations for Terence's *nullus sum* (v. 599) trace an interesting example of the translator's art. In the first version Machiavelli wrote *sono spacciato*, "I'm done for," then crossed it out and wrote *diventato nonnulla*, "I've become a mere nothing"; he finally settles on *Io sono diventato pichino*, more like "I'll eat humble pie" or "I'll eat crow."

17. Machiavelli muddies some subtleties of theme and characterization. He omits *in nuptias conieci erilem filium* (v. 602), "hurled my master's son right into a wedding." Furthermore he obscures *insperante hoc atque invito Pamphilo* (v.603), "beyond the hopes of the father and against the wishes of Pamphilus." Machiavelli's translation, in effect, minimizes Davo's perception of the importance of the father in the father-son relationship, a point vital to Terence's meaning. Perhaps Machiavelli does so with the expectation that, because the audience must inevitably realize Davo's shortcomings on this score, it will supply a respect for the primacy of the father. In so doing, of course, it involves itself in the play's thematic movement and simultaneously fulfills the tidy function of advancing a principle Machiavelli also cherishes.

18. By elaborating on Terence's mere *aliquid* (v. 616), "something," Machiavelli indicates his desire to emphasize a narrator's viewpoint whenever possible; cf. p. 405 and p. 406 below.

19. This speech represents Machiavelli's attempt to deal with Terence's fourteen-line *canticum*, or lyrical monologue, that mixes four different meters—the dactyllic, iambic, cretic, and bacchiac—to achieve a poetic equivalent for Charinus' emotional outrage at Pamphilus, a technique more typical of Plautus than Terence.

20. Translates *conari manibus pedibus* (v. 676); see p. 403 above.

21. Translates *Io vo pensando*; perhaps with intentional irony Machiavelli echoes the opening line of a famous *canzone* by Petrarch (*In Morte* #264). The last four lines of this scene closely parallel an exchange between Ligurio and Callimaco in *Mandragola* IV, 2 ("Let me think . . . I've got it) where the operative phrase is *Io voglio un poco pensallo*.

22. Most Latin texts of Terence assign this speech to Pamphilus not Charinus.

23. Translates *imprudente*; it is actually a mistranslation of *eho tu inpudens* (v. 710), "you ought to be ashamed." By translating badly, Machiavelli loses a joke because the Latin word is customarily an epithet for slaves.

So, the audience would get a rise out of the slave Davus calling the upper-class Charinus someone "with cheek."

24. Rather than risk an anachronism, Machiavelli translates *ex ara* (v. 726), "from the altar," more neutrally—if not more accurately.

25. Translates *quae haec est fabula* (v. 747) for which Machiavelli uses *favola*. Thus, one might conclude that, because both dramatists are using words that mean "nonsense" and "plot," they are self-consciously calling attention to the comic nature of their respective plays; see Introduction, pp. 7–8, p. 404 above, and p. 405 below.

26. Terence draws these speeches out a little more, thereby intensifying the comedy; Machiavelli flattens the comic interchange by making Davo more assertive sooner.

27. A translation that has more to do with Terence's word *sycophantam*, "informer," "deceiver," "flatterer" than it does with Machiavelli's *spione*, "secret agent" or "spy." To justify ignoring Machiavelli's word choice requires pointing out that he is caught in a typical translator's dilemma—and squirming in it. In the first draft he used another word, only the first part of which is clear, *pappa*, meaning one who "scrounges" or "sponges"—hence, akin to "parasite." The second part may be *-lefave*, so that the whole word refers to a weak, ineffectual person. Obviously, Machiavelli is troubled by a lexicon giving him equivalents that are too many and too varied. The original Greek word, *sukophantes*, refers to an "accuser," usually a false one, thus the sense of "rogue." As the word comes through Latin, it gains the sense of "informer" with the added meaning of "parasite" or "flatterer." The Greek word literally means "a person who who shows forth figs" for a variety or reasons, one of which Machiavelli may have known from Plutarch's "Life of Solon," chapter 24. As Partridge says in *Origins*, "orig such an informer as denounced those who sold contraband figs or who stole fruit from the sacred fig-trees, as the ancients explained it; a rogue, because . . . he was addicted to the indecent gesture indicated by . . . 'to make the fig'." Machiavelli was probably closer to a good derisive term, even one etymologically rich, in his rough draft; his second thought, at least in this case, results in a blander choice.

28. The son has become a father illegitimately; thus he has defiled a Roman tradition and offended its staunchest supporter in the play; see Introduction, pp. 10–11.

29. Machiavelli plays for all it is worth Terence's meager *metuo ut substet hospes* (v. 914), "I'm afraid the stranger will not stand up to this"; in the first version Machiavelli wrote *si cachi sotto*, "shit in his pants," cf. p. 403 above.

30. Translates *spione* for Terence's *sycophanta*; see n.27 above.

31. Machiavelli elaborates Terence's *fabulam inceptat* (v. 925), "here the comedy starts"; hence both dramatists are trying to capitalize on the multivalencies of their respective *fabula* and *favola*; see the Introduction, pp. 7–8, and p. 404 and p. 405 above.

32. Terence has Pamphilus, not Crito, supply the name; Ramnusio, below, means from a deme, a district or township, in Attica called Rhamnus.

33. Translates *nodum in scirpo quaeris* (v. 941), "you'd find a difficulty where there is none" (literally, "you'd look for knots in a bullrush"). Machiavelli uses a slangy idiom, *tu cerchi cinque piè al montone* meaning "to look too closely into a thing."

34. Translates *at mihi nunc sic esse hoc verum lubet* (v. 958), "because I feel like having it be true, all the same." Machiavelli appears to downplay this interiorized psychologizing, although *pare*, "seems," for the original version's *piace*, "pleases," may result from a fault of Machiavelli as copyist.

35. For the ending of the play, see the Introduction, p. 12.

NOTES FOR *THE MANDRAKE*

1. This opening *canzone*, along with the four songs between the acts, was added by Machiavelli for a performance of *The Mandrake* to be given by his friend Guicciardini, then Governor of Romagna, at Faenza, during the Carnival of 1526.

2. A complimentary reference to Guicciardini.

3. Boethius, the author of the *Consolations of Philosophy*, seems to be named here solely for the sake of a pun on the first syllables of his name (*bue*=ox).

4. Generally taken to be that of the order of the *Servi*, detested by Machiavelli.

5. The name of a medicinal plant supposedly endowed with magical powers, in part because of its "man-" like shape (the pun does not, however, exist in Italian).

6. Because of his exile from Florence.

7. King Charles VIII of France invaded Italy in 1494, to conquer the Kingdom of Naples (see also *Clizia*). The action thus takes place in 1504.

8. A title of respect reserved in Machiavelli's time for jurists.

9. To a watering-place, or spa.

10. Spas not far from Florence.

11. The cupola, designed by Brunelleschi, of the cathedral of Santa Maria del Fiore, in Florence.

12. Prato (near Florence), Pisa and Leghorn are all in Tuscany.

13. This pun in English, an anachronism here, replaces an untranslatable one in Italian: *carrucola* (pulley) vs. *Verrucola* (from *Verruca*, a mountain visible from Pisa).

14. "Good day, Doctor."

15. "And to you, too, attorney."

16. "To our subject."

17. "For the causes of sterility are: either in the semen, or in the womb, or in the seminal vessels, or in the penis, or in an extrinsic cause."

18. The exact text and sense of this comparison is controversial; its intention seems clearly phallic.

19. This reading, which is not the usual one, is based on that suggested by Mario Martelli in "La versione machiavelliana dell' *Andria*," *Rinascimento*, ser. 2, 8–9 (1968–69), 212, note 1.

20. "For a woman's urine always has greater grossness and whiteness and less beauty than men's. Among other things, furthermore, the cause of this is the width of the canals, and the mingling of what comes out of the womb with the urine."

21. In Italian, "a case for the Eight," i.e. for the eight High Justices of Florence.

22. The church of the *Servi* (see note 4).

23. The fall of Constantinople in 1453, and the sack of Otranto in 1480, had spread fear of an invasion of Italy by the Turks.

24. In Italian, "to the tax collector," implying "into my pocket."

25. In Italian, "as the toad said to the harrow," a proverbial expression for an unwelcome return. Machiavelli explains this saying in a letter to Guicciardini.

26. In the original, Nicia is referring to a similar adventure of Ogier le Danois, a hero of medieval romance.

27. In the original, seven o'clock is "one," ten o'clock is "four," the hours of the day counting from 6 p.m.

28. In the original, "hypocras," a sweetened wine spiced with cinnamon, almonds, musk and amber.

29. The devil.

30. In Italian, "Monna Ghinga," apparently the protagonist of contemporary smutty stories.

31. In Italian, "Va'-qua-tu" ("Come-along-you"), the nickname of a well-known jailer.

32. In Italian, "corno" ("horn"), which connotes both the wing of a military company and the traditional symbol of the cuckold. "Saint Cuckoo," in the next sequence, also has the latter connotation (in French).

33. This phrase is not in the original text.

34. "Churching," a ceremony reserved for women attending services for the first time after childbirth: Messer Nicia's request is somewhat premature.

35. "Good day."

NOTES FOR *CLIZIA*

1. Here Machiavelli, through his Prologue, is summarizing the action of Plautus's *Casina*, on which the *Clizia* is largely based.

2. Ramondo, the *deus ex machina*, Clizia's father.

3. See *The Mandrake*, note 7. The Count of Foix was the commander of the French armies in Italy.

4. Site of an important battle, at Fornovo di Taro (July 6, 1495), in

which the army of the League failed to bar Charles VIII's return route to France.

5. This is the same song as that following Act One of *The Mandrake*.

6. In the original, "el Mirra," a traditional name in anecdotes.

7. In the original, "Altopascio," a fertile area near Lucca in Tuscany.

8. In Italian, "we both know how far away Saint Blaise's day is"—referring to a saint's day (February 3) which was moved to avoid coinciding with Candlemas (February 2).

9. In the original, a play on the word "soffiona," a blast of wind or gas.

10. Cf. *The Mandrake*, in which Friar Timoteo, Messer Nicia and Madonna Lucrezia figure.

11. In Italian, a proverbial expression: "Even the Duke worked as a mason."

12. The tradition of kicking a ball through the streets of Florence during Carnival, an early form of soccer.

13. See *The Mandrake*, note 27.

14. These last words, absent in the Italian text, are added here for clarity, since the reference would be unfamiliar to an English-speaking audience.

15. This is the same song as the one following Act Three of *The Mandrake*.

16. In the original, the *ithyphallus*, an obscene gesture crooking the left hand in the elbow of the bent right arm.

NOTES FOR *THE MANDRAKE* APPENDIXES

1. This free, doggerel version of the Prologue, aimed at a modern audience rather than that of Machiavelli's original, was written for the production by the Dartmouth Players, under the direction of Professor Errol Hill, for which this translation was originally undertaken, in the spring of 1976.

2. This verse closing was written to provide a more effective envoy, in the spirit of the prologue and the poetic intermezzi, for the Dartmouth Players' production.